THE WARRIORS & WIZARDS COMPENDIUM

THE WARRIORS & WIZARDS COMPENDIUM

A Young Adventurer's Guide

WRITTEN BY JIM ZUB AND STACY KING

with ANDREW WHEELER

California | New York

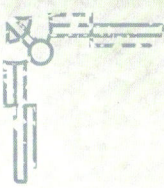
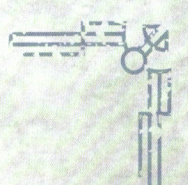

CONTENTS

Introduction 1

CHARACTER CLASSES 3

Barbarian 4
LEGENDARY BARBARIAN
Wulfgar the Warhammer 6
Bard 8
LEGENDARY BARD
Florizan Blank 10
Cleric 12
LEGENDARY CLERIC
Bel Vala 14
Druid 16
LEGENDARY DRUID
Dawan Pax 18
Fighter 20
LEGENDARY FIGHTER
Bruenor Battlehammer 22
Monk 24
LEGENDARY MONK
Whey-Shu 26
Paladin 28
LEGENDARY PALADIN
Redclay 30

Ranger 32
LEGENDARY RANGER
Minsc the Mighty 34
Rogue 36
LEGENDARY ROGUE
Shandie Freefoot 38
Sorcerer 40
LEGENDARY SORCERER
Damini Mahajan 42
Warlock 44
LEGENDARY WARLOCK
Zanizyre Clockguard 46
Wizard 48
LEGENDARY WIZARD
Mordenkainen 50

MARTIAL CLASS FLOWCHART 52
MAGICAL CLASS FLOWCHART 54

ORIGINS 57

Backgrounds 58
Character Details 60

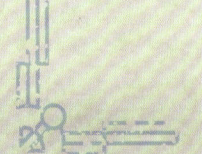
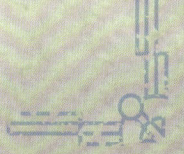

SPECIES 63

- Aasimar 64
- Dragonborn 66
- Dwarf 68
- Elf 70
- Gnome 72
- Goliath 74
- Halfling 76
- Human 78
- Orc 80
- Tiefling 82

TYPES OF MAGIC 85

- Rituals & Scrolls 86
- Spellcasting 87
- **CANTRIPS** 88
- **FIRST LEVEL** 92
- **SECOND LEVEL** 96
- **THIRD LEVEL** 100
- **FOURTH LEVEL** 104
- **FIFTH LEVEL** 108
- **SIXTH LEVEL** 112
- **SEVENTH LEVEL** 116
- **EIGHTH LEVEL** 120
- **NINTH LEVEL** 124

IN YOUR PACK: ITEMS FOR TRAVEL & EXPLORATION . . 129

CLOTHES: ANATOMY OF AN ADVENTURER'S OUTFIT 131
- What to Wear When You're Adventuring! 132

WEAPONS: BE READY FOR COMBAT 135
- Swords 136
- Polearms 138
- Other Melee Weapons 140
- Ranged Weapons 142
- Special Weapons 144

ARMOR: THE FOUNDATION OF DEFENSE 147
- Light Armor 148
- Medium Armor 150
- Heavy Armor 152
- Shields 154
- Survival Gear 156
- Adventuring Gear 158

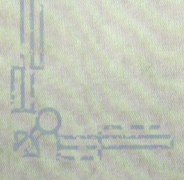

MAGIC ITEMS 161
Weapons 162
LEGENDARY WEAPONS 164
LEGENDARY SWORD
The Sunsword 166
Staffs 168
LEGENDARY STAFF
Staff of the Magi 170
Wands 172
LEGENDARY WAND
Wand of Wonder 174
Potions 176
PARTICULAR POTIONS 178
Rings 180
Cloaks 182
Wondrous Items 184
Guardian Gear 188
Curative Contraptions 190
Infused Instruments 192
Sneaky Supplies 194
Tremendous Tomes 196
Useful Oddities 198

CURIOUS CONSTRUCTS 201
Constructs Overview 202
Golems 204
Clockworks 206
Household Constructs 208

TRAVELING THE REALMS ... 211
Finding Your Way 212
Travel Methods 214
Inns & Waystations 218
Making Camp 220
ENCOUNTER Which Way to Go? ... 223
Foraging & Hunting 224
Dangers on the Road 226
Allies on the Road 228

A REALM OF YOUR OWN ... 231
Dungeon Concept 232
Populating Your Dungeon 234
Mapmaking 239
Exploration & Quests 244
Treasure 246
Building Your World 248
Mapping Your World 250
Inhabitants 256
Monsters & Lairs 258

Using Characters to
Tell Your Own Stories 261

INTRODUCTION

This is a fantasy story.

You are the main character.

Who are you?

What do you do?

This book is a way to answer those two very important questions. It compiles all the information you'll need to start dreaming up your own DUNGEONS & DRAGONS characters and imagining their adventures. Inside these pages, you'll find information about character classes, weapons, equipment, and magic items. You'll learn about traveling across dangerous lands and even how to create dungeons and worlds of your very own.

You can read this book from start to finish or open it up at any spot, get pulled in by the exciting illustrations, and start brainstorming from there. The more you read, the more character ideas and stories of exploration will spring from your imagination.

Every character is unique. Even when two of them share the same species and class, the decisions they make will take them on an exclusive journey that is yours to tell. DUNGEONS & DRAGONS is all about building memorable characters and imagining their exciting journey. Turn the page and the legends of your grand deeds will begin.

Have fun!

BARBARIAN

FIGHTER

MONK

PALADIN

RANGER

ROGUE

BARD

CLERIC

DRUID

SORCERER

WARLOCK

WIZARD

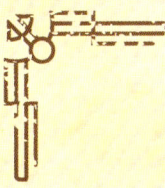

CHARACTER CLASSES

The class you choose for your character is more than a profession—it's a calling! Classes shape not only what they can do, but what kind of person they are, as well as the way your character thinks about the world and interacts with others. For example, a barbarian might see the world as a constant struggle for survival, where brute strength and cunning are all that matter, while a paladin would filter interactions through the lens of faith, always aware of the holy battle between good and evil. A rogue would have contacts among thieves, spies, and other nefarious types, while a ranger would know foresters and innkeepers spread across the wild lands.

Your class provides special features, such as a fighter's mastery of weapons and armor, or a rogue's expertise with stealth. When you first start out, your skills won't be specialized, but as you gain experience, your character will grow and change, unlocking new abilities and powers. Choose your class wisely, for it will shape the hero you become!

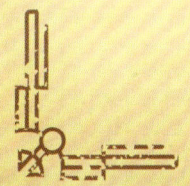
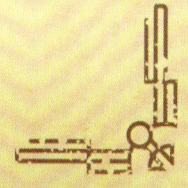

BARBARIAN

ARE YOU FEARLESS IN THE FACE OF DANGER?

DO YOU PREFER NATURE INSTEAD OF BIG CITIES?

DO YOU SOMETIMES LOSE YOURSELF IN ANGER?

YOU MIGHT MAKE A GOOD **BARBARIAN!**

PRIMAL PATHS Although all barbarians share a rage they call upon in times of need, where that anger comes from and how they feel about it can be quite different. Some barbarians consider their anger a curse, others see it as a blessing. Depending on what their belief entails, a barbarian may prescribe to a certain primal path.

PATH OF THE WILD HEART
Inspired by wildlife, Wild Hearts communicate with animals and channel their strengths during battle.

PATH OF THE WORLD TREE
This path connects with the cosmic world tree, Yggdrasil, drawing on it for power and dimensional travel.

PATH OF THE BERSERKER
Berserkers thrill at combat and let their anger overwhelm them in a joyous display of violence.

PATH OF THE ZEALOT
Guided by faith, these barbarians gain powerful blows and healing from divine sources.

Barbarians are warriors of rage. They call upon deep wells of anger from within or draw on the fury of their ancestral spirits to grant them power and strength in their times of need. When your enemies outnumber you and things look lost, a barbarian's fearless combat abilities can turn the tide.

During combat, barbarians will charge into the fray without any hesitation. They know their place is up front, making sure all eyes are on them as they scream a war cry or roar with unmatched fury.

A barbarian's intense emotions guide their actions. Some are very protective of their communities and stay close to home, while others wander far in search of adventure and the thrill of battle.

EQUIPMENT AND ATTRIBUTES

Armor Barbarians wear light or medium armor (see pages 148 and 150). They want to make sure that any armor they do wear won't impede their movement in battle.

Weapons Barbarians tend to have large and loud weapons that work well with their rage-fueled attacks—hammers, battle axes, two-handed swords, and the like. They appreciate weapons that intimidate their foes and make them look even more fearsome than they already are.

Rage Barbarians have a primal ferocity they call upon in times of great stress. This rage helps them focus their attacks and enhance their strength. It also helps them shrug off blows and ignore pain for as long as their fury lasts. A raging barbarian is a scary sight to behold if they're your enemy, but their courage and passion in the heat of battle is also very inspiring to their allies.

Danger Sense Barbarians may seem reckless, but their senses are quite sharp. They're deeply in touch with their emotions and intuition, and it gives them an uncanny sense of when things around them aren't as they should be. When a barbarian perceives something wrong, get ready!

LEGENDARY BARBARIAN

WULFGAR THE WARHAMMER

TEMPERED RAGE Like all barbarians, Wulfgar calls upon his internal anger to aid him in battle and shrug off wounds, but Wulfgar is not the type to relish these moments of rage. The time he spent with Bruenor Battlehammer (see page 22), a dwarven fighter who started as his enemy but over time became like a father to him, taught Wulfgar a lot about self-control and honor in battle.

Wulfgar is a famous human barbarian warrior who grew up in a northern land called Icewind Dale. As a member of the Tribe of the Elk, he learned how to hunt, forage, survive harsh winters, and defend his people from creatures and invading armies.

Facing Wulfgar in combat is a terrifying prospect—he stands almost seven feet tall and weighs 350 pounds. His strength is incredible to behold, especially when swinging Aegis-Fang, his magical warhammer. With that mythic weapon at his side, Wulfgar has driven back invaders and defeated dragons. Facing Wulfgar head-on is a recipe for disaster, so only the most agile and careful have a chance of holding their own against him.

PLAYING WULFGAR Wulfgar is not subtle or careful. He's direct, focused, confident, and always ready for combat. Growing up in a barbarian tribe has left him without much knowledge of cities, especially those in the south, and he feels ill at ease around too many people. Wulfgar thrives in cold open air and it is where he feels most at home.

AEGIS-FANG

Aegis-Fang is a legendary weapon for a legendary warrior. Forged by Bruenor Battlehammer and imbued with powerful dwarven magic, the head of the hammer is made from pure mithral with a diamond coating magically adhered during the forging process and an adamantine shaft. Its head is engraved with the magical inscriptions of Clangeddin, the dwarven god of battle, as well as the symbols of Moradin, the dwarven god of creation, and Dumathoin, keeper of secrets under the mountain.

Most people would have difficulty even lifting Aegis-Fang, but Wulfgar is well trained with the weapon and able to swing it with ease. Even more amazing, it will magically return to Wulfgar's hand at his command, allowing him to throw it at enemies and then get right it back, pummeling those who dare to stand in his way.

BARD

DO YOU BELIEVE THERE IS MAGIC IN MUSIC?

DO YOU OFTEN FIND YOURSELF THE CENTER OF ATTENTION?

DO YOU LOVE TO PERFORM?

YOU MIGHT BE A BARD!

BARDIC COLLEGES Bards may learn music and magic on the road, from a mentor, or with formal schooling. All bards belong to informal associations called Colleges, through which they share their stories and traditions. The four main Colleges are Dance, Glamour, Lore, and Valor.

Traveling from town to town, singing songs and telling tales, bardic life is traditionally associated with the adventures of other people spun into stories that a bard will tell or sing in exchange for a few coins. Yet there are many bards who pursue a life of adventure themselves. After all, what could be more glorious than singing songs where *you* are the star?

Bards understand that story and song have the power to reshape reality. There is magic in these gifts, and bards harness that magic to achieve great deeds. A talent for music is something all bards share, but playing an instrument and singing songs are not the only styles of performance available to them. You might prefer to be a poet, an actor, an acrobat, a dancer, or a clown.

Although most bards prefer to assist their allies from the sidelines, they are able to defend themselves with spells that enhance both weapons and armor. That said, their magic leans toward charms and illusions rather than destructive power. The end of a life is the end of a story, after all, and bards tend to believe that there is always a chance for redemption so long as a story continues to be told.

EQUIPMENT AND ATTRIBUTES

Armor Bards tend to travel light, using only leather or studded-leather armor.

Weapons They favor graceful defenses such as rapiers, swords, and hand crossbows, along with daggers, hand axes, and slings.

Musical Instruments Almost all bards play some sort of musical instrument, from a simple reed flute to an elegant harp, and their instruments can be used in spellcasting.

Music as Magic A bard's magical music can have many effects, including healing the sick, charming others, or freeing people from mind control.

Inspirational Gifts Bards use music and song to inspire others around them to perform great deeds. If a member of your party is struggling, a bard will often know exactly what they need to hear to turn their fortunes around!

LEGENDARY BARD

FLORIZAN BLANK

PLAYING FLORIZAN BLANK Florizan hates bullies and tyrants, and loves beauty and art. He's warm, charming, and quick to adapt to new situations. He enjoys talking to people to get a sense of their stories and experiences. Having seen life from both the palace and the gutter, Florizan knows that truth and kindness are free to every person, no matter their possessions or wealth.

As the youngest son of a royal family in a small southern kingdom, Florizan Blank studied music, poetry, and dance from an early age. When he was 10 years old, his family was overthrown by traitors; Florizan was the only survivor. Smuggled out of the palace by his music teacher, he was given a new identity and raised in a traveling circus, where he learned bardic magic. He gained a reputation as a great actor, and it was in this role that fortune brought him back to the palace where he had lived as a child.

Florizan saw an opportunity. He wrote and performed a play that exposed the tyrant's crimes and incited a revolution. When offered the chance to retake his throne, Florizan refused, preferring life on the road.

DANDY DUELIST Florizan's stylish appearance and way with words have led many opponents to underestimate him as a fighter, yet his dance training has made him an excellent swordsman. His favorite move is to cast a dancing enchantment on his foe, so that a fight to the death becomes a flamboyant two-step—to the amazement and amusement of anyone watching—until Florizan delivers the finishing blow!

BLANK MASK

Florizan carries a simple pink carnival mask that was given to him by a grateful witch after he used his powers of persuasion to save her from execution. When Florizan wears the mask, he can magically alter his appearance for up to an hour. He uses this mask to impersonate other people or to create fictional individuals from his own imagination.

CLERIC

DO YOU HAVE A CLEAR PURPOSE IN LIFE?

DO YOU SEEK TO INSPIRE THOSE AROUND YOU?

DO YOU DESIRE TO SERVE A HIGHER POWER?

YOU MIGHT BE A CLERIC!

DIVINE DOMAINS Each cleric is devoted to one specific god and each god is devoted to one particular idea or principle. The magic on which clerics draw is tied to these divine domains. Most divine magic falls into one of four domains.

LIFE
Gods that care most for the preservation of life. These clerics are expert healers.

LIGHT
Gods of beauty, rebirth, and the sun. These clerics use cleansing fire and blinding light.

TRICKERY
Gods of mischief and subversion. These clerics may alter their appearance or slip between shadows.

WAR
Gods of chivalry and battle. These clerics use magic to strike their enemies hard and fast!

Gods are a very real presence in the worlds of DUNGEONS & DRAGONS, and they can bestow blessings and power upon their most faithful followers. Among these faithful are the clerics who act as earthly servants of their chosen deity, and who are able to channel divine magic to heal the injured, protect the weak, and smite the wicked.

A cleric's magic is defined by the nature of the god they serve. They wear their gods' symbols, fight in their gods' name, and live every day according to the principles of their faith. This doesn't necessarily mean that they're reserved or quiet characters. Some gods are very raucous and wild!

Clerics will often follow their god's call to set off on an adventure, perhaps to right a wrong, vanquish a foe, or bring home a lost relic. Wherever they go, clerics take their god and their faith with them.

EQUIPMENT AND ATTRIBUTES

Armor Clerics are the chosen warriors of their gods, and often don heavy armor.

Weapons They carry formidable instruments of war, such as swords, hammers, or crossbows.

Holy Symbols Each god has a symbol that is sacred to its faith, and clerics will not only wear these symbols on their armor but also carry physical representations of them, such as a talisman or an engraved shield.

Channeling Divinity Clerics draw on the powers of their gods to cast their magic. The effects vary according to the type of god they serve, and can include powers of healing, destruction, deception, and light.

Destroying the Undead Clerics are the scourge of undead creatures, whose existence is an insult to all the gods. Clerics can channel their divine powers through their holy symbols to drive the undead away or to destroy them.

LEGENDARY CLERIC: BEL VALA

PLAYING BEL VALA Bel Vala is a devout follower of Corellon, the patron god of elves and the protector of life, and she takes her faith very seriously. She believes that Corellon is the source of her strength and her survival. She also considers life to be a holy gift that one must never be quick to take away, even in combat.

HEALING OVER HARM Bel Vala is not enthusiastic about martial combat. She prefers to play the role of healer, focusing her time and energy to ensure her friends and allies prosper. The exception is when she faces the undead. In those instances, Bel Vala is a remorseless warrior who channels a divine light that can eradicate their evil.

Bel Vala was a young novice healer in Tower Crystalis when the earthquake came. Inexperienced and unsure of her strength, Bel found herself trapped among the sick and dying after the tower collapsed. Next came the flood waters, bringing with them an ancient evil. Suddenly, the dead were walking again. The broken tower was filled with abominations seeking to feed on the few remaining survivors.

Bel Vala prayed to her god, Corellon, for guidance. Inspired, she channeled a cleansing light through her body into the fallen shards of the crystal tower, where it refracted a thousand times. The undead were destroyed by this incredible burst of divine power.

Bel Vala woke years later from a deep sleep. She had lost her sight but gained a new clarity of purpose. She was Corellon's humble champion, protector of the living and bane to all undead.

DIVINE VISION Though completely blind, Bel Vala has refined her divination skills to an extraordinary degree, allowing her to sense the thoughts and intentions of those around her. Bel Vala believes that Corellon will guide her through danger and lead her to where she needs to be.

THE CHALICE, THE BOOK, AND THE DAGGER

Bel Vala has been named the caretaker of a set of linked items, said to have belonged to Corellon, which she can summon from a fold of light.

The chalice is Taker, and anyone who drinks from it can be relieved of all mundane injuries and illnesses. The book is Keeper, which keeps a record of those afflictions. The dagger is Giver, and it can pass those afflictions on to anyone it touches. Bel Vala must balance the book by each new moon, or any afflictions recorded in the book will pass on to her.

DRUID

DO YOU FEEL A STRONG CONNECTION TO NATURE?

DO YOU CARE PASSIONATELY ABOUT THE ENVIRONMENT?

DO YOU LOVE ANIMALS SO MUCH THAT YOU WISH YOU COULD BE ONE?

YOU MIGHT BE A **DRUID**!

DRUID CIRCLES Most druids belong to groups called circles, each with unique abilities.

CIRCLE OF THE LAND
Attuned to the earth, these druids tap into ancient knowledge while on their home turf.

CIRCLE OF THE MOON
Inspired by the moon's phases, these druids are skilled shape changers.

CIRCLE OF THE SEA
Drawing on the ocean's power, these druids specialize in elemental and storm magic.

CIRCLE OF THE STARS
Connected with the cosmos, these druids track heavenly omens and transform into constellations.

Druids are champions of the natural world. By attuning themselves to the elements, or by serving the gods who protect nature, they can unlock great mystical powers, including the ability to transform into beasts.

Druids care most about living in peace with nature and maintaining a balance between earth, air, fire, and water. They often defend wildernesses and sacred sites from unwanted intruders, fighting those who would try to control, abuse, or corrupt the natural world—especially undead abominations and unnatural monsters.

Druids are most likely to pursue a life of adventure when they feel the balance of nature is disturbed or that the harmony of their existence is under threat. They feel a sacred duty to the life force that runs through all things, and they will pursue that duty to the best of their ability.

EQUIPMENT AND ATTRIBUTES

Armor Druids use armor and shields made from natural materials such as wood and leather.

Weapons They prefer light, simple arms that have everyday uses in the wilderness, such as spears and slings for hunting or knives and sickles for harvesting. They also favor wooden weapons, or weapons with wooden handles.

Nature Magic Druidic spells harness the power of the natural world, such as exerting control over the weather and the elements, summoning and speaking to animals, and controlling the surrounding environment.

Wild Shape Druids can transform into animals and take on that animal's abilities. This can include land animals such as tigers and bulls, swimming creatures such as dolphins and sharks, and flying creatures such as eagles and bats, or even a swarm of bees! Most druids can't use their other skills, such as spellcasting, while in animal form.

DAWAN PAX
LEGENDARY DRUID

PLAYING DAWAN PAX Dawan Pax is both a devoted ally of nature and a powerful orc fighter. These aspects of his character manifest in the fierce and sometimes brutal way he defends and avenges his animal friends. He prefers the company of animals; and he does not eat meat, which is unusual for an orc.

WIND THROUGH THE GRASS Despite his considerable size, Dawan Pax can move silently and stealthily through wild terrain, at times even becoming magically invisible. He retains the grace and athleticism of the beasts into which he transforms.

Many strange stories have been told about Dawan Pax, an orc also known as The Hunter's Curse for his sabotage of sporting hunts. Some say he was raised by beasts, and that's why he protects them. Others say he's a simple-minded brute who knows no other life. Still others believe that he doesn't exist at all, and he's merely a superstition created to scare strangers away from the wilds. None of these stories are true, and many of them were designed to belittle the fearsome druid—because few hunters have ever found any other way to defeat him.

The truth is, Pax lived an unremarkable life in a small orcish village, where he was raised to be a hunter. His closest friend was an old gray wolf who lived near the village in peace and harmony with the people.

One day, outsiders slaughtered the wolf. Pax found the body. In that moment, he devoted himself to search out the hunters and end their sport. In the pursuit of this end, he has traveled to many lands, becoming a great warrior and honing his druidic arts.

HONORING THE BEASTS Dawan Pax often uses his wild shape to live among the animals he protects. He has also been known to pursue hunters in the forms of animals they have killed. To this day, he still sometimes takes the shape of the old gray wolf.

THE SOUL OF THE EARTH

Dawan Pax carries an ancient piece of polished volcanic stone called the Soul of the Earth, which allows him to cast a particularly advanced form of *scrying* spell. If Pax recovers an arrow or other projectile from an injured creature, he can use the Soul of the Earth to summon a vision of the person who attacked the animal. He retains this vision even when in animal form, allowing him to track down his new enemy.

FIGHTER

DO YOU LIKE THE IDEA OF CHARGING INTO BATTLE?

ARE YOU UP FRONT AND READY FOR ACTION?

CAN YOU KEEP A COOL HEAD WHEN THINGS GET INTENSE?

YOU MIGHT MAKE A GOOD FIGHTER!

MARTIAL ARCHETYPES With so many different fighters out there, having a focal point for your skills can be valuable. There are many archetypes, but here a few examples to help inspire you.

BATTLE MASTER
These fighters carry on enduring traditions of combat and weapon mastery passed down through generations. Studying the techniques of the past gives them knowledge they bring to future conflicts.

CHAMPION
These fighters focus on raw power and strength, honing their physical prowess to deadly perfection.

ELDRITCH KNIGHT
These fighters supplement their battle skills with a bit of magic knowledge, wielding spells that can enhance their abilities and surprise their enemies.

Soldiers, warriors, gladiators, mercenaries, bodyguards—there are as many different types of fighters as there are conflicts needing to be fought with weapon in hand. What all of these occupations share is a mastery of melee combat and a desire to stare down death and not give up.

Fighters encompass a wide range of combatants. There are those who use size and strength to gain the upper hand in battle, yet a number are dexterous or stealthy. Some are adept at long-range fighting with bows or spears, while others wade into hand-to-hand combat with a sword and shield, a polearm, or any other weapon in which they're trained. Whatever their methods or equipment, fighters are almost always at the front line of combat, charging forward to engage their enemies and protect their friends from harm.

EQUIPMENT AND ATTRIBUTES

Armor Fighters are trained to wear any type of armor, from light cloth or hide all the way up to full plate with a shield. Whatever is required, a fighter can wear it.

Weapons Fighters are trained with all regular and martial weaponry, giving them a deep pool from which to choose. Many also have specialized training with unusual weapons, so feel free to get creative.

Second Wind After long days of adventure and combat, when most other adventurers would be exhausted and lose momentum, fighters can dig deep within themselves to regain their strength and keep going. Their resolve inspires the rest of their group to push past adversity.

LEGENDARY FIGHTER

BRUENOR BATTLEHAMMER

MASTER BLACKSMITH More than just a warrior, Bruenor is also a brilliant smithy, able to forge powerful dwarven weapons from even the most difficult materials. The art of crafting a weapon from raw materials and building each component to its proper strength and balance is his lifelong pursuit. Bruenor trained for many years to understand how weapons are made, and it gives him a greater appreciation for how they're used in combat.

Bruenor Battlehammer is a famous dwarven fighter known for his gruff demeanor and impressive fighting skills. Loyal to his friends and vicious to his enemies, Bruenor longed for the day when he and his people could reclaim their ancestral home, the dwarven fortress known as Mithral Hall, from the evil shadow dragon known as Shimmergloom. In time, Bruenor would find a way to make that dream a reality, and it would lead him to be crowned King of Mithral Hall.

In his prime, Bruenor was known for wearing a one-horned helmet, wielding a single-bladed axe, and carrying a shield emblazoned with a foaming mug sigil (the symbol of Clan Battlehammer).

PLAYING BRUENOR Bruenor is abrupt and stubborn, even more so than regular dwarves, who are already known for their dour attitude. In conversation, he doesn't waste time, and that direct approach carries through all his interactions, social and physical.

A headstrong curmudgeon, Bruenor is hard on his friends and family, expecting them to do their best no matter what situation they find themselves in. He's just as hard on himself, pushing his physical limits and charging first into battle so others don't get hurt. Bruenor is a true hero, courageous and caring, even if he doesn't let it show on the surface.

FLAMETONGUE

Bruenor's magic axe, Flametongue, bursts into flame upon his command, creating light and burning foes even as its blade cuts deep. Bruenor becomes the center of attention in combat when he fearlessly raises Flametongue as magical fire pours forth; allies rally around as they rush into battle. A dwarven army at Bruenor's command is an awe-inspiring sight on the battlefield.

MONK

DO YOU WANT TO HARNESS THE MYSTICAL POWER THAT LIES WITHIN?

ARE YOU NIMBLE YET STRONG?

CAN YOU HANDLE THE RIGORS OF A MONASTIC LIFE?

YOU MIGHT MAKE A GOOD MONK!

MONASTERY LIFE Monasteries are typically small, walled communities where monks live a simple, structured life focused on training, study, and, sometimes, farming. While some compounds are isolated, others interact freely with their neighbors, trading their services for food and goods.

Many monks enter the monastery as children, sent to live there because they had been orphaned or their parents could no longer feed them. Others are sent by their parents in gratitude for some service the monks had performed to help their family.

Monks dedicate their lives to the study of a mystical force called ki, which flows through all living creatures in the world. They learn to harness this energy within their own bodies, channeling it into powerful blows and elegant dodges that display uncanny speed and strength. These graceful fighters shun complex weapons and armor, relying upon the power that lies within to achieve their victories!

The life of a monk begins in childhood, when they live in tight-knit communities and their daily training follows a rigid routine. Becoming an adventurer means leaving this structure behind, a harsh transition that few undertake lightly. Adventuring monks generally do not value gold or glory, focusing instead on the pursuit of self-improvement and spiritual enlightenment.

EQUIPMENT AND ATTRIBUTES

Armor Monks choose not to wear any type of armor, since it interferes with the flow of ki.

Weapons Monks can use simple weapons and shortswords. They favor inexpensive weapons such as staffs and clubs that can move with the flow of their martial attacks.

Ki A monk's training allows them to harness the mystical power of ki. This energy allows them to make extra unarmed blows after an attack, improve their ability to dodge, or even disengage from battle with a powerful jump. In the beginning, access to ki is limited, but as monks become more skilled, the amount of ki they harness also grows. Experienced monks are capable of astonishing, supernatural feats using their ki!

Martial Training Most monks begin training in the martial arts at a young age. They may have studied broadly, gaining a basic competence in a wide range of fighting styles, or chosen to focus their training on a single skill, mastering a specific weapon or unarmed attack. Their training emphasizes a flowing, dexterous approach to combat; witnessing a monk in battle is like watching a complex, elegant dance.

WHEY-SHU

LEGENDARY MONK

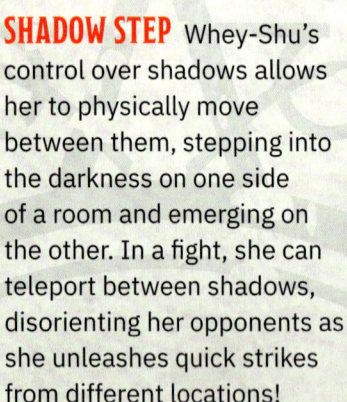

SHADOW STEP Whey-Shu's control over shadows allows her to physically move between them, stepping into the darkness on one side of a room and emerging on the other. In a fight, she can teleport between shadows, disorienting her opponents as she unleashes quick strikes from different locations!

CLOAK OF SHADOW Through the power of her ki, Whey-Shu can become one with the darkness. Unless in a very brightly lit space, she can magically wrap shadows around her body, concealing her from view. In combat, she uses this ability to devastating effect, striking unseen and then vanishing again before her opponent can land a single blow!

KENKU'S CURSE Generations ago, an evil curse took away the kenku's voice and their ability to fly. They can only speak by mimicking words or sounds they have heard before.

PLAYING WHEY-SHU Whey-Shu is quiet but confident, willing to let others talk while she observes and plans. Once she decides to act, she is swift and determined. Her goal is to end a conflict as quickly as possible. If she miscalculates her enemy's strength, she will retreat and reassess before trying again. What matters most to her is the result, not individual setbacks along the way.

There is a famous kenku monk known as Whey-Shu, but that's not her actual name. It's just the closest sound most humanoids can make to her true name, the sound of a soft slipper sliding across a wooden floor. Whey-Shu's name reflects both her monastic training and her quiet presence, behind which she conceals considerable power.

After her kenku flock was saved from a goblin invasion by dwarven monks, Whey-Shu's parents gave her, their youngest child, to the monastery in gratitude. Her inability to communicate relegated her to the role of a lowly servant, and she was assigned to cleaning duties and making copies of sacred texts. Her kenku gift for mimicry soon led her to spend nights practicing the techniques from the scrolls she spent the day transcribing. By the time the monks discovered Whey-Shu's secret training regiment, she had developed incredible control over ki power that rivaled many adults. Despite her youth, Whey-Shu is now widely regarded as one of the masters of the Way of the Shadow, a monastic tradition that emphasizes stealth and subterfuge.

THE WAY OF THE SHADOW

One monastic tradition focuses on the use of ki energy to manipulate shadows and darkness—the Way of the Shadow. Known as shadowdancers, such monks often serve as spies and assassins. Like mercenaries, they are hired by any who can afford their fees. Whey-Shu doesn't mind working for others for money. The one exception is fighting goblins—she still has vivid memories of the invasion that endangered her family and eagerly battles goblins free of charge.

PALADIN

DO YOU LONG TO SERVE A NOBLE CAUSE?

ARE YOU EQUALLY HAPPY HELPING FRIENDS AND SMITING ENEMIES?

DO YOU WANT TO BE THE BEST AT BEING GOOD?

YOU MIGHT BE A PALADIN!

SACRED OATHS Paladins use magic with power derived from a commitment to their gods. To that end, all paladins must swear a holy oath that grants them special spells and abilities. If paladins fail to live up to their pledge, they may be cut off from these powers.

OATH OF THE ANCIENTS
Paladins who take this oath are dedicated to love and kindness. They have the power to channel the wrath of nature and use other nature-based spells.

OATH OF DEVOTION
Paladins who take this oath are dedicated to the causes of honesty, virtue, and compassion. They can bless their weapons and use spells of protection and revelation.

OATH OF VENGEANCE
Paladins who take this oath are dedicated to punishment and retribution. They can grant themselves advantage in battle and use other spells to help destroy their enemies.

Some adventurers seek glory, some seek wealth, and some seek excitement, but paladins pursue a life of adventure in service to a higher calling. They are warriors and champions of righteousness who fight the wicked and save the innocent because they've been called by their god or gods to do so. And their gods imbue them with divine gifts to make them better servants. However, if a paladin ever fails to live up to their gods' ideals, they may find their divine powers leaving them.

Paladins are skilled warriors with expertise in many weapons and fighting styles, but they're also adept spellcasters who channel the power of their gods to help or heal those around them, or to smite their foes with a single devastating blow. Paladins are typically very disciplined fighters who head into battle with clear purpose and unshakeable principles.

EQUIPMENT AND ATTRIBUTES

Armor Like fighters, paladins are trained to wear any type of armor, from light cloth or hide all the way up to full plate with a shield.

Weapons Paladins are trained with all regular and martial weaponry, so they have many options when heading into battle.

Healing Touch Paladins are blessed with the ability to heal wounds, cure disease, or remove poisons by laying on hands. Paladins are immune to disease because of the power flowing through them.

Divine Powers Devotion to their gods gives paladins special abilities, including the power to sense whether a person is wicked or good and the power to channel divine energy into a strike known as Divine Smite. Some paladins can also project an aura that protects or inspires those around them.

Martial Prowess Paladins are soldiers of faith, and they are well trained in the ways of battle. Some choose to be great defensive fighters, protecting those in trouble. Others choose to be great offensive fighters, putting all their energy into smiting!

LEGENDARY PALADIN REDCLAY

CLEANSING FIRE As a dragonborn with fire dragon ancestry, Redclay was born with the ability to breathe fire, but as a master paladin she has a much more devastating ability. For brief periods of time, Redclay can surround herself, and her allies, with a wall of divine flame that destroys nearby enemies while leaving those enclosed untouched by the blaze.

PRAYER OF HEALING Redclay is a devotee of Bahamut, the draconic god of justice. Through her prayers to him, Redclay can heal the sick and injured. She offers particular care to those afflicted by madness or delusion, believing the mad should be restored, not punished.

An orphan dragonborn raised in a remote mountain monastery dedicated to the draconic god Bahamut, Redclay first came to notice one brutal winter when her home was besieged by an army of orcs seeking control of the mountains. A month into the siege, with food almost all gone, Redclay slipped out of the monastery and passed through the enemy camp undetected. She returned leading an army of Bahamut faithful and headed a cavalry charge that broke the siege apart. She was 13 years old.

After becoming a celebrated figure, Redclay was named a general of her clan. Yet she found that neither the life of a soldier nor the life of a monk quite suited her, so she became a paladin, seeking out those most in need of aid and giving them hope when all seemed lost.

Though still quite small for a dragonborn, and so youthful that she retains her childhood name, Redclay is widely respected for the strength of her faith and the scale of her accomplishments.

PLAYING REDCLAY Redclay is a devout and humble warrior who lives a simple life of service to others. Her chosen cause is to help people of good character who are suffering from injustice and have nowhere else to turn. Though she is content to pursue her crusade alone, she will gladly accept the aid of traveling companions if they are also above repute. She will always put the needs of others ahead of her own.

THE WAR DRUM OF BAHAMUT

Redclay's fame makes her an inspiring figure, but she also possesses a drum, given to her by the monks, that can magically inspire all those who fight at her side. Any ally of Redclay within earshot when she plays the drum before battle receives a boost to their courage that makes them fearless and resistant to mind control during the fight.

RANGER

ANIMAL COMPANIONS While some rangers prefer to be solitary hunters, many find friendships with animals in their travels, and some even form lasting fellowships with these animal allies. Here is a short list of possible animal companions.

DO YOU FEEL MORE AT HOME IN THE OUTDOORS?

DO YOU LOOK CAREFULLY AT YOUR SURROUNDINGS WHEREVER YOU GO?

ARE YOU FOCUSED AND METHODICAL?

YOU MIGHT MAKE A GOOD RANGER!

BADGER
Quick, able to burrow, and has a sharp sense of smell.

BAT
Able to fly, can locate things in the dark, and has a keen sense of hearing.

BOAR
Can charge and attack with their sharp tusks.

CAT
Quick, athletic, and has sharp claws.

GIANT WOLF SPIDER
Can spin webs, climb walls, and sneak around.

LIZARD
Quick, stealthy, and can give a nasty bite.

OWL
Able to fly, keen hearing and sight, and has sharp talons.

PANTHER
Sneaky, able to pounce, and has sharp claws and teeth.

RAT
Tiny and easily able to hide, can see in the dark, and has an annoying bite.

WOLF
Keen sense of smell and hearing, with a strong, powerful bite.

Rangers are hunters, scouts, trappers, or nomads. They're warriors of the wilderness who specialize in stopping monsters that threaten civilization. Rangers feel comfortable in nature and can befriend local wildlife, but when it comes to taking down a specific target, they can be deadly and unrelenting.

In combat, rangers know how to use the immediate environment to their advantage. Any tree can be a hiding spot as they sneak up on their prey. Every field can be used to set a trap or snare. With practice, rangers learn how to wield simple nature spells to enhance their stealth, increase their speed, or strengthen their focused attacks.

EQUIPMENT AND ATTRIBUTES

Armor Rangers tend to wear light or medium armor (see pages 148 and 150) so they don't impede their movement or make too much noise.

Weapons Rangers prefer quick weapons to large and bulky ones. Swords, spears, knives, and axes in close combat and bows for ranged combat are the norm. Some rangers specialize in nonlethal capture of their prey, in which case they may use ropes, nets, snares, and even darts with mixtures that knock out their targets.

Favored Enemy Almost all rangers choose a type of monster on which to focus their hunting skills. Some rangers build their entire identity around hunting specific beasts—giant killers, dragon hunters, demon stalkers, or vampire slayers.

Natural Explorer Rangers may also specialize in making the most of a particular type of terrain: arctic, desert, forest, grassland, mountain, swamp, or the strange subterranean land known as the Underdark. Once the ranger enters their preferred environment, that training kicks in and they can be even more effective.

LEGENDARY RANGER

MINSC THE MIGHTY

PLAYING MINSC Minsc is unwavering in his desire to battle evil and he will never back down from fighting for what he believes is good and right, even against enemies many times his size. He is fearlessly courageous, almost to the point of being suicidal. Everything Minsc does, he throws himself into with reckless abandon.

The legendary ranger is an eternal optimist, believing the best of himself, his allies, and everything around him. In Minsc's mind, the world is a very simple place of heroes and villains—either you're good or you're evil. Everyone he considers good should be his friend and everyone he considers evil needs a swift boot in the butt. Minsc's quest to prove he's a legendary hero never ends.

Minsc, and his hamster animal companion Boo, are fabled heroes known throughout a well-traveled part of the land called the Sword Coast. Over the years they have "kicked butt for goodness" many times, defeating monsters big and small while saving lives and building their reputation as great heroes.

The legendary ranger and his hamster are more than 100 years old thanks to an unexpected turn of events. During one of their adventures, the two were turned into a statue by evil magic and then, many decades later, turned back to flesh and blood. Minsc has always been a bit confused about where he is or who his friends are, and this bizarre time shift has only served to enhance his discombobulation.

BOO THE HAMSTER

Minsc is absolutely convinced that Boo is more than the small rodent he appears to be. Minsc tells his allies (and anyone else who will listen) that Boo is a "miniature giant space hamster," which sounds impressive but doesn't make a whole lot of sense. Whether or not Boo has this impressive lineage, he's definitely smarter than the average hamster and is capable of impressive problem solving. What's also apparent is that Boo is fiercely loyal to Minsc and, when things are dire, quite proficient at viciously fighting to defend his closest friend. An angry Boo will rapidly race around his opponent, biting, scratching, and attacking vital areas, including eyes, ears, the nose, and even "down below." Most enemies assume a hamster is not much of a threat, but a bum-bite from Boo quickly changes their minds.

ROGUE

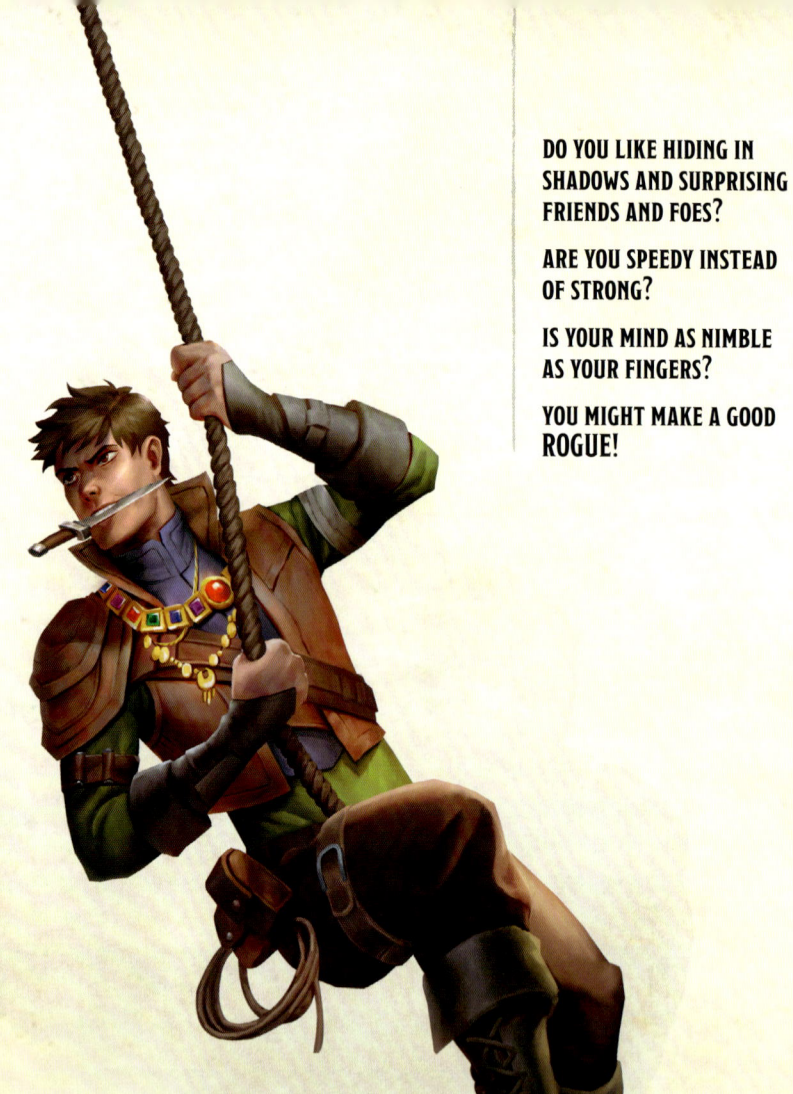

DO YOU LIKE HIDING IN SHADOWS AND SURPRISING FRIENDS AND FOES?

ARE YOU SPEEDY INSTEAD OF STRONG?

IS YOUR MIND AS NIMBLE AS YOUR FINGERS?

YOU MIGHT MAKE A GOOD ROGUE!

THIEVES AND ASSASSINS When you have a reputation for sneaking around, picking locks, and going where you're not welcome, it's easy to see why common folk consider rogues as criminals. In many cases, they're not wrong. Many rogues break the law and take things that aren't theirs, but not all of them are evil. Some rogues do what they do for the thrill of adventure, enjoying the challenge of solving puzzles and exploring dangerous places.

Rogues are problem solvers. They rely on stealth and dexterity over big weapons and bigger muscles. When you need to get in somewhere without making a sound, pick a complex lock on a treasure chest, or set off a deadly trap without anyone getting hurt, you call in a rogue.

When it comes to combat, rogues rarely charge into battle. Remember, they're not fighters or paladins. A rogue would rather sneak up on a bad guy and make a precise strike that will impair the target. Successful rogues are versatile and resourceful, always looking for a solution that keeps them out of danger while getting them closer to filling their pouches with gleaming treasure.

EQUIPMENT AND ATTRIBUTES

Armor Rogues wear light armor (see page 148) so they can keep moving quickly while staying quiet.

Weapons Rogues tend to use small and fast weapons—daggers, rapiers, short-swords, small crossbows, and so on. They value weapons that they can easily conceal and pull out at a moment's notice.

Sneak Attack Rogues specialize in distracting or surprising enemies in order to strike them in a vulnerable spot. In combat, rogues leave the loud and flashy attacks to their heavily armored friends while moving in from the sidelines like a cat ready to pounce at the perfect time.

Thieves' Cant Rogues have their own special form of communication. A combination of hand movements, facial expressions, symbols, and slang, it allows them to carry on a conversation without non-rogues knowing what they're really talking about. It's a good tool for gaining information in a seedy part of town or helping out a friend who shares the same profession.

LEGENDARY ROGUE

SHANDIE FREEFOOT

TRICK SHOTS Shandie's skill with a bow has reached such incredible levels that she can fire arrows into darkness and hit her target based solely on sound, or shoot into a windstorm and compensate for the violent changes in trajectory. Once Shandie sets her mind to hitting a target, her arrows almost always find their mark.

BOWYER AND FLETCHER Shandie decided she didn't just want to master firing a bow, she wanted to understand every aspect of its creation. She studied how to craft her own bow from a single piece of wood and even whittle her own arrows. Controlling every part of the process has given Shandie even more confidence with her favorite weapon.

Shandie Freefoot is an infamous thief and archer based in Baldur's Gate, a coastal city with a reputation for secrets and scoundrels. She grew up on the rough and tumble streets of the Lower City and quickly learned that if she wanted to survive, she needed to be fast on her feet and even faster with her wit and weaponry. The first time Shandie saw a bowman gracefully launch an arrow into a bull's-eye, she knew she had to master archery. Halfling elders told her that her small size would make it too difficult to carry a bow and strike targets across a battlefield, but she took that as a challenge. With years of practice, Shandie learned how to rapidly climb to high vantage points and effortlessly fire arrows while constantly staying on the move. Any opponents underestimating this stealthy halfling rogue soon realize how dangerous she is as a volley of arrows bear down on them from unexpected rooftops or shadowy corners.

PLAYING SHANDIE Shandie is confident and cool under pressure. She's been through enough scrapes to know that she can figure a way out of almost any situation. Once she draws back an arrow and prepares to fire, she is completely focused, holding perfectly still while she decides how much speed and power she'll need to strike her target.

THE QUIVER OF EHLONNA

Over the course of her adventures, Shandie acquired a magical quiver. A regular quiver can hold approximately twenty arrows and weighs about 2 pounds. The Quiver of Ehlonna looks like a well-crafted piece of equipment, but few people realize it can hold up to sixty arrows in the exact same space and with the same weight as a normal quiver. When Shandie draws an arrow, the quiver magically replenishes, keeping her well stocked in combat and surprising foes who assume she's run out of ammunition.

SORCERER

DO STRANGE THINGS HAPPEN WHEN YOU'RE AROUND?

DO YOU COPE POSITIVELY WITH UNCERTAINTY AND CHAOS?

DO YOU TRUST YOUR INTUITION?

YOU MIGHT BE A SORCERER!

DRACONIC BLOODLINES

Draconic-bloodline magic comes from the intersection of a dragon's magic with either you or your ancestors. As you learn to channel this magic, the imprint of the dragon will begin to manifest. At first, you will be able to speak draconic, the ancient language of dragons. As your power grows, dragonlike scales will appear on your skin, increasing your resistance to damage. Powerful draconic-bloodline sorcerers have even been known to sprout dragon wings that allow them to fly!

Your draconic ancestor can be one of any of the different types of dragons, and your magic will be influenced by the dragon you select. See *The Monsters & Creatures Compendium* for more details about dragon types and their powers.

Sorcerers are born with an innate magic, one they did not choose but cannot deny. This magic may come from a draconic bloodline, an otherworldly influence, or exposure to unknown cosmic forces. In some cases, the sorcerer may have no idea why or how their magic developed, leading them on a lifelong quest to uncover the source of their power. This wild magic can be unpredictable and dangerous, with startling side effects at the most awkward moments.

Most sorcerers find themselves drawn to a life of adventure sooner rather than later. The magic in their veins does not like to lie dormant. Those who don't learn to channel their power may find their gifts spilling out anyway, in unexpected and often unpleasant ways.

EQUIPMENT AND ATTRIBUTES

Armor Too much gear can interfere with a sorcerer's magic, so they wear no armor.

Weapons They can use only simple armaments such as daggers, darts, quarterstaffs, and light crossbows.

Font of Magic The deep wellspring of magic within each sorcerer allows them to cast magical spells at will. Fledgling sorcerers begin with the power to cast a few spells each day. As they gain more understanding of their inner magic, that number increases.

Metamagic Unlike spells learned by rote memorization, a sorcerer's magic is intuitive and flexible. With a little experience under their belts, they can learn to alter spells to suit their needs. Some examples of metamagic include shielding allies from a spell's effects, extending the range of damage done, or allowing the spell to be cast silently rather than spoken aloud.

LEGENDARY SORCERER

DAMINI MAHAJAN

PLAYING DAMINI MAHAJAN

Like her draconic ancestor, Damini can be proud. She does not tolerate disrespect, especially from those who need her help. When approached politely, she is warm and welcoming, surprisingly down-to-earth for a sorcerer who literally spends all day with her head in the clouds. The air around her cackles faintly with energy and a pale blue light, reflecting the magic held within her diminutive frame.

LIGHTNING ELEMENTALS

Damini can summon lightning elementals to fight on her behalf or to assist with her occult research. These creatures, formed from actual lightning into a humanoid shape, remain for up to one hour after summoning and only obey Damini's commands. These dangerous elementals are attracted to metal and will damage any living flesh that they touch.

Born to a long line of draconic sorcerers descended from a powerful blue dragon, Damini Mahajan displays an extraordinary control over lightning. Her powers manifested at an early age, and she spent her childhood learning to transform tiny sparks into crackling bolts of electricity. Now in her seventies, her mastery over this volatile element has reached the level of legend.

Damini is best known for her leadership in the war against the Batiri, a tribe of goblin fighters lead by Queen M'bobo to invade the neighboring kingdom. In a desperate last stand, when the rest of her party had been knocked unconscious, Damini summoned a lightning storm so powerful that it killed more than eighty goblins with a single blast. The backlash from her spell left the distinctive spiral scar that still marks one side of her face.

Although her three children did not inherit her magic, the power has manifested in two of her grandchildren. Damini has dedicated her remaining days to training them as the next generation of Mahajan sorcerers.

MAHAJAN TOWER

Damini lives in Mahajan Tower near the peak of Mount Pentos, where she can be close to the clouds that fuel her research. Two of her grandchildren reside with her in the spiraling column, learning to control their own magical abilities. From time to time, Damini takes on students from outside her family line, teaching them to understand and master their newfound mystical talents.

WARLOCK

ARE YOU DRIVEN TO PURSUE KNOWLEDGE, WHATEVER THE COST?

ARE YOU ABLE TO BACK UP YOUR MAGIC WITH PHYSICAL FIGHTING SKILLS?

ARE YOU PREPARED TO SERVE SOMEONE ELSE'S WILL IN TRADE FOR POWER?

YOU MIGHT BE A **WARLOCK!**

PACT BOON A warlock's magic can include access to several class-exclusive magical skills, if their patron deems them worthy.

PACT OF THE BLADE
The warlock learns to create a magical melee weapon out of thin air, so they are never unarmed.

PACT OF THE CHAIN
The warlock can summon a magical familiar, a spirit that looks like a small animal and obeys the warlock's commands.

PACT OF THE TOME
The warlock can create a magical book, called a grimoire, that contains three spells the warlock can always cast, so long as the book is in their possession.

Warlocks are driven by the pursuit of knowledge above all other things. Their power comes not from innate talent or long study, but by making a lifelong pact of service to an otherworldly force. These patrons, as they are called, can take a variety of shapes, from ancient magical creatures to dark beings from forgotten places.

Whether good, evil, or simply indifferent to mortal affairs, all patrons require a price from those they aid. This may be as simple as a few tasks here and there, or as complex as running a vast following devoted to the patron. In trade for their service, the warlock is given access to arcane wisdom and magics beyond the realm of most mortals.

Some warlocks enjoy a good relationship with their patron, like that between a teacher and a favored student. Others struggle with the demands placed on them by their pact. In either case, their powerful spells and deep occult insight make warlocks a valuable addition to any party, even if their true loyalty may sometimes be uncertain.

EQUIPMENT AND ATTRIBUTES

Armor Warlocks don't shy away from getting their hands dirty, and can wear light leather armor to get the job done.

Weapons They wield a range of simple weapons, such as daggers, shortbows, crossbows, and hand axes.

Eldritch Invocations Fragments of occult lore uncovered during a warlock's studies, these powerful incantations allow the warlock to cast certain spells with ease.

Pact Magic A warlock starts their adventures knowing two cantrips (see page 88) and two regular spells, taught to them by their patron, and learn more as they gain experience.

LEGENDARY WARLOCK

ZANIZYRE CLOCKGUARD

PLAYING ZANIZYRE CLOCKGUARD Zanizyre is naturally curious and cheerful, but the weight of her patron's evil often weighs on her, inspiring fits of melancholy. She does her best to help others and always takes the opportunity to do a good deed. However, she is unable to refuse her patron's requests. Since Tiamat is a creature bent on destruction, this means Zanizyre sometimes finds herself committing terrible crimes. Even so, she will refuse any attempts to be freed from Tiamat's service.

Fearsome warlock Zanizyre Clockguard is among the few mortals gifted with the patronage of Tiamat, the legendary Queen of Evil Dragons. There are many rumors as to how Zanizyre gained Tiamat's attention, but the most persistent tale is that she rescued an injured dragon hatchling and brought it to one of Tiamat's temples. Zanizyre refuses to answer questions on the matter, saying only that it was fate.

Driven to explore the world in her endless quest for knowledge, Zanizyre rarely stays in one place for long. She is known for using her magical powers to help the oppressed and downtrodden, and many a small town is grateful for her well-timed help against an invading force. Some say she is making amends for the terrible service demanded by her patron, for Tiamat is an evil creature dedicated to wiping out all mortal life.

DOMINATE DRAGON This powerful spell is a variation on the *dominate monster* spell (see page 120) and allows Zanizyre to force a dragon to do her bidding. Dragons are notoriously difficult to subdue with magic, between their resistant hides and own innate magical natures. Although Zanizyre rarely uses this spell, it always makes an impression. The sight of a three-foot-tall gnome charging into battle on the back of a mighty dragon is not easily forgotten!

TIAMAT'S FANG

Zanizyre's pact boon is a magical shortsword known as Tiamat's Fang. This weapon can deliver damage related to each of Tiamat's five heads, allowing Zanizyre to choose between acid, lightning, poison, fire, or freezing effects each time she summons the weapon. This ability to tailor attacks to her opponent's weakness makes Zanizyre a deadly and unpredictable foe.

WIZARD

DO YOU ENJOY READING AND STUDYING NEW THINGS?

DO YOU YEARN FOR A LIFE OF MAGIC AND ADVENTURE?

DO YOU DESIRE MAGICAL POWER?

YOU MIGHT BE A WIZARD!

A WIZARD'S SPELLBOOK A good spellbook is crucial to any wizard. You can write new spells in your book, expanding your powers with each new entry. Spellbooks can range in appearance from plain, travel-worn volumes to ornate tomes decorated with precious gemstones. No matter how fancy, the true value of a spellbook lies in the magic words written upon its pages!

If your spellbook is ever destroyed, you can recover only the spells you have currently memorized. For this reason, many wizards create a backup copy of their book, stored in a safe place while they are off adventuring.

Wizards are the supreme magic users, steeped in occult knowledge and trained extensively in the art of spellcasting. Fire and lightning are within their grasp, along with deceptive illusions and powerful mind control. The mightiest can command powers beyond imagination, including visions of the future and gateways that connect to strange dimensions beyond our reality.

For wizards, improving their spellcraft is their driving motivation; all else is secondary. They learn from many sources, including experimentation, libraries, mentors, and even ancient creatures willing to trade insight for personal favors. Most wizards spend years in intense study before embarking on their adventures.

However, unlike warlocks, wizards refuse to be bound in service to any creature or ideal. Their greatest personal treasure is their spellbook, where they make note of all the rituals, magical words, and arcane knowledge that they uncover during their travels.

EQUIPMENT AND ATTRIBUTES

Armor To effectively cast spells, a wizard must be able to move freely. Most wear no armor.

Weapons They use only simple defenses such as darts, slings, daggers, quarterstaffs, and light crossbows.

Spellbook Wizards begin with just six spells written in their spellbook, and can memorize two for quick use during a battle. They can switch up which spells they have memorized, but only when they have a few hours to rest and prepare.

Spellcasting Wizards have limits in their spellcasting power, although this grows as they gain experience. To begin with, a wizard can cast only a few spells before needing rest.

MORDENKAINEN
LEGENDARY WIZARD

PLAYING MORDENKAINEN Brilliant and well-read, Mordenkainen does not tolerate fools. He prefers to listen rather than talk and is skilled at encouraging others to share their thoughts with him. When he does speak, his words evoke authority and confidence. He can be stubborn and difficult, and rarely changes his mind once he decides on a course of action.

A one-man peacekeeping force, Mordenkainen has created some of the most powerful spells known throughout the realms. His strong opposition to moral absolutes means that he can appear as a friend or foe, depending on his current goals and fickle mood. Above all, he is driven by a desire for balance, never letting the cosmic scales tip too far toward either good or evil.

Mordenkainen's origins are unknown, although he is thought to have been born along the Wild Coast of Greyhawk, an untamed land filled with hardship and danger. He came to prominence as the founder of the Citadel of Eight, a collective of magic users who sought to keep peace throughout the lands of Oerth. The Citadel disbanded after a hard-fought battle at the Temple of Elemental Evil, where one member lost his life. Two years later, Mordenkainen founded the Circle of Eight, which continues to operate under his guidance.

A skilled leader and political manipulator, Mordenkainen is always looking to expand his arcane understanding of good and evil as an agent of true neutrality.

MORDENKAINEN'S SPELLS

As one of the most powerful wizards to have ever lived, Mordenkainen is responsible for creating many new spells, including the following:

MORDENKAINEN'S MAGNIFICENT MANSION

This incantation creates an extradimensional dwelling that exists for up to twenty-four hours. The house appears with enough food to feed one hundred people and contains a staff of one hundred ghostly servants, although these specters cannot attack or leave the mansion.

MORDENKAINEN'S FAITHFUL HOUND

This spell summons a phantom watchdog that can see through illusions yet remains invisible to every creature but the spellcaster. The hound will remain for up to eight hours, although it will vanish if the spellcaster moves more than one hundred feet from the spot where the summoning occurred.

MORDENKAINEN'S SWORD

Casting this invocation conjures a shimmering elemental sword made of pure force, which hovers in the air before the spellcaster. The sword will deliver melee attacks against chosen targets on command. It lasts for one minute before dissolving.

MARTIAL CLASS FLOWCHART

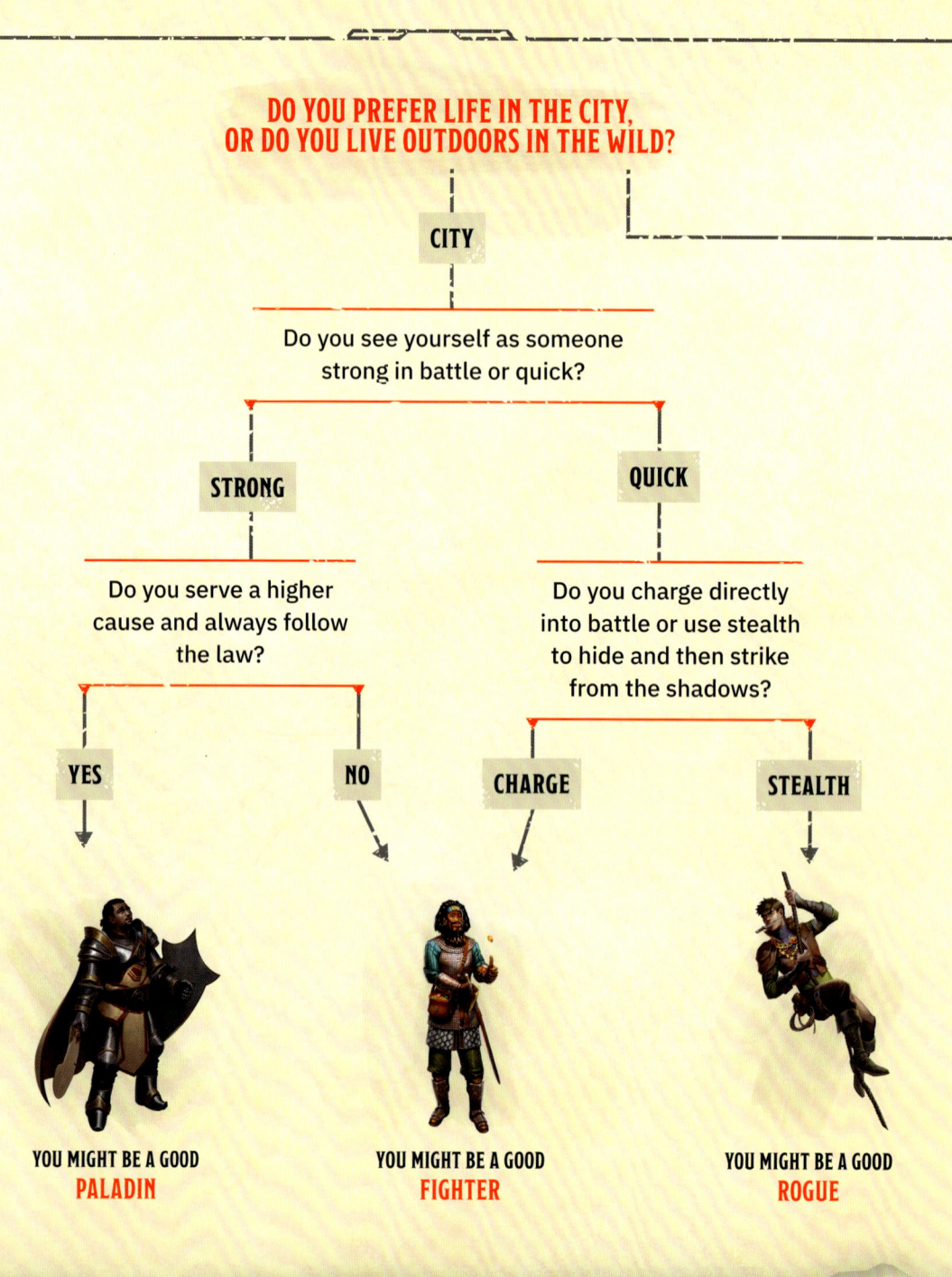

DO YOU PREFER LIFE IN THE CITY, OR DO YOU LIVE OUTDOORS IN THE WILD?

CITY

Do you see yourself as someone strong in battle or quick?

STRONG

Do you serve a higher cause and always follow the law?

- **YES** → YOU MIGHT BE A GOOD **PALADIN**
- **NO** → YOU MIGHT BE A GOOD **FIGHTER**

QUICK

Do you charge directly into battle or use stealth to hide and then strike from the shadows?

- **CHARGE** → YOU MIGHT BE A GOOD **FIGHTER**
- **STEALTH** → YOU MIGHT BE A GOOD **ROGUE**

Choosing a character class can be difficult. Answer these questions for help choosing a character who excels in combat.

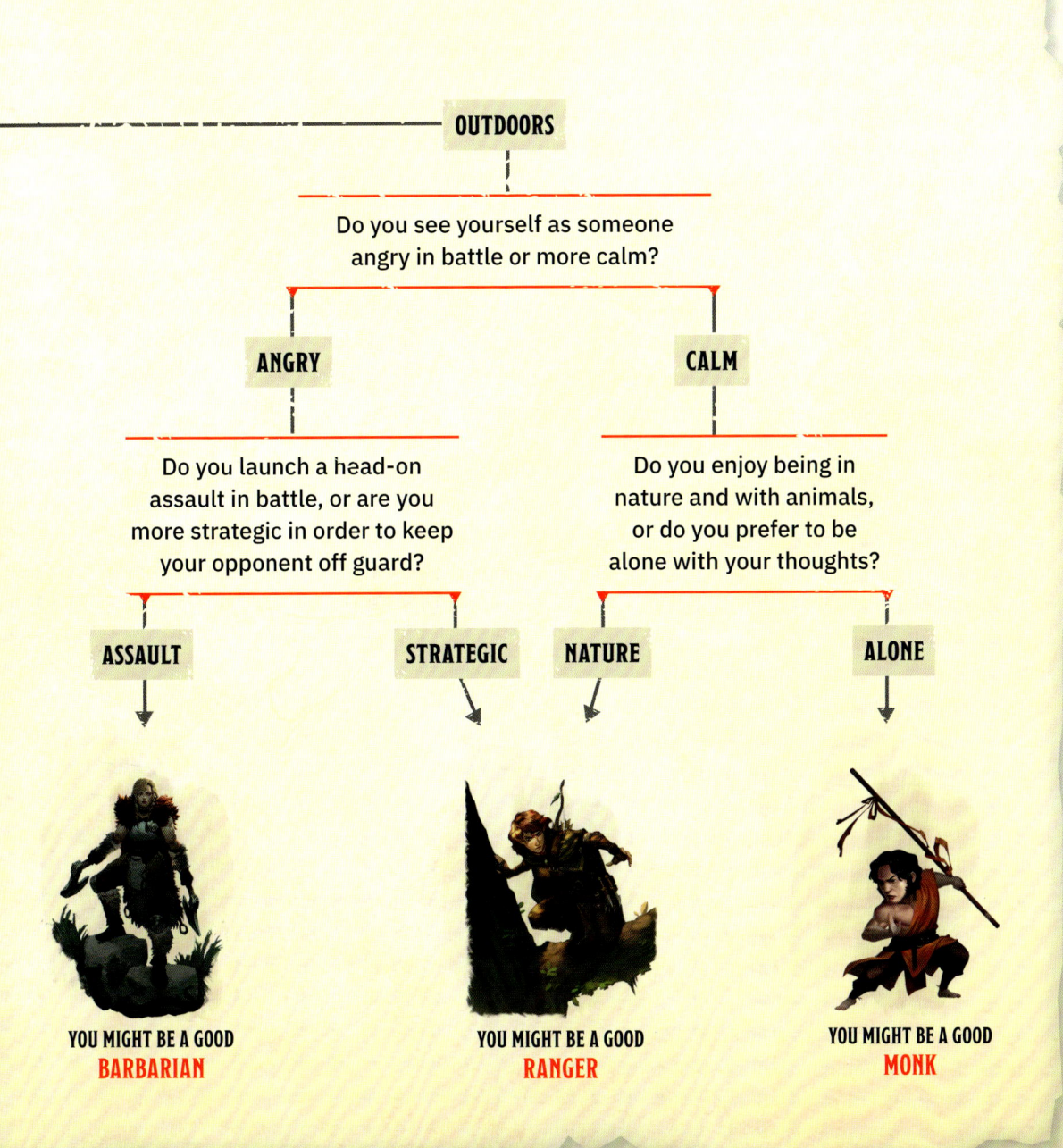

OUTDOORS

Do you see yourself as someone angry in battle or more calm?

ANGRY — **CALM**

Do you launch a head-on assault in battle, or are you more strategic in order to keep your opponent off guard?

Do you enjoy being in nature and with animals, or do you prefer to be alone with your thoughts?

ASSAULT — **STRATEGIC** — **NATURE** — **ALONE**

YOU MIGHT BE A GOOD
BARBARIAN

YOU MIGHT BE A GOOD
RANGER

YOU MIGHT BE A GOOD
MONK

MAGICAL CLASS FLOWCHART

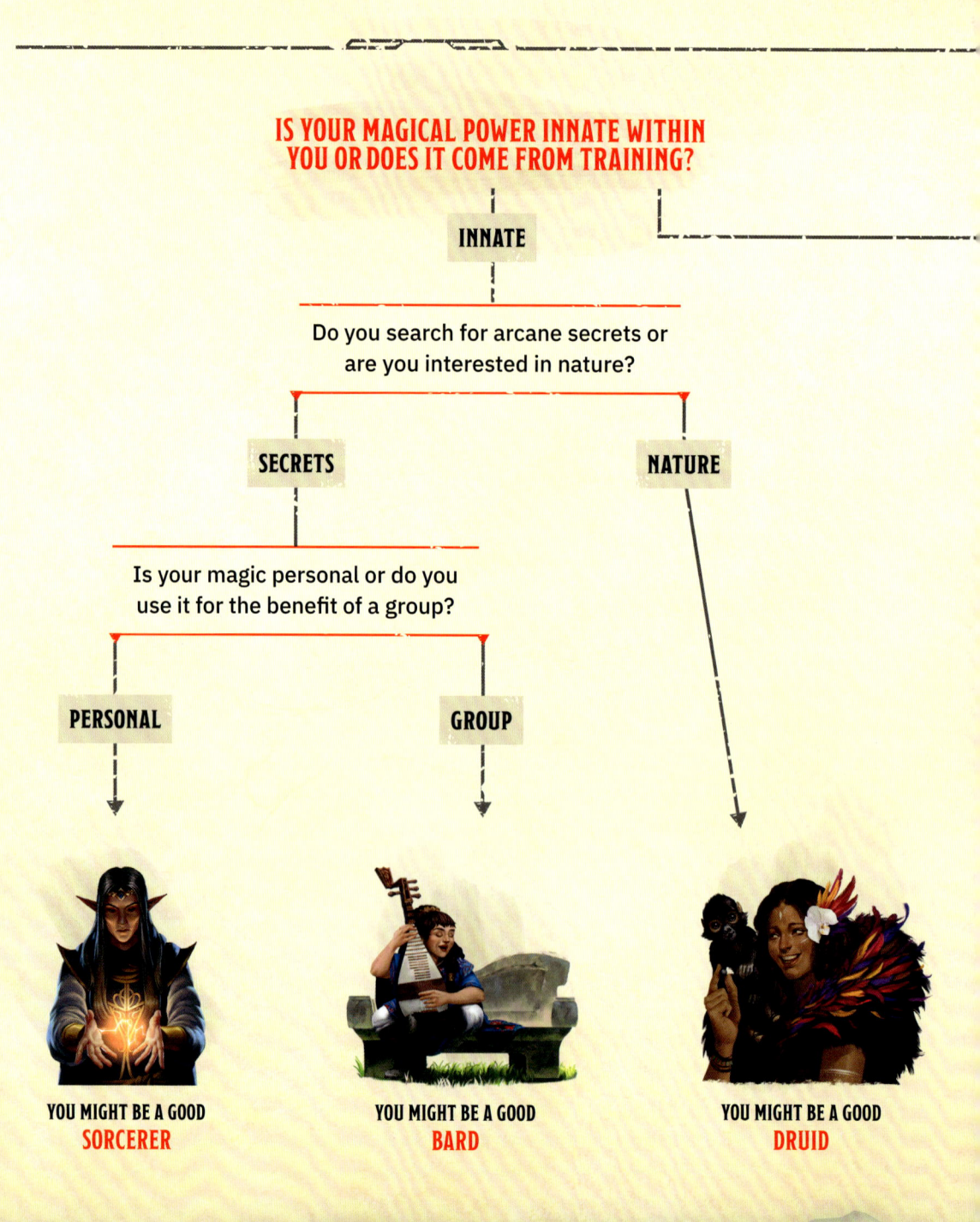

IS YOUR MAGICAL POWER INNATE WITHIN YOU OR DOES IT COME FROM TRAINING?

INNATE

Do you search for arcane secrets or are you interested in nature?

SECRETS — **NATURE**

Is your magic personal or do you use it for the benefit of a group?

PERSONAL — **GROUP**

YOU MIGHT BE A GOOD
SORCERER

YOU MIGHT BE A GOOD
BARD

YOU MIGHT BE A GOOD
DRUID

Choosing a character class can be difficult. Answer these questions for help choosing a character who excels in using magic.

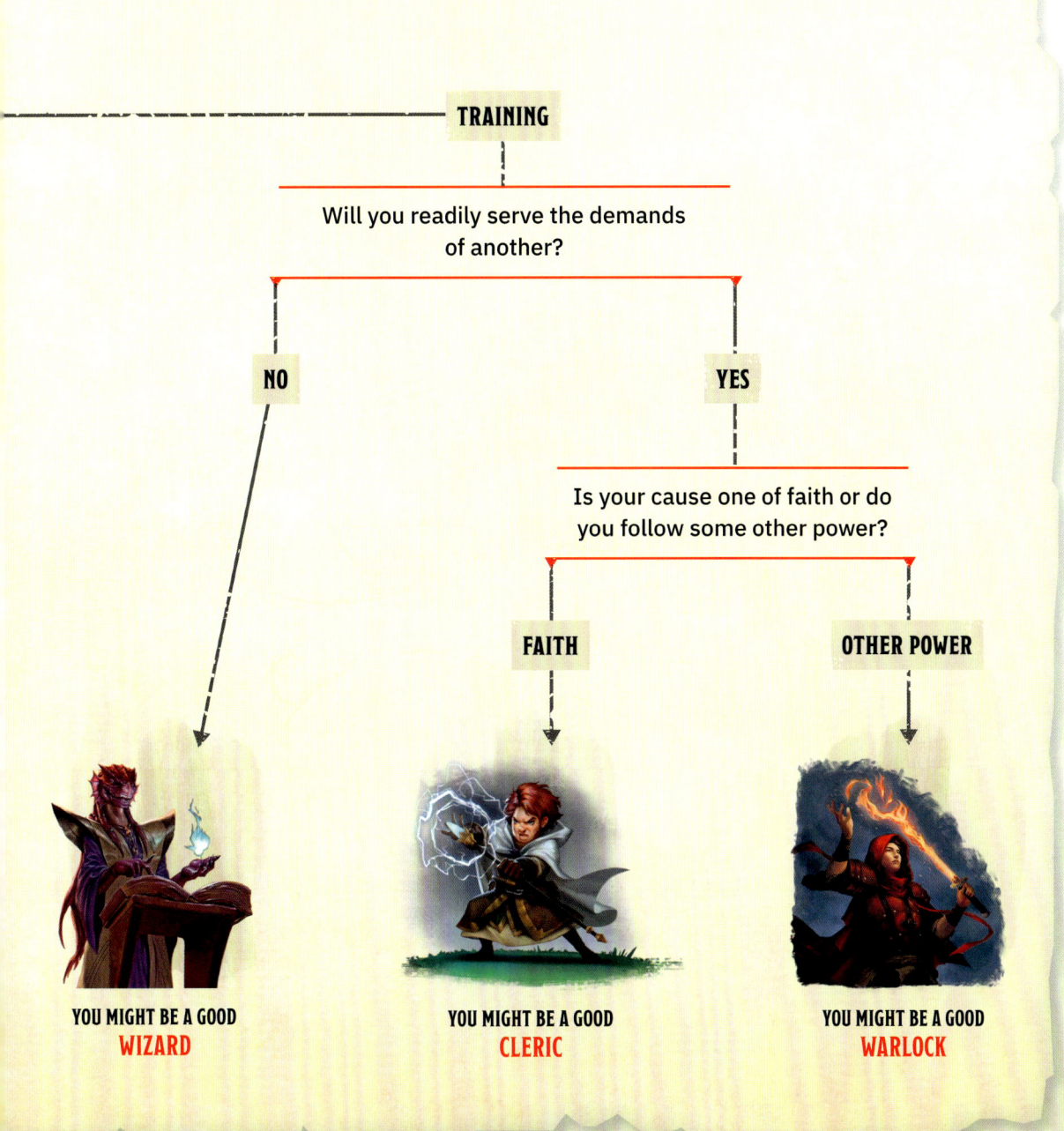

TRAINING

Will you readily serve the demands of another?

NO

YES

Is your cause one of faith or do you follow some other power?

FAITH

OTHER POWER

YOU MIGHT BE A GOOD
WIZARD

YOU MIGHT BE A GOOD
CLERIC

YOU MIGHT BE A GOOD
WARLOCK

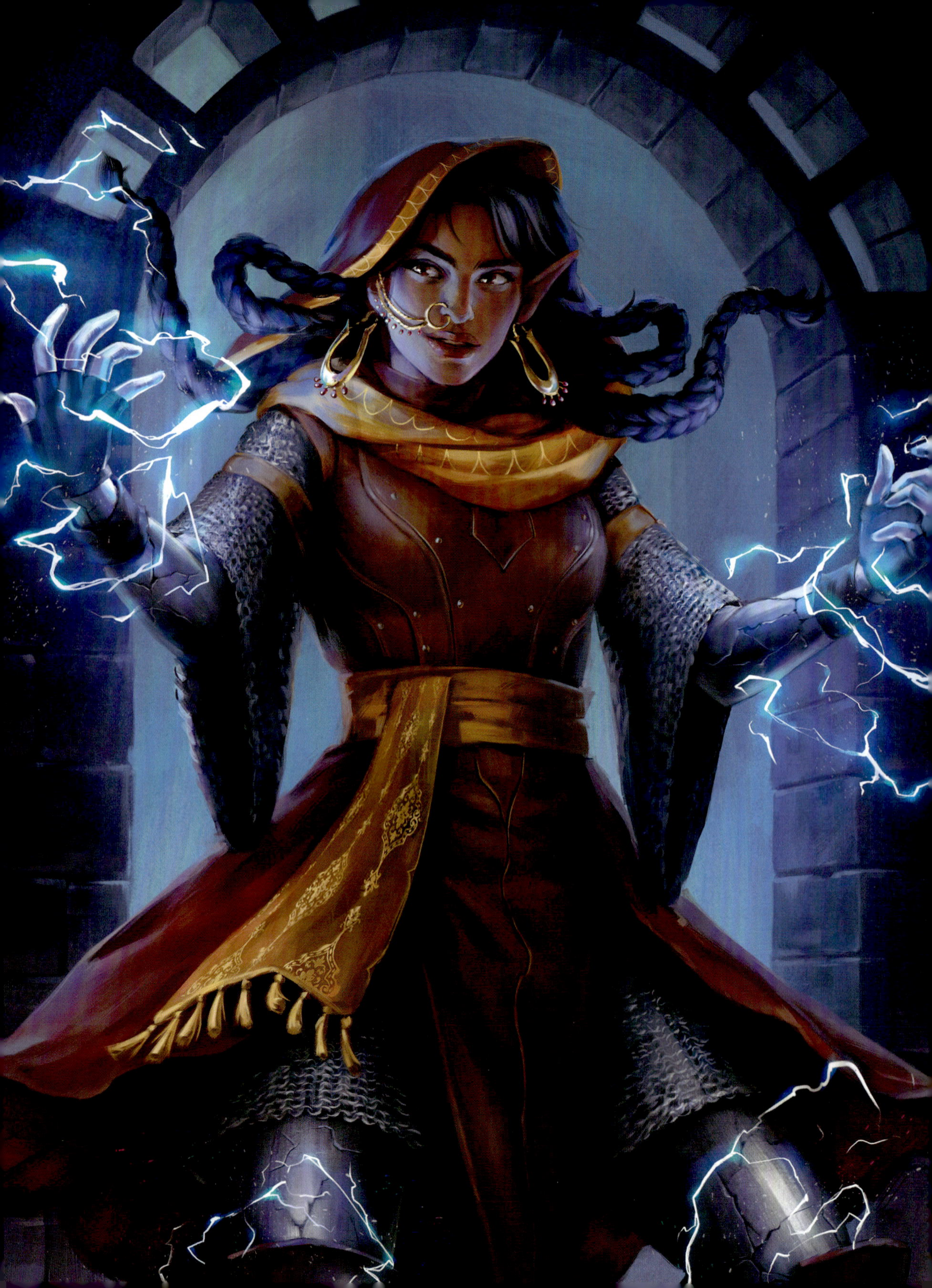

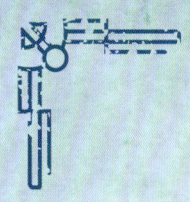

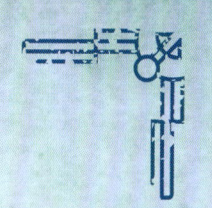

ORIGINS

Every person is shaped in part by their upbringing and experiences. The characters in Dungeons & Dragons are no exception. The game uses two different categories to describe a character's origins: background (page 58) and species (page 63). A background represents your character's formative years prior to the start of their adventures. This includes their education, occupation, and where they grew up. Species represent their family, including their ancestors, cultural traditions, and physical traits.

Remember that no two characters are ever quite the same, even if they come from the same class, background, and species. One outlander elven druid might be proud and solitary, uncomfortable anywhere but their home forest. Another could relish the chance to escape their isolated upbringing, eager to make new friends and explore different environments. The final decision about how your character's origins affect their personality and goals is up to you!

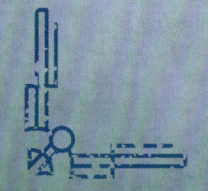

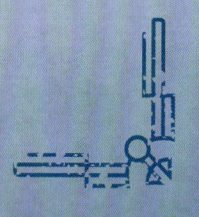

BACKGROUNDS

Backgrounds describe your character's life prior to the start of their adventure. Their skills, abilities, training, and equipment can be affected by their upbringing and experience. If the sixteen options provided here don't seem quite right, you can also collaborate with your Dungeon Master to create your own.

ACOLYTE Raised in a religious setting, your character knows the sacred rites and customs of that faith. Are you still friends with the church? Do you go on quests to raise funds for it?

ARTISAN Apprenticed to a craftsperson at a young age, you learned their trade and how to deal with customers. Did you learn blacksmithing, woodworking, or a different craft? Who was your teacher, and how do you feel about them?

CHARLATAN You became a hustler at an early age, earning your living through scams, lies, and forgeries. Were you inspired by greed, desperation, or something else? How do you feel about the people you deceived?

CRIMINAL You've been a troublemaker for a long time, working as a pickpocket or petty thief. Do you still commit crimes or are you trying to mend your ways? Do you have criminal contacts who might still be looking for you?

ENTERTAINER You thrive in front of an audience, especially one that appreciates your performance. What kind of entertainment do you specialize in—dance, music, poetry, singing, or something else? Are you just getting your start or are you well known?

FARMER You were raised on the land, tending animals, growing food, and learning the patterns of nature. How large was your community? Did you experience hardships like drought or monster attacks, and how did you overcome them?

GUARD You have years of experience with standing watch, patrolling streets, or protecting merchant caravans. Did you protect something specific, like a city, important person, or special place? What friends or enemies did you make?

GUIDE Raised far from settled lands, you grew up immersed in wilderness. You learned to fend for yourself and eventually help others travel the land. What memories, wonderful or frightening, do you carry from those days?

Backgrounds can be used to create links between different characters in a party. Before the adventure begins, they might have been friends, rivals, coworkers, or even enemies. Two soldiers may have fought in the same war, for example, or a merchant may have hired a guard and a guide for a dangerous trip. What other connections between different backgrounds can you imagine?

HERMIT You've lived away from towns and cities for a long time, whether that was in a monastery or completely on your own. What has brought you back from your isolation? Are you excited to reconnect with the world or do you want to get back to solitude as soon as possible?

MERCHANT Your youth was steeped in commerce, learning the flow of goods and money. Your apprenticeship may have been with a caravan, shopkeeper, or other tradesperson. What type of business did you do? Are you still connected to those people?

NOBLE You were raised in a castle, surrounded by wealth and politics. You were well educated on many topics, from leadership and court manners to martial skills. Were you a minor aristocrat or heir to a great kingdom? Do you flaunt your famous name or try to hide your background?

SAGE You've always felt more comfortable reading books and studying scrolls. You have a lot of knowledge, but you've yet to put it into practice in the wider world. What has prompted you to leave your books and go on an adventure? How do you feel about war and conflict?

SAILOR As a seafarer, you've spent more time on water than you have on dry land. You may have been part of a merchant crew, a pirate vessel, or a fishing vessel. Were you a willing crew member or a conscript? Are there any ports where you wouldn't be welcome?

SCRIBE You were trained to carefully copy important documents and books, perhaps at a monastery or government office. Was the work enjoyable or dull to you? Did you copy anything that might get you in trouble, like secret details of a political plot or magical research?

SOLDIER War has always been a part of your life, whether with a mercenary company or as a recruit in a full-size army. Either way, you understand armed conflict and following orders. Are you still hungry for battle or has your opinion changed? Did you earn a high rank or desert your post?

WAYFARER You grew up on the streets, poor and homeless, and learned to fend for yourself. Despite these hardships, you held onto hope for a brighter future. What was the name of the city you grew up in? Do you still have contacts there? If so, how do they feel about you now?

THE WARRIORS & WIZARDS COMPENDIUM

CHARACTER DETAILS

Once you've figured out your main features and where your character came from, it's time to work out the details that will make them unique and interesting.

NAME
Names are important. They create an impression and build expectations. A powerful-sounding name, like "Battlehammer," tells people you're a capable warrior, while a name such as "Fenius" can sound mysterious or sly.

Silly or serious, bubbly or brutal, whatever you choose, make sure it's something that exemplifies the key traits of your character.

HEIGHT AND WEIGHT
You don't need to work out your exact height and weight, but it can be useful to know which species tend to be taller than others.

Every hero has a distinctive element that helps them stand out from the crowd. It might be something internal, like a secret they keep or a piece of ancient lore they discovered, or it might be external, like a special birthmark, an item they carry, or an expertise they have. When coming up with ideas for your character, figure out what makes them special while not overlapping too much with other characters. Everyone in the group deserves to have their own unique feature.

Give your character a big goal to accomplish or a faraway place to visit and you'll see how easy it can be to build a story around their adventures.

OTHER PHYSICAL CHARACTERISTICS You can decide if your character is young or old, as well as the color of their skin, hair, and eyes. Speaking of hair—how much of it do they have and how short or long do they keep it? Do they have any tattoos, scars, or other markings?

Close your eyes and imagine how your character might look. The more distinctive and interesting you can make them, the better.

DON'T FORGET FLAWS

It may seem counterintuitive when you're creating someone heroic, but adding weaknesses can help make someone distinctive. It's fun to think about flaws and make them part of your character's personality.

Is your character afraid of something? Do they have something they hate? Are they dimwitted, quick tempered, disorganized, or scatterbrained? Are they allergic to cats, loose with their money, or do they have an old injury that gives them a hard time?

Give your character at least one flaw and you might be surprised at how enjoyable it can be to incorporate it into their history.

THE WARRIORS & WIZARDS COMPENDIUM

AASIMAR

DRAGONBORN

DWARF

ELF

GNOME

GOLIATH

HALFLING

HUMAN

ORC

TIEFLING

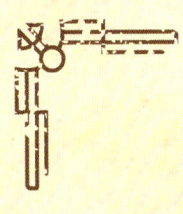

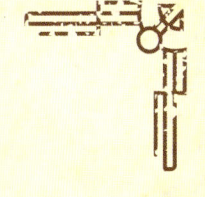

SPECIES

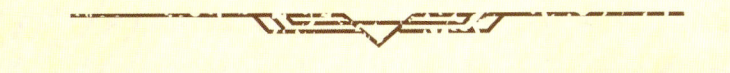

Creating a new character involves understanding the traits they share with you and the traits they don't. Your character can be human, but they could also be one of a wide range of fantasy species. Each member of a species shares some common traits, such as general physical appearance and unique abilities. Even so, that doesn't mean they're all exactly alike.

Clichés about each species are common, such as the idea that all elves are artistic, or all dwarves enjoy mining. Exceptions that disprove these clichés are equally common. Your character's personality and choices are always yours to make. Each of the ten species options presented here is filled with potential that you can unlock when you decide to incorporate it into your character's story.

These include the kenku, flightless bird people; the tabaxi, humanoid cat folk; and the tortles, who resemble giant tortoises.

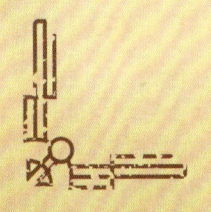

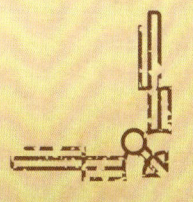

AASIMAR

ARE YOU DRAWN TO LIGHT AND HEALING?

DO YOU HAVE QUIRKY FEATURES LIKE ODD FRECKLES OR GLOWING EYES?

DO YOU SEEM TO HAVE A "CERTAIN SPARK"?

YOU MIGHT BE AN AASIMAR!

AGE Aasimar live up to 160 years, regardless of their parents' species. They mature at the same speed as any non-aasimar siblings, with their celestial abilities appearing as they approach adulthood.

SIZE Aasimar can be born to any other mortal species, and they have the physical traits of their parents. This means they can be found in a range of sizes, from petite halflings to towering goliaths.

Aasimar (pronounced AH-sih-mar) can be born among any group of mortals. Each one carries a spark of the Upper Planes, the realm of celestial beings and holy power. By tapping into this connection, they can create light, power their healing magic, and unleash heavenly might.

Physically, aasimar resemble their parents, except for small details that suggest their heavenly connection. These traits can include metallic freckles, glowing eyes, a halo, or an unusual skin color like silver, shimmery green, or coppery red. Such marks are subtle in childhood, becoming more pronounced once their celestial heritage is revealed.

Divine heritage can be a burden as well as a gift. Some aasimar struggle with the expectations placed on them, both by their communities and by themselves. Siblings may be jealous or resentful. Parents can create pressure with their lofty ambitions. Matters of luck and fate are widely debated among aasimar, who can never be sure if their spark arose from divine intent or random chance.

CELESTIAL REVELATION Once per day, a trained aasimar can briefly transform into one of three different celestial forms. Heavenly Wings creates ghostly wings on an aasimar's back, granting them the ability to fly. Inner Radiance radiates light from the aasimar's eyes and mouth, damaging creatures caught within their glow. Necrotic Shroud can frighten nearby creatures with the sight of an aasimar's dark-filled eyes and huge (non-flying) wings.

ATTRIBUTES

Healing Hands Once per long rest, aasimar can heal a creature by touching them.

Celestial Resistance Aasimar are less affected by damage from holy and unholy or undead sources.

Light Bearer Aasimar can cast the light spell anytime, causing an object to emit bright light for one hour.

DRAGONBORN

ARE YOU PROUD AND DEFIANT?

DO YOU ALWAYS PUT FAMILY FIRST?

DO YOU PUSH YOURSELF HARDER THAN THOSE AROUND YOU?

YOU MIGHT BE A DRAGONBORN!

AGE Dragonborn mature quickly, reaching full adulthood by the age of 15 years. They live to around 80 years old. Dragonborn commonly have one simple name in childhood and take on a different moniker to mark their transition into adulthood.

DRAGONBORN COLORS Most dragonborn scales are brass or bronze in tone. Red, rust, copper-green, and gold hues are also common. A few clans still have a strong bloodline connection to their founding dragon and, in these rare cases, brighter colors, including blue, green, and shining white, can be found.

SIZE Dragonborn are usually taller than most humans, and much more heavily built, with thick hides that make them heavier still. They lack the wings and tails of their dragon relatives, however.

Dragons are some of the most powerful and terrifying creatures you might ever meet. Their humanoid kin, the dragonborn, are a lot more approachable, but still kind of scary!

Descended from dragons and shaped by draconic magic, dragonborn are a noble warrior species, with dragonlike features and powers inherited from their ancestors. These skills are tied to specific types of destructive energy, which are often reflected in the color of the dragonborn's scaly hide. They live in clans that are often linked to a specific class of dragon ancestor, and they proudly worship their dragon gods. Clans are the heart of dragonborn society, and all dragonborn know their duty and strive to serve to their best abilities, whether that means being a great warrior, a great craftsperson, or a great cook. Failure brings shame to the clan, and excellence brings honor. As descendants of arguably the most noble and mighty of all creatures, they feel they have a lot to live up to.

Dragonborn will rarely look beyond their clans for assistance, yet they find that sometimes the best way to serve their clan and honor their gods is to leave everything behind and set out on an adventure, pursuing a great quest or bringing glory to their people.

ATTRIBUTES

Strength Draconic heritage imbues all dragonborn with great physical power.

Breath Weapon Dragonborn can exhale the type of destructive energy associated with their ancestry! Some dragonborn breathe fire, but others expel bolts of lightning, bursts of cold, streams of acid, or clouds of poison.

Resistance Dragonborn have a natural resistance to whatever destructive energy they possess, so a dragonborn who breathes fire is immune to fire, and a dragonborn who breathes acid is invulnerable to acid.

DWARF

AGE Dwarves are recognized as adults by age twenty, but are still considered "young" until age fifty. They live to an average age of 350 years.

DO YOU VALUE HARD WORK AND FAMILY?

DO YOU SOMETIMES HOLD A GRUDGE?

ARE YOU ALWAYS ON THE LOOKOUT FOR TREASURE?

YOU MIGHT BE A DWARF!

SIZE Adult dwarves stand four to five feet tall and weigh around 150 pounds.

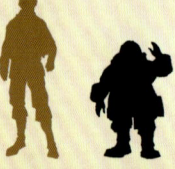

Stout and endlessly loyal, dwarves are a people who value tradition and the bonds of clan and family. They are short but strong as well as resilient due to a harsh life on the mountains, making them quite adept for their demanding work as miners.

Dwarven culture is built around mining. Its rewards inform why dwarves have such a powerful appreciation for the splendor of gold and jewels (and the value of solid iron weapons), and its challenges explain why they form such tight-knit communities that are often hostile to possible rivals, most notably goblins and orcs.

Dwarves can be stubborn and single-minded, which means feuds between rival clans can last for generations. Dwarves that bring their crafting skills to cities far from home will never forget where they come from. In fact, honoring a clan tradition or avenging an ancient wrong are common reasons for dwarves to head out on adventures, though they might also go exploring for the sake of personal glory, in service to one of their industrious gods, or simply for the chance to get more gold!

DWARVEN FEUDS Dwarves have a strong sense of justice and deep loyalty to their clan traditions. A wrong done to one dwarf is considered a slight against the entire clan, which means one insult, if not apologized for quickly enough, can become a full-blown clan feud lasting for generations.

ATTRIBUTES

Tough Physically robust, dwarves can take a lot of hits, and they have a natural resistance to poison.

Handy Dwarves love to develop their expertise in certain crafts, whether it's forging weapons or cutting stone. They know the tools of their trade inside out.

Strong Dwarves that live in tough terrain, like cold and rugged mountains, are particularly noted for their physical strength.

Wise Dwarves that live in less hostile terrain tend to be highly perceptive. Away from the shelter of their mines, they've learned to keep their wits about them.

ELF

DO YOU LOVE MAGIC AND ARCANE MYSTERIES?

DO YOU FEEL OLDER AND WISER THAN YOUR YEARS?

DO YOU PREFER DIPLOMACY RATHER THAN PHYSICAL CONFRONTATION?

YOU MIGHT BE AN ELF!

AGE Elves mature at about the same rate as humans but consider themselves childlike and inexperienced until about their 100th birthday. They typically live for more than 700 years.

SIZE Elves are generally a bit shorter than humans. They are typically very slender and beautiful!

There are places in the world that don't quite seem real; areas of breathtaking beauty where the magic of other realms spills through into our own. It's in these locations that you're most likely to encounter elves, a species known for their elegance, grace, and gifts of enchantment.

Born of otherworldly magic, elves live for centuries, and often seem unfazed by the presence and actions of more short-lived creatures. They prefer to remain in their own secluded communities, but may venture out to share their artistic gifts or martial skills with the world, or to expand their understanding of other cultures. Elves cherish diplomacy and avoid violence if they can, preferring to rely on civility and cunning to resolve conflicts. An elf might master swordplay without ever engaging in actual battle!

Elven society generally falls into three categories. High elves are the most refined, the most haughty, and the most devoted to magic. Wood elves are in touch with the natural world and the skills needed to survive in the wild. Dark elves, also called drow, have adapted to life underground. Though some have a reputation for wickedness, one must never be too quick to judge. After all, being predictable is boring, and elves hate to be boring.

FAVORED WEAPONS Elves excel at armed combat and specialize in different weapons, such as longswords, longbows, crossbows, and rapiers.

ATTRIBUTES

Grace Elves are as dexterous in combat as they are in dance.

Magic Naturally gifted in magic, many elves can perform some simple spells without any study, and all elves have a high resistance to enchantment.

Vigilance Elves have refined senses. They can see clearly in the dark and are very alert to strange sights and sounds. Elves do not need sleep, which makes them excellent at performing watch duties!

GNOME

ARE YOU FASCINATED BY HOW THE WORLD WORKS?

DO YOU SOMETIMES TALK TOO MUCH?

DO YOU LONG TO SEE THE WORLD AND MAKE NEW FRIENDS ALONG THE WAY?

YOU MIGHT BE A GNOME!

AGE Gnomes reach adulthood by about age twenty and live for 350 to 500 years.

SIZE Adult gnomes stand just over three feet tall, about half the height of a tall human. They weigh about 45 pounds.

The small bodies of gnomes hold big personalities, filled with humor, happiness, and positivity that shine forth from their smiling faces. They live in bustling communities carved out of hillsides, where the sounds of hard work and laughter fill the air, though many of them will travel far and wide to seek out adventure and get as much excitement out of life as they can. They always see the best in other people and will often be enthusiastic to join an adventuring party, though their talkativeness can be exhausting for some. They have a lot to say and are happy to share it all!

Gnomes' love of learning makes itself known in their passion for taking on hobbies—and because they live long lives, they can hone their skills in fine crafts, such as woodworking, engineering, inventing, or the study of magic and alchemy. Gnomes never worry about making mistakes, because every error is another opportunity to learn and grow. If there is a bright side to any situation, or a positive way to look at any encounter, a gnome will find it.

GNOMISH NAMES Gnomes love names, and most have a half-dozen or so! These range from the formal, three-part names they use around non-gnomes to affectionate nicknames bestowed by family and friends. Gnomes favor names that are fun to say, such as Zook, Boddynock, Ellyjobell, or Stumbleduck.

ATTRIBUTES

Intellect Gnomes are known for their wit, charm, and smarts, and will often try to talk their way out of difficult situations.

Industrious Many gnomes are natural tinkerers who build wonderful clockwork toys and devices.

Dexterity Gnomes have strong reflexes and an excellent sense of balance. They might prefer to duck out of a fight rather than fight back.

Tricky Many gnomes have a gift for stealth and illusion, allowing them to mask their presence or easily slip away from trouble.

GOLIATH

ARE YOU A VERY PHYSICAL PERSON?

DO YOU FEEL THE WEIGHT OF FAMILY HISTORY ON YOUR SHOULDERS?

DO YOU LIKE TO BE NOTICED BY EVERYONE AROUND YOU?

YOU MIGHT BE A GOLIATH!

AGE Goliaths age at the same rate as humans and might live for about eighty years.

SIZE Goliaths are at the high end of the medium size category, standing up to a couple of feet taller than the average human—maybe as much as eight feet tall.

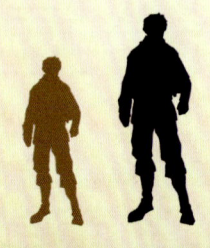

Descended from mighty giants, goliaths are usually tall and imposing. They often have a reputation as big as their powerful frames. Goliaths' gigantic ancestors are dragon slayers, and the wars between giants and dragons are the stuff of legends, so being related to giants is a *big* deal.

Besides their size, goliaths share other features in common with their ancestors. Their skin color and markings might evoke the appearance of a frost giant or a stone giant, for example, and each line of goliaths can access a unique power that they inherited from giants (see Attributes box).

Goliaths are not limited or defined by their ancestors, of course. Some goliaths think that the endless wars of giants sound like a kind of chaos they don't want any part in! They would rather find their own reason to stand out in a crowd.

GETTING BIGGER! Experienced goliaths can tap into an extra ability from their giant ancestry to grow much bigger for up to ten minutes a day, making them faster and stronger during that time.

ATTRIBUTES

All goliaths inherit one of the following special powers from their ancestors:

Cloud's Jaunt Cloud giant descendants can teleport a few times a day.

Fire's Burn/Frost's Chill Fire giant descendants can deal extra fire damage on some attacks, and frost giant descendants can do the same with cold damage.

Hill's Tumble Hill giant descendants are more likely to knock opponents off their feet.

Stone's Endurance Stone giant descendants can sometimes reduce the damage they take from an attack.

Storm's Thunder Storm giant descendants can react to an attack by unleashing thunder.

HALFLING

DO YOU SEE THE GOOD IN EVERYONE?

DO YOU VALUE FAMILY AND FRIENDS OVER FAME AND FORTUNE?

ARE YOU BRAVE ENOUGH TO FACE DANGERS MANY TIMES YOUR SIZE?

YOU MIGHT BE A **HALFLING**!

AGE Halflings are considered adults by age twenty and can live up to 150 years.

SIZE Adult halflings stand about three feet tall and weigh 40 to 45 pounds.

Halflings are friendly, cheerful people inspired by the values of family, home, and simple pleasures. Short and stout, they like to wear bright colors that contrast with their ruddy skin, brown to hazel eyes, and brown hair. Most live in small, peaceful communities within the kingdoms of other species. Displays of wealth and status don't impress them, and there is no halfling royalty. Instead they are ruled by the wisdom of their elders, although there is always room for capable young halflings to make a name for themselves.

Halflings are a curious people, interested in even the most ordinary details about the world. This curiosity, rather than a love of gold or glory, is the inspiration for most young halflings who become adventurers. Others are driven by a danger to their community, putting themselves at risk to protect their families and their friends. Halflings excel at finding simple, practical solutions to problems and bring a touch of home comforts wherever they go. Many an adventuring party has been grateful for the warmth and good cheer that a halfling companion can create in even the most desolate of dungeons!

THE UNSEEN HALFLING Their small size and innate stealth help halflings excel at avoiding unwanted attention. They can slip through busy crowds without being noticed, giving them a great advantage when gathering information or sneaking away from a fight!

ATTRIBUTES

Luck Their knack for finding practical solutions can sometimes give halflings a second chance to correct their mistakes.

Bravery Stout of heart as well as of body, halflings will face dangers that cause other adventurers to flee.

Nimbleness Because they are so small, halflings can evade the attacks of larger creatures!

Stealth Their short stature makes it easy for halflings to hide and avoid unwanted attention.

HUMAN

DO YOU LONG TO MAKE YOUR MARK ON THE WORLD?

DO YOU LIVE IN THE MOMENT YET PLAN FOR THE FUTURE?

ARE YOU BRAVE AND AMBITIOUS?

YOU, YES YOU, MIGHT BE A **HUMAN**!

AGE Humans reach adulthood after about two decades and generally live less than a century.

SIZE Adult humans vary wildly in height and build, but most stand between five feet and just over six feet tall and weigh between 100 and 250 pounds.

Humans are the youngest of the common species, late to appear in the world and short-lived compared to dwarves, elves, and halflings. Ambitious and far-reaching, humans make the most of their short lives, whether by exploration, innovation, or the founding of great empires. They are the most adaptable of all the species, and can be found in the remote corners of the world, from vast deserts and tropical islands to mighty mountains and snow-swept plains.

Diversity is a hallmark of the human species. There is no typical appearance—they may be pale to dark skinned, tall or short, with hair that crosses the spectrum of both shade and texture. Their customs, morals, and tastes vary too. Where they settle, they stay—building cities and kingdoms that persist long after their mortal lifespans have ended. Unlike other species, human communities tend to be welcoming of outsiders as mingling places for all.

Humans who seek adventure are the most daring and ambitious members of a daring and ambitious species. Many are driven by the desire for glory, adventuring to amass power, wealth, and fame. Others are inspired by personal causes, such as a desire to protect their home from danger, to seek out hidden knowledge, or to satisfy their curiosity about the world.

VARIETY IS THE SPICE OF LIFE Humans come from the most varied backgrounds of all characters, giving them access to more knowledge, more languages, and more homeland choices than the other fantasy species.

ATTRIBUTES

Adaptable Humans' flexible nature means that they can easily learn new skills and abilities, giving them an edge when studying or training.

ORC

DO YOU THROW YOURSELF INTO ACTION?

DO YOU SHRUG OFF OTHER PEOPLE'S IDEAS ABOUT YOU?

ARE YOU FULL OF ENERGY AND ALWAYS THE LAST TO TIRE OUT?

YOU MAY BE AN ORC!

AGE Orcs have similar lifespans to other humanoids, maturing in their late teens and living into their eighties.

SIZE Orcs can come in many different shapes and sizes, but they are generally a bit taller and broader than most humans, with an average height of between six and seven feet.

Orc society is rooted in exploration and adventure, as orcs typically live in wandering communities rather than settling in villages and towns. Orcs have journeyed to every corner of the map and beyond, but this instinct for exploration also exposes them to danger. For this reason, orcs believe they were gifted their toughness by the god Gruumsh.

Even orcs who have now settled in towns can still feel that pull to adventure. They may set off into the unknown to chart distant lands, hunt for treasures, or fight terrifying monsters. There appears to be nowhere that orcs won't go!

Orcs have a reputation for anger. Centuries of tense encounters between wandering orcs and other communities have certainly left a lot of people with that impression. Not all orcs are fighters, however. An orc is as likely as anyone to be an artist, poet, teacher, or protector.

APPEARANCE Orcs have some striking physical features, including gray skin and pointed ears, but they are perhaps best known for their impressive teeth. Their lower canine teeth are very prominent and look like the tusks of hippos or boars.

ATTRIBUTES

Darkvision Orcs have impressive eyesight. They can see twice as far as elves in the dark, and just as well as dwarves.

Adrenaline Rush Generations of hunting and fighting have given orcs the ability to call on sudden bursts of energy during times of danger. This allows them to move faster and stay on their feet a little longer.

Relentless Endurance When seriously injured, orcs can draw on reserves of strength to avoid slipping into unconsciousness. Even when an orc appears defeated, they may get back up and keep on fighting.

TIEFLING

DO YOU SOMETIMES FEEL LIKE YOU DON'T FIT IN?

ARE YOU USED TO RELYING ONLY ON YOURSELF TO GET THINGS DONE?

DO YOU TRUST THOSE CLOSE TO YOU, BUT KEEP OTHERS AT ARM'S LENGTH?

YOU MIGHT BE A TIEFLING!

AGE Tieflings age at the same rate as humans and live a little longer.

SIZE Tieflings are similar in size to humans, although their horns and imposing auras may make them seem taller than they are!

Tieflings are linked to the Lower Planes, the home of fiends and devils. Some were born in those dark lands, while others carry the blood of a demonic ancestor.

With their long tails, horns, sharp teeth, and strange pupil-less eyes, tieflings are cursed to resemble devils. Some are defiantly proud of their appearance, decorating their horns or tails with jewels or precious metals, while others try to disguise these features. Their diabolical traits include a natural talent for magic.

Tieflings face considerable prejudice. They are often rejected by their communities, or even their families, so they head out into the world on their own, mistrusted by everyone they encounter. In turn, they tend to be distrustful of others as well.

Despite what superstitious strangers may think of them, tieflings are not inclined toward evil. Their cursed bloodlines determine their appearance, not their character. Yet, because of how they look, they are often denied work, lodging, or a fair chance to prove themselves. The life of an adventurer offers one path for tieflings determined to prove their virtue.

TIEFLING NAMES Some tieflings are given names that reflect their infernal heritage and bring to mind dark magics. Others are named after a virtue or ideal, hoping they will live up to the values embodied by their moniker.

ATTRIBUTES

Presence Tieflings are noted for their magnetic charm. Even people who don't like or trust them will usually find them fascinating.

Fire Resistance Their infernal blood gives tieflings a natural resistance to fire and heat.

Hellfire Attacking a tiefling can be a dangerous gamble, as they can sometimes strike back instantly, consuming their attacker in flames!

Darkness Tieflings have the innate magical ability to create a cloud of shadow that's impenetrable, even to those with darkvision!

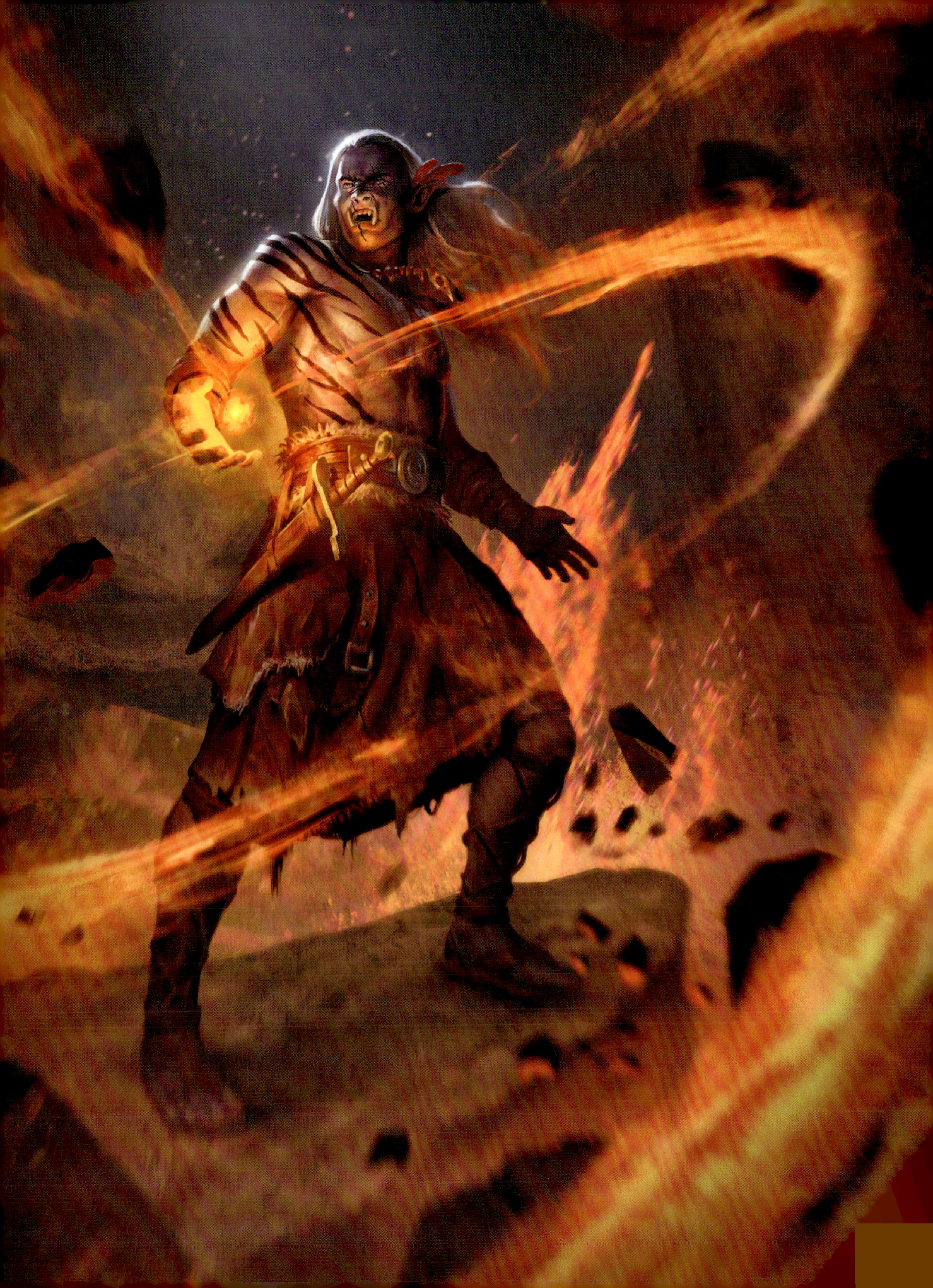

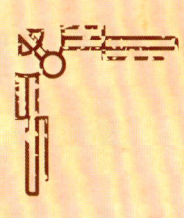

TYPES OF MAGIC

Academies of magic and eldritch researchers have grouped spells and their effects into eight categories called the schools of magic. A magic user can learn spells from multiple schools, although they may find that certain types suit their aptitude and personality better than others.

Abjuration: Block attacks or negate harmful effects.

Conjuration: Transport objects and creatures or bring them into existence from thin air.

Divination: Reveal information such as forgotten secrets, the location of hidden things, or glimpses of future events.

Enchantment: Influence or control others through entrancement or commands.

Evocation: Manipulate magical energy to create a desired effect, including the creation of fire, lightning, or beams of light.

Illusion: Deceive the senses with magical trickery, right in front of one's eyes or sometimes inside the mind.

Necromancy: Use the cosmic forces of life, death, and undeath to strengthen or drain energy from a target.

Transmutation: Alter the nature of things or creatures from their original form.

There's another important way magic can be categorized: Arcane or Divine.

Arcane magic, used by wizards, warlocks, sorcerers, and bards, draws directly upon magical energies to produce their effects. Divine magic, used by clerics, druids, paladins, and rangers, is mediated by divine powers—gods, the primal forces of nature, or a paladin's sacred oath. Both types of magic can be quite potent.

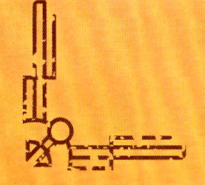

RITUALS & SCROLLS

Most spells are cast in the moment and unleash an immediate magical effect, but there are other ways to cast or store magic—via rituals and scrolls.

A *ritual* is a longer and more involved magical-casting process. It can be used to create increased and sometimes even permanent effects, such as warding a room against intruders. Some rituals involve rare components, carefully chosen locations, or even specific times of the day or alignments of stars and planets in the sky above.

A *scroll* is a spell stored in written form, waiting to be unleashed. Once used, the scroll is destroyed and cannot be used again.

Any creature who can understand a written language can activate a scroll. An adventuring party without a spellcaster can use scrolls to help with healing, protection, or other enchantments needed for their quest.

SPELLCASTING

Of the many different types of magic found in the worlds of DUNGEONS & DRAGONS, the most common are *spells*. A spell is a distinct magical effect created by a caster that alters the normal world in some fashion. Spells can be quite subtle or literally world-shaking in their purpose and power. A well-timed spell can turn the tide of a losing battle or save an adventuring party from ruin. As your hero travels, their magical abilities will grow as they learn new spells by training with a mentor, discovering ancient writings, or exploring their inner power.

Beginning spellcasters can use only cantrips and first-level spells, and they gain access to more powerful levels of magic as they test their abilities and grow in experience. Some spells can be used with any type of magic, while others require a connection to either Arcane or Divine power to be cast. Magic is complex, and so are the rules of which classes can cast specific spells.

Though magic-wielding adventurers can access only a handful of spells at any one time, hundreds are available to them; and many more are waiting to be discovered or even created. There's no way to cover every spell imaginable, so our focus is on four spells for each level that will most benefit spellcasters as their powers develop.

CONCENTRATION

In the following profiles, there are spells where "concentration" is indicated. These spell effects can last longer than the instant they're cast, but only while a spellcaster maintains absolute focus on the magic being used.

CANTRIPS

Cantrips take very little power and concentration, allowing them to be used at will, unlike higher-level spells, which require the caster to rest after using their allotment. In this way, a spellcaster always has a bit of magic to help themselves or their allies in a tough situation.

MESSAGE SCHOOL: TRANSMUTATION

When you cast a *message* spell, you can point your finger at a creature or person within one hundred twenty feet of you, and they'll hear a message from you and be able to respond briefly. No one else can hear the messages, so it's the perfect way to communicate a quick idea in secret.

SPELL TIPS

- You can cast this spell if you know the location of your recipient, even if they're on the other side of a barrier.
- This spell can be blocked by thick stone, metal, or wood if they don't contain any gaps. But a *message* spell can travel around corners or through tiny openings.
- The creature you target with this spell needs to understand your language in order to communicate with you. This spell doesn't translate words, it only sends a message in a language you already know.

LIGHT *SCHOOL: EVOCATION*

This basic spell makes an object glow with bright light for up to one hour. The target can be up to ten feet wide, creating a stationary light source. Alternatively, it can be something handheld that you carry with you. A *light* spell is a classic bit of spellcasting for good reason—it's always helpful to see where you're going in the dark!

SPELL TIPS

- The light can be any color you choose, so don't be afraid to get imaginative.
- Although the light this spell gives off is bright, it can be covered by a cloak or other obscuring material if necessary.

THE WARRIORS & WIZARDS COMPENDIUM

PRESTIDIGITATION

SCHOOL: TRANSMUTATION

Novice spellcasters use this minor magical trick to practice their spellcasting abilities. With *prestidigitation*, you can create one of these situations.

- An instant, harmless, and obviously magical effect such as a shower of sparks, puff of wind, faint musical notes, or a strange smell.
- Light or snuff out a candle, torch, or small campfire.
- Make a small object clean or dirty.
- Chill, warm up, or add flavor to food (about one cubic foot's worth).
- Mark with a symbol or add color to an object for up to an hour.
- Create a trinket or a small magical illusion in your hand for a few seconds.

SPELL TIPS

▶ If you cast this spell three times, you can have up to three different *prestidigitation* effects going simultaneously.

▶ This spell is an easy way to show off to commoners and build your reputation as powerful and mysterious. An imaginative use of *prestidigitation* can amuse or frighten people or creatures who don't know the ways of magic.

SHOCKING GRASP SCHOOL: EVOCATION

The *shocking grasp* spell conjures a bit of electricity to deliver a jolt to the next creature or person you touch. It may look like a practical joke but, if you're lucky, this shock can knock down small creatures in one hit. Use it wisely and its zap will be one your foes remember!

SPELL TIPS

- This spell only works if you can touch your target (unlike *call lightning* on page 101, which is a more powerful spell that can hit targets farther away).

- If your opponent is wearing metal armor, this shock can be even more powerful, so pick your target wisely to maximize its effect.

FIRST LEVEL

These spells for novice magic wielders will give your character a bigger taste of the power that magic can offer.

CURE WOUNDS — SCHOOL: EVOCATION

With *cure wounds*, a target you touch is healed. Their wounds knit without scars or bruises left behind. More severe injuries may require multiple castings of the spell to heal fully.

SPELL TIPS

- A *cure wounds* spell can heal injuries received in battle, including burns or other traumas, but it cannot halt poison, cure disease, or return life to the dead. More powerful magic is needed for such tasks.
- Although this spell can be cast at first level, it can also be empowered at a higher level in order to mend more grievous injuries. The more power a caster uses, the more damage that can be healed.

DISGUISE SELF   SCHOOL: ILLUSION

Disguise self makes you look like someone else for one hour, fooling people into thinking your appearance has changed. This includes your clothes, armor, and possessions. They're not real physical changes though, so if someone tries to grab an illusionary hat, they'll reach right through and touch your head instead! If you're careful about how you use it, this basic illusion can be very effective.

SPELL TIPS

- Your new appearance must be relatively close to your actual form. You can't make it look like you're a giant or turn from a tall person into a halfling with this spell.
- Stay out of reach, or people quickly realize that your physical form doesn't match what they see!
- This spell affects only your visual appearance. Your voice, scent, and other physical cues will still be your own.
- Intelligent creatures may be able to see through your disguise, so don't assume you'll be able to trick everyone with this.

MAGIC MISSILE **SCHOOL: EVOCATION**

A *magic missile* spell creates three glowing darts of magical force that you can send hurtling toward a target. These missiles don't cause a lot of damage individually, but if you get zapped by all three they can really hurt. This is a classic combat spell used by many wizards to defend against threats.

SPELL TIPS

- These aren't physical darts, so they effortlessly move through wind, rain, and even armor. All a wizard has to do is point toward their target, and *zap*!
- After about forty yards, these missiles fizzle, so make sure your target is within range before you cast the spell.
- Powerful wizards can create more than three missiles at a time. So if you see a wizard with four or more missiles floating nearby, watch out.

SPEAK WITH ANIMALS

SCHOOL: DIVINATION

The *speak with animals* spell allows you to understand and verbally communicate with beasts for up to ten minutes at a time. Striking up conversations with local wildlife is a good way to find out what's happening in the area.

SPELL TIPS

- Most animals aren't very smart compared to people. Don't expect complex conversations or detailed descriptions.

- Just because you can speak to an animal doesn't mean they'll be your friend. Some animals are angry, hungry, or just want to be left alone!

SECOND LEVEL

Second-level spells are sure to dazzle the untrained; but a skilled spellcaster probably won't be impressed.

BARKSKIN — SCHOOL: TRANSMUTATION

Casting this spells gives yourself (or another willing creature) tough, barklike skin that protects you as if you're wearing armor made of wood. This bark protection can last up to an hour, as long as you maintain concentration.

SPELL TIPS

- Barkskin doesn't have the weight or bulkiness of metal armor, so it's a good temporary option for rogues, rangers, or other adventurers trying to stay sneaky.
- Having rough barkskin can also help you hide in a forest.
- Since this skin protection is magical, it's not actual wood, so you don't have to worry about termites (any more than you would normally).

INVISIBILITY — SCHOOL: ILLUSION

A creature you touch (either yourself or someone else) becomes invisible for up to an hour, as long as you maintain concentration. Anything the target is wearing or carrying is also invisible as long as the *invisibility* spell lasts.

SPELL TIPS

- Attacking a target or casting another spell while invisible will end the effect.
- More powerful spellcasters can turn multiple targets invisible at the same time.
- Invisibility is great for sneaking around, just remember that the spell only hides you from being seen. It doesn't make you silent or muffle your footsteps.

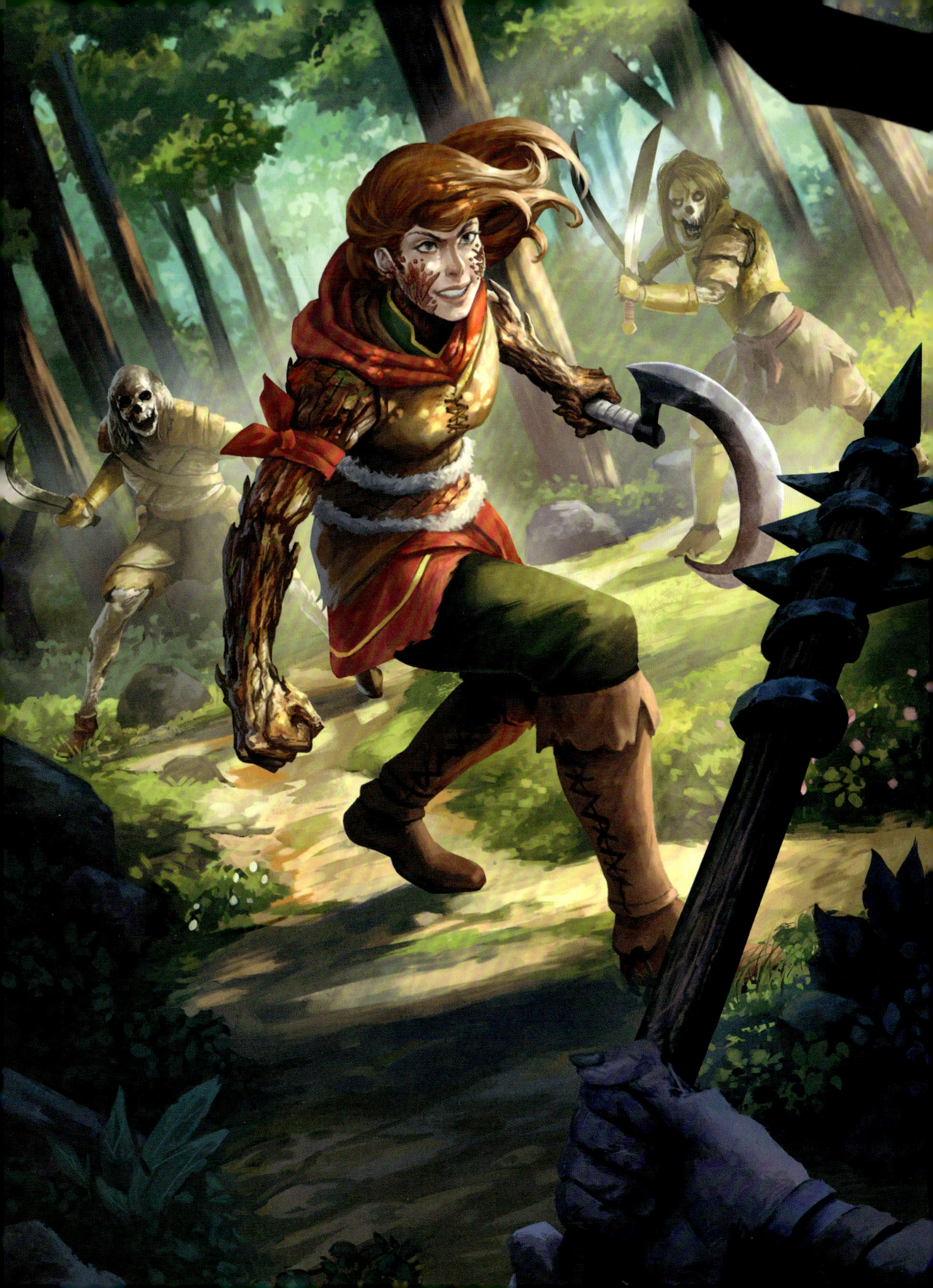

MIRROR IMAGE SCHOOL: ILLUSION

The *mirror image* spell creates three illusionary versions of the caster that mimic their movements, constantly shifting position so observers can't figure out which one is real. Enemies can try to attack these illusions and destroy them, reducing the duplicates until the original is the only one left, but doing so wastes precious time—and in combat, every second counts.

SPELL TIPS

- This spell lasts for exactly one minute, so make sure you cast it only at the most opportune time.
- Attacks that strike a large area may destroy multiple mirror doubles at the same time, dispelling the illusion.
- Creatures whose senses don't rely on sight, like those with extraordinary hearing or an advanced sense of smell, can tell the difference between mirror doubles and reality.

WEB
SCHOOL: CONJURATION

Casting a *web* spell creates a mass of sticky webbing in front of you, anchoring on any walls, trees, or other spaces to which it can attach. Creatures who try to move past the webs may be caught in them and get stuck. Very nimble or strong creatures may be able to break free, but most regular humanoids will find themselves caught for up to an hour, or until the caster stops concentrating and lets the *web* spell dissipate.

SPELL TIPS

- Make sure you have surfaces to anchor your *web* spell. Otherwise, the webbing you create will just collapse on itself.
- These magical webs are flammable, so lighting them on fire can be a quick way to get rid of them. Doing so will also burn anything still caught in the strands.
- *Web* spells are normally used against enemies, but a quick-thinking spellcaster can also use them to save people who are falling or to detect invisible creatures.

THIRD LEVEL

More impressive in their effect, these spells also demand more power to cast and more time to master.

FLY — SCHOOL: TRANSMUTATION

With the *fly* spell, you, or someone you touch, gains the ability to fly through the air. You can move about as fast as you would normally run, so birds and other naturally flying creatures can easily outrace you, but it's still a lot better than trudging along on the ground.

SPELL TIPS

- A *fly* spell lasts for only ten minutes, so make sure you're close to the ground when time is running out.
- Powerful magic users can cast this spell on multiple targets at once, allowing an entire group to fly at the same time.

CALL LIGHTNING **SCHOOL: CONJURATION**

Casting a *call lightning* spell creates a storm cloud in the sky above. Every few seconds, you can choose a spot and lightning will rain down from the cloud to hit that area. If you maintain concentration, you can launch lightning this way toward different spots, striking enemies or sending them running for cover to try and avoid being blasted.

SPELL TIPS

- This spell only works outside or in areas with a ceiling one hundred feet or higher. Without that much space, there isn't enough atmosphere to conjure a storm cloud.

- If you cast this spell while there's already a storm raging, you'll take control of the existing storm clouds instead and can enhance their power.

- This spell can be quite powerful, but concentrating on controlling the cloud can leave you vulnerable to attack. Make sure you have other adventurers around to help protect you.

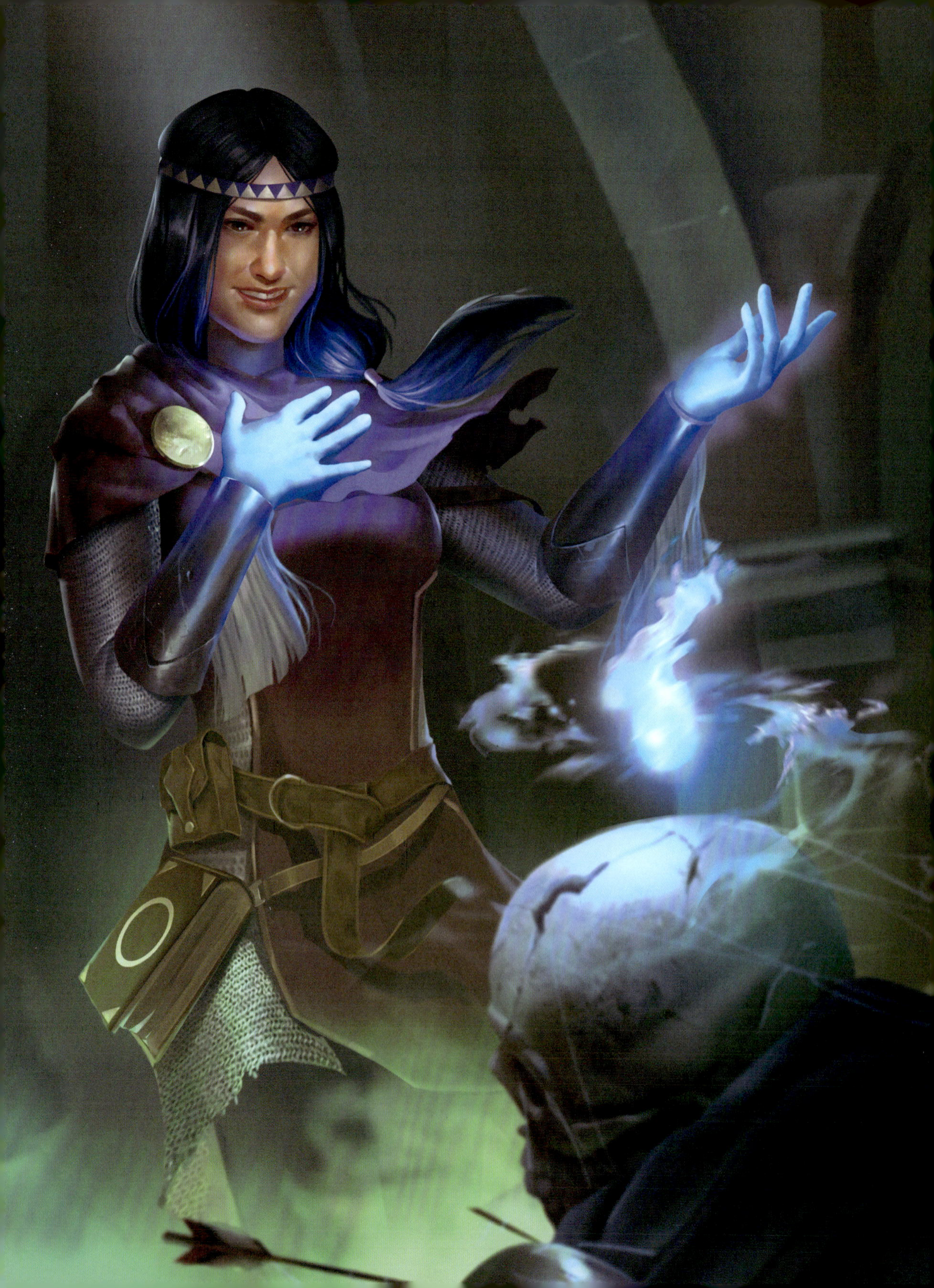

SPEAK WITH DEAD
SCHOOL: NECROMANCY

Casting a *speak with dead* spell allows you to converse with the spirit of a deceased creature or person and ask them up to five questions. Finding out how someone died and what to look out for can help you and your fellow heroes from meeting the same fate during a quest.

SPELL TIPS

- An apparition summoned with this spell can only speak languages and give information based on what it knew in life. Translation is not included as part of this spell.
- This spell doesn't work on undead creatures, since they're not actually dead!
- The dead aren't compelled to tell you the truth just because you ask them something. They can lie, tell riddles, or refuse to give information if they don't trust you.

WATER BREATHING
SCHOOL: TRANSMUTATION

This spell gives up to ten creatures (you and/or your allies) the ability to breathe underwater for up to twenty-four hours. Anyone affected by this spell also retains their normal breathing abilities as well, so if you normally breathe air, you can still do that while this spell is active.

SPELL TIPS

- Being able to breathe underwater is a powerful ability, but it doesn't automatically mean that you know how to swim or can do it well. If you're planning to adventure underwater, you'll want to get additional training in how to move and fight underwater.
- Breathing underwater doesn't let you communicate with fish or other aquatic creatures, but you could combine this with a *speak with animals* spell (see page 95) to travel underwater *and* chat with the locals at the same time.

FOURTH LEVEL

A spellcaster needs real experience under their belt to cast these spells.

FIRE SHIELD — SCHOOL: EVOCATION

Once a *fire shield* spell is cast, a barrier of fire appears around your body, lighting up the nearby area and protecting you at the same time. You can choose to activate this spell as a "warm shield" to protect against ice, snow, and cold climates or attacks, or as a "chill shield" to protect against fire and heat.

SPELL TIPS

- This spell can last up to ten minutes, which makes it useful for combat against fire- or ice-based enemies; however, it isn't going to keep you safe for a long time if you're outside in a snowstorm or exploring a volcano.
- You can use the light that this spell emits instead of carrying a torch, freeing up your hands for other things.

ICE STORM — SCHOOL: EVOCATION

Casting an *ice storm* spell summons a torrent of rock-hard ice chunks that rain down from above, pounding the ground in a twenty-foot circular area of your choosing. Targets within the area are hit by these hailstones and their skin begins to freeze.

SPELL TIPS

- An *ice storm* spell not only hurts enemies, it also slows them down as they struggle to move against the wind and keep their footing on the slippery and uneven frozen ground created by its power.

- This spell can put out fires, just as long as you're not worried about damaging anything within the area of effect.

THE WARRIORS & WIZARDS COMPENDIUM

POLYMORPH SCHOOL: TRANSMUTATION

The *polymorph* spell transforms a creature in your field of vision, along with all the gear and weapons they're carrying when the spell activates, into a non-magical beast. If you maintain concentration, this transformation will last up to an hour.

SPELL TIPS

- You can use this spell against enemies to turn them into something harmless or as a way to help friends escape by skittering or flying away.
- If a transformed target is knocked unconscious, they turn back to their original form.
- Transformed people can't speak, cast spells, or perform actions that require complex hand movements or speech, which means that casting *polymorph* on another spellcaster can be a powerful way to stop them from casting spells on you or your friends.

STONE SHAPE SCHOOL: TRANSMUTATION

After casting a *stone shape* spell, you can touch a small stone object or area of stone five feet across or deep and form it into any shape you choose. That means you can make a small passage, mold stone to make a small statue, or even make a small weapon out of rock.

SPELL TIPS

- Get creative! You could pull up a section of stone from the floor to block a door while trying to escape from creatures chasing you, hide an item in a space you carve out in a wall, or drill a small peephole into a barrier to see what's on the other side.
- If you use *stone shape* to make a hole, remember that you'll need to cast the spell again if you want to close it afterward.

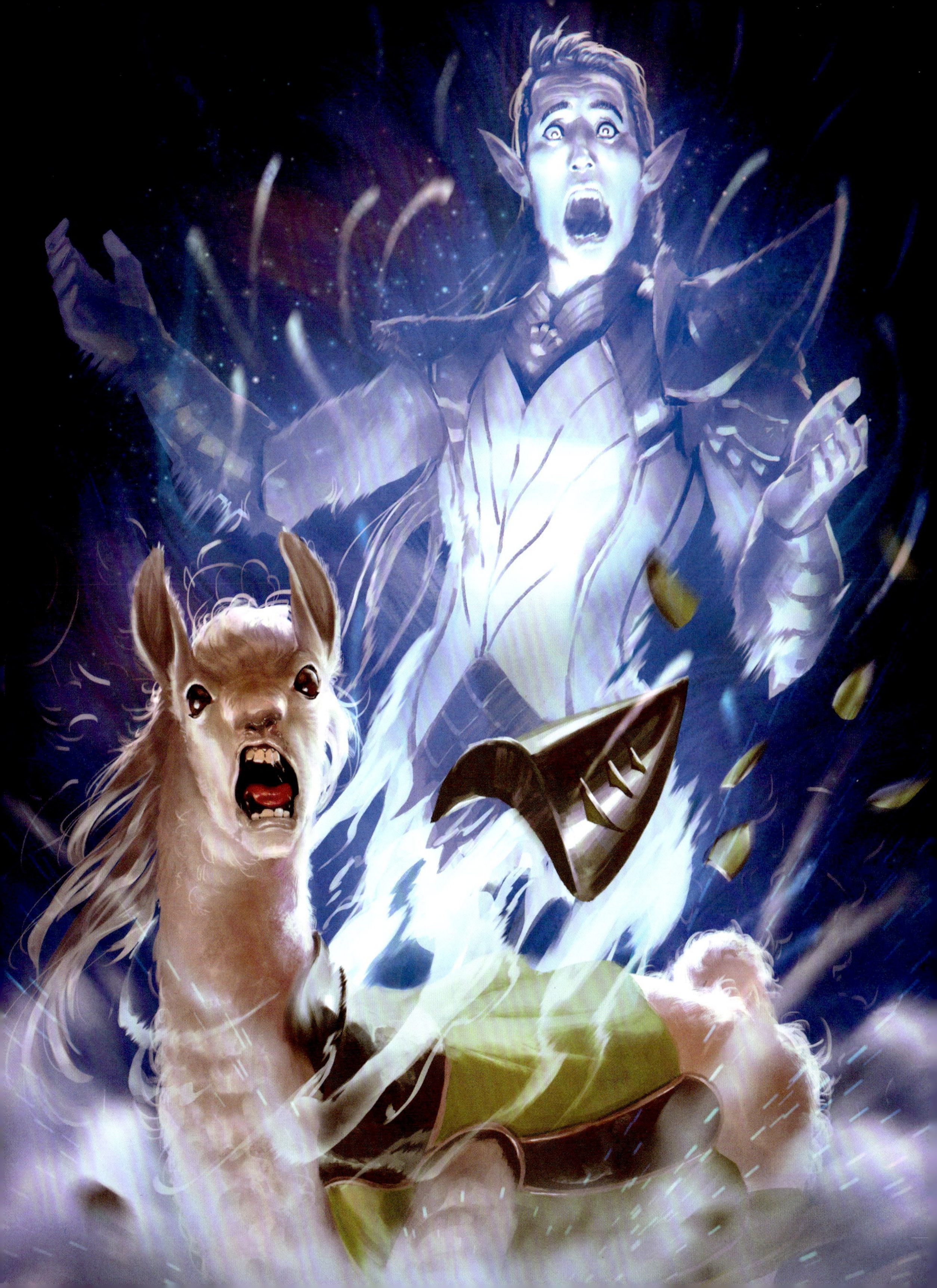

FIFTH LEVEL

Mastery of these powerful spells reflects hard work, study, and a deep internal store of magical power.

ANIMATE OBJECTS — SCHOOL: TRANSMUTATION

After casting an *animate objects* spell, you can choose up to ten small objects (or smaller numbers of larger objects) to come to life and follow your command. Doors will open or slam shut, chains will try to ensnare creatures, and free-floating objects will guard, attack, or defend as you direct them, for up to a minute as long as you maintain concentration.

SPELL TIPS

- Animated objects don't have any personality. They can't speak and won't be able to relay any information.
- If an enemy smashes an object, it reverts to its original form and is no longer animated.

FLAME STRIKE **SCHOOL: EVOCATION**

The *flame strike* spell summons a vertical column of fire that drops down from above, burning anything within a ten-foot radius of where you direct it. This spell is particularly effective against undead creatures, as it hurts them with both holy light and fire at the same time.

SPELL TIPS

- Area-of-effect spells such as *flame strike* can hurt multiple enemies at the same time if you plan carefully. Look for areas where enemies are gathered close together and use it there for maximum effect.
- Flashy spells such as this one can be quite impressive on the battlefield, but they also call a lot of attention to themselves. That can make you a target for enemies who want to avoid being hit by future spells.

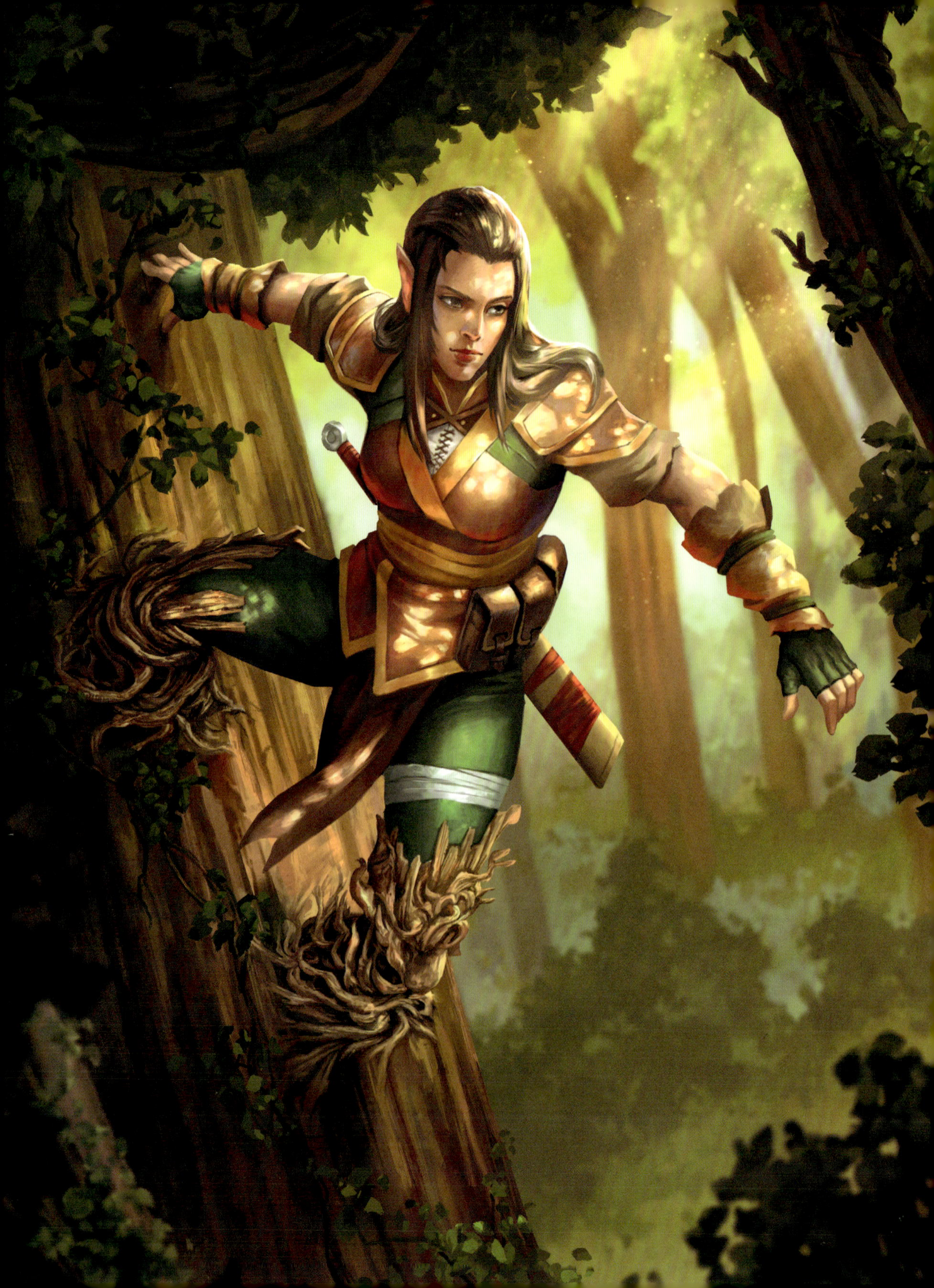

TREE STRIDE
SCHOOL: CONJURATION

Casting a *tree stride* spell allows you to step into a tree and then instantly step out from another tree of the same type up to five hundred feet away. You can do this as many times as you want for up to a minute, shifting between trees at will. This power is used by forest creatures and fairy folk to spy on targets or to escape from attackers. Some druids and rangers have learned to do this as well.

SPELL TIPS

- Use this spell to sneak up on an enemy in a forest or to get to the top of an incredibly tall tree faster than you could climb it.

- As soon as you step into a tree with this spell, you sense where all the trees of the same type are within five hundred feet; so you can plan your movement and stay ahead of anyone trying to keep an eye on you.

HOLD MONSTER
SCHOOL: ENCHANTMENT

When you cast a *hold monster* spell on a creature, it will magically paralyze them, keeping the beast from moving or attacking for up to a minute, as long as you maintain concentration.

SPELL TIPS

- Using this spell on a powerful foe is a good way to keep it from attacking while your allies defeat smaller and less-dangerous creatures, giving you a strategic advantage.

- Creatures with strong minds may be able to overpower your will and escape, so be careful against highly intelligent monsters.

SIXTH LEVEL

Spellcasters of this level have a well-earned reputation that precedes them on their travels, and likely a few heroic ballads to celebrate their achievements.

CREATE UNDEAD — SCHOOL: NECROMANCY

The *create undead* spell can only be cast at night; when cast, it turns up to three humanoid corpses into undead creatures called ghouls! After being created, ghouls feed on humanoid flesh. They hunt in packs and tend to lurk near places where bodies can be found—graveyards, crypts, and battlefields. These ghouls will follow your commands for twenty-four hours.

SPELL TIPS

- If you want to maintain control of the ghouls for another twenty-four hours, you'll need to recast the spell.
- A ghoul's touch can paralyze their target, leaving you helpless for up to a minute. That's more than enough time for a ghoul pack to turn you into their latest feast, so watch out!

FLESH TO STONE   SCHOOL: TRANSMUTATION

Casting a *flesh to stone* spell at a target attempts to petrify their flesh, turning them into stone. Every few seconds, the creature may try to resist the effect. But if its will is weaker than yours, the target will harden and turn to stone. If you can maintain concentration for a full minute, then the stone transformation is permanent (until it is dispelled through more powerful magic).

SPELL TIPS

- Turning a creature to stone permanently can be quite difficult. But if a creature is even temporarily slowed down by this spell, it can lend a strategic advantage to an adventuring party in combat.

- If a petrified creature is damaged while in stone form, it will have that same damage when returned to its original form.

HEROES' FEAST   SCHOOL: CONJURATION

Casting a *heroes' feast* spell creates a huge banquet of food that up to a dozen creatures can enjoy at the same time. It will take more than an hour to get through this enchanted meal, but at the end of this repast everyone who has eaten will feel healthy and cured of sickness.

SPELL TIPS

- Spells such as *heroes' feast* may not seem as powerful as conjuring fire or speaking with the dead, but group morale is very important. A magical meal like this can lift spirits and ready an adventuring party for difficult times ahead.

- Magical food has benefits that last beyond the duration of the meal itself. For the next twenty-four hours, anyone who ate feels stronger and braver.

OTTO'S IRRESISTIBLE DANCE   SCHOOL: ENCHANTMENT

When you choose a target and cast *Otto's irresistible dance*, that creature begins a comic dance on the spot, shuffling and tapping its feet for up to a minute, if you maintain concentration. Not only does this look ridiculous, it can also create confusion among enemies as they wonder why their cohort won't stop dancing around when they should be fighting you and your allies!

SPELL TIPS

- Like *hold monster* (see page 111), *Otto's irresistible dance* can be a useful way to keep powerful enemies occupied while your allies deal with lesser threats.

- A creature that's dancing can still try to attack anyone who gets close to them, but it's much more difficult than normal.

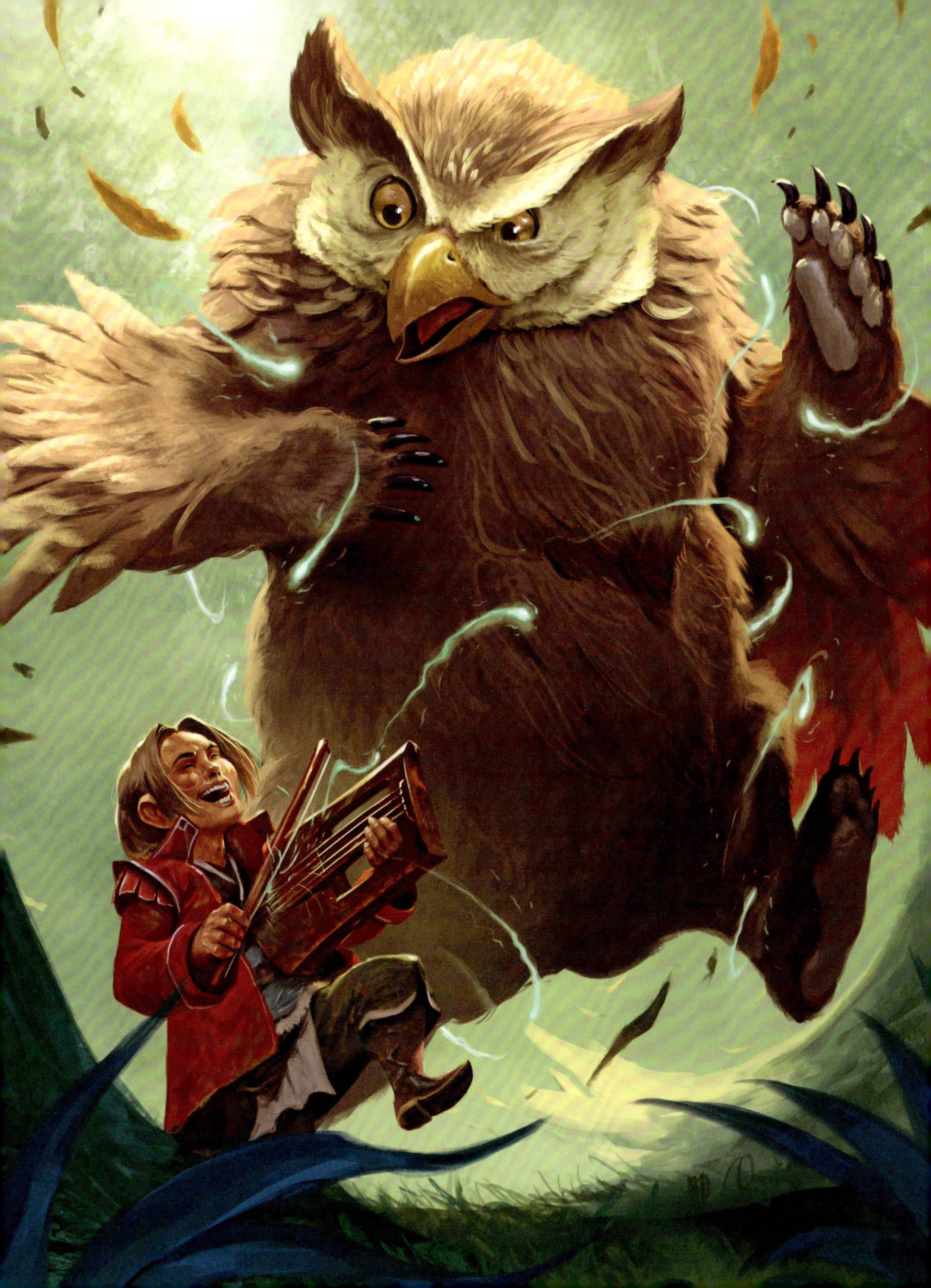

SEVENTH LEVEL

Nearing the peak of magical power available to mortals, these spells are truly impressive.

PRISMATIC SPRAY SCHOOL: EVOCATION

The *prismatic spray* spell conjures seven multicolored rays of light that flash from your hand, blasting enemies with powerful magic. Each ray is a different color and has a different power.

Red: Fire

Orange: Acid

Yellow: Lightning

Green: Poison

Blue: Ice

Indigo: Paralysis

Violet: Blindness

SPELL TIPS

- Not all creatures are vulnerable to the same kinds of magic, so do your research on monsters and creatures so you know which kind of *prismatic spray* to cast against them.
- This spell can't tell friend from foe, so make sure your allies aren't in range when you let it blast.

RESURRECTION
SCHOOL: NECROMANCY

There are many lesser healing spells, but the ultimate curative power is to bring a fallen ally back from death itself. As long as a soul is free and willing to return, and they did not die of old age, this spell restores a being to life and cures them of all damage that afflicted them before they passed. Even still, returning from the dead is quite exhausting and it can take several days for a person to return to full strength.

SPELL TIPS

- This powerful spell can resurrect beings who have been deceased for fewer than 100 years; but the longer a target has been dead, the more draining it is on the caster.
- Many spells have components, special ingredients required to fuel their magic. A *resurrection* spell requires a valuable diamond as its component, and casting the spell destroys the diamond instantly. Powerful magic can get quite expensive.

PLANE SHIFT **SCHOOL: CONJURATION**

Casting a *plane shift* spell allows you and up to eight other creatures who link hands to teleport to another dimensional plane. A physical component is necessary to complete this spell; in this case, a forked metal rod. There are many dimensions beyond our own and great treasures to be found in those worlds, but great danger as well. Such a trip is not to be taken lightly.

SPELL TIPS

- You can specify a destination in general terms with this spell, but not land with pinpoint accuracy.
- This spell can be cast on unwilling targets as well, banishing them from your current dimension.

PLANES OF EXISTENCE

There are a multitude of worlds, as well as myriad alternate dimensions of reality, called the planes of existence. Some are made of pure energy or raw elemental forces (earth, air, fire, and water), others are realms of pure thought or ideology, and others still may be home to deities or the demonic. Saving a city or a country can make an adventurer a hero, but questing in other worlds and saving entire dimensions can make a legend.

DIVINE WORD

SCHOOL: EVOCATION

This potent spell calls forth a tiny piece of the power that shaped creation. Any enemies you choose within thirty feet that can hear this sound are struck by its magical force, which may deafen, blind, or stun them. Weaker creatures may even be destroyed completely by its might.

SPELL TIPS

- In addition to damaging regular creatures, *divine word* may cause targets who are from a different plane of existence to be sent back to their home dimension.

- Area-of-effect spells such as *divine word* are an incredibly useful way to stop large groups of smaller creatures from overwhelming an adventuring party.

THE WARRIORS & WIZARDS COMPENDIUM

EIGHTH LEVEL

Few spellcasters reach this level of power, but those who do are nearly unstoppable.

CLONE — SCHOOL: NECROMANCY

The curious *clone* spell grows an inert duplicate of a living creature to act as a safeguard against death. Once the process begins, it takes about four months for the clone to be fully grown. After that, if the *original* creature is killed, then their soul will transfer to the duplicate and they will live again. Pretty neat, huh?

SPELL TIPS

- The clone has all the memories, personality, and abilities of the original being from which it was copied, but none of their equipment, so make sure the clone has clothes and weapons once it wakes up.
- A clone can be created to reach maturity at a younger age than the original. Some spellcasters charge a fortune to rich patrons looking to extend their life using this powerful magic spell.

DOMINATE MONSTER — SCHOOL: ENCHANTMENT

After casting a *dominate monster* spell on a creature, you attempt to exert your will upon it and take control of its mind and actions. If you succeed and can maintain concentration, then the monster is yours to command for up to an hour. The creature will follow your directions to the best of its ability.

SPELL TIPS

- If a creature is hurt while under this spell, it will be easier for its mind to fight back and break your control over it.
- Creatures without proper minds, including constructs, oozes, and some undead, are immune to charm spells such as this.

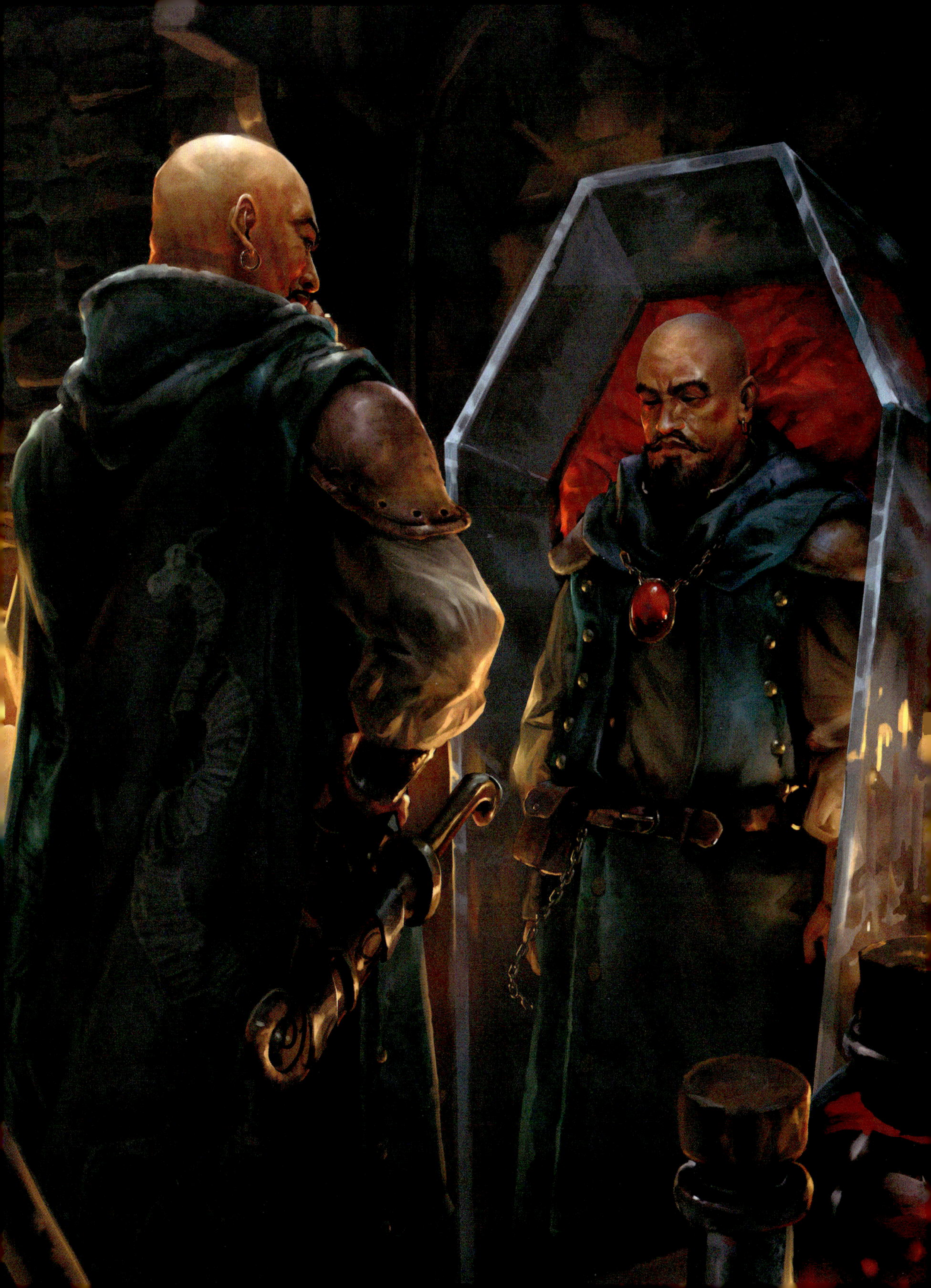

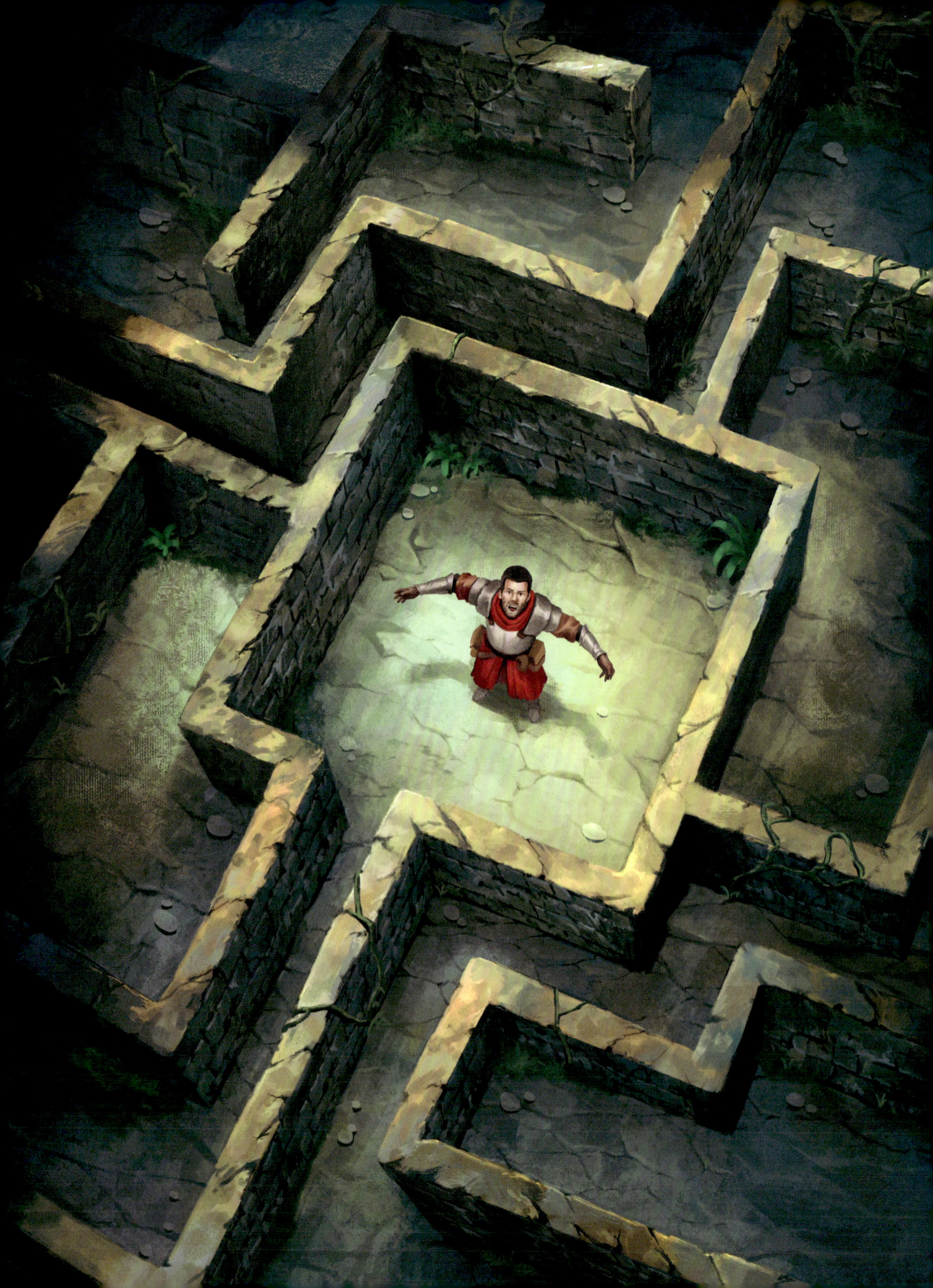

EARTHQUAKE
SCHOOL: EVOCATION

The powerful *earthquake* spell creates a massive seismic disturbance. Any creatures in its area of effect may be knocked off their feet, thrown into the air, or fall into fissures that open up in the ground beneath them. If this spell is cast in an area where there are buildings or other structures, they are damaged as well and may collapse, causing even more destruction and danger for anyone within range.

SPELL TIPS

- Large-scale destructive spells such as *earthquake* are extremely potent but must be directed with caution, otherwise your allies may end up feeling the effects and be hurt by it as well.

- Casting this spell while inside a building is also extremely dangerous, as the structure may end up collapsing on top of you!

MAZE
SCHOOL: CONJURATION

Casting a *maze* spell sends the target creature to a pocket dimension filled with a complex labyrinth. If you can maintain concentration, this labyrinthine banishment will last up to ten minutes, more than enough time to finish off other foes during a battle and prepare for your enemy's return.

SPELL TIPS

- If the target trapped in the maze can find their way to the exit, they'll return to the point from which they vanished.

- Minotaurs can automatically solve these magical mazes, so don't waste this powerful spell on them.

NINTH LEVEL

The most potent spells imaginable, these awesome powers defy the laws of the universe.

METEOR SWARM SCHOOL: EVOCATION

The mighty *meteor swarm* spell summons blazing orbs of burning stone that plummet to the ground with unmatched force, destroying almost anything unfortunate enough to be in their way. Every creature in a forty-foot radius is pummeled and burned by the heat of these meteors, and anything combustible an individual is wearing may burst into flame.

SPELL TIPS

- *Meteor swarm* is one of those "go for broke" spells that can cause massive destruction, but also change the course of a desperate battle.
- A poorly aimed spell with this kind of power can easily wipe out allies or ravage buildings and terrain, so choose your targets carefully.

TIME STOP

SCHOOL: TRANSMUTATION

When the impressive *time stop* spell is cast, the flow of time is halted for everyone but the caster. For up to thirty seconds, you can move and use your equipment without anyone within one thousand feet even knowing that it's happening. When time resumes, those within that space will believe whatever changed did so instantaneously.

This spell ends if you interact with anything you're not personally carrying, including other creatures, or if you move beyond one thousand feet from where the spell was cast.

SPELL TIPS

- A *time stop* spell is the perfect way to make your escape when things have gone wrong. It's also a useful way to change your position in a battle or drink a much-needed healing potion.

- Unfortunately you can't stop the flow of time for anyone else, so using this spell with your allies is impossible.

SHAPECHANGE SCHOOL: TRANSMUTATION

Casting a *shapechange* spell causes you to transform into a beast or magical creature. You can keep changing form into different creatures for up to an hour, as long as you maintain your concentration throughout. You will take on any of the physical attributes of the creature you have become, but keep your own mind and personality throughout any and all transformations. With this spell, you could temporarily become a dragon, a unicorn, a beholder, or any other creature you've encountered on your travels.

SPELL TIPS

- When the spell activates, decide if your clothing and equipment falls away, merges into your body, or is worn (only if it fits). Clothes and equipment won't change size or shape.
- You can only speak if your chosen form also has the ability to speak.

WEIRD SCHOOL: ILLUSION

A *weird* spell creates a potent illusion that reaches into the minds of your enemies and creates a vision of nightmare creatures formed from their deepest fears. These imaginary monsters attack inside your opponents' minds, but your adversaries can't tell what's real and what isn't as they struggle to escape. All your targets within a three-hundred-foot radius will be hurt by these mental terrors until they either muster the willpower to resist or are destroyed.

SPELL TIPS

- Since this is a psychic attack happening within your target's imagination, you can't see what it is they're fighting.
- Although targets of this spell are not being physically attacked, if they die in their mind they will also die in the real world.

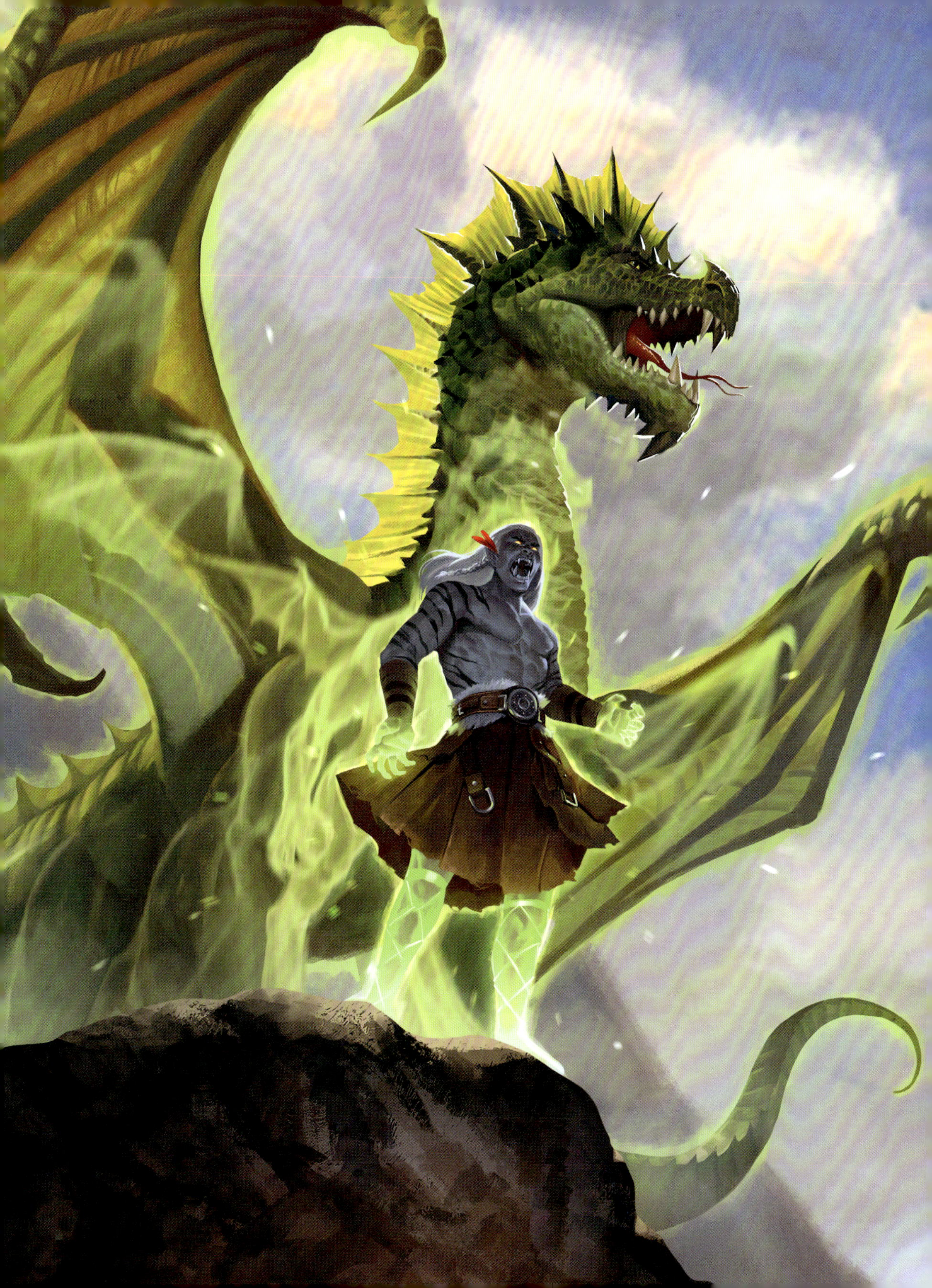

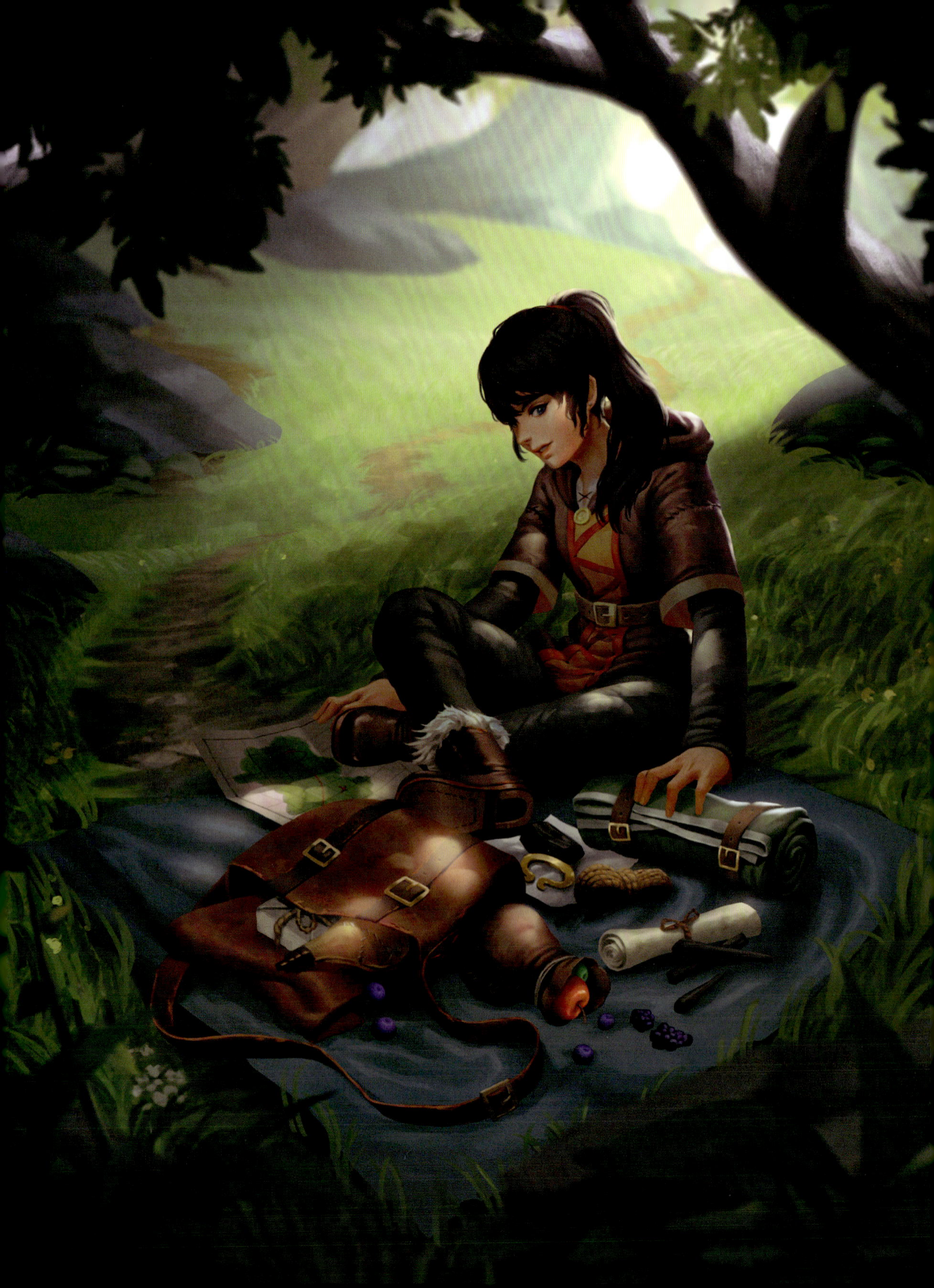

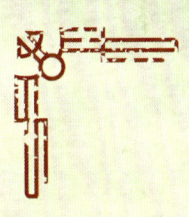

IN YOUR PACK: ITEMS FOR TRAVEL & EXPLORATION

Being a dungeon delver requires courage, a desire to explore, and the right tools for the challenges ahead. What you carry determines your success against tough terrain, worrisome weather, and creepy creatures.

Adventuring packs are an easy way to get all the gear you need for a particular task or quest, usually at lower cost than buying all the equipment individually. Your character class will probably inform the kind of starting equipment you'll want to take on your journey, and these packs might be just what you're looking for.

Even so, you can't take it all. Getting packed for an epic journey means making choices about what to bring and what to leave behind. Every bit of equipment or weaponry can slow you down, tire you out, or leave less room to carry the treasures you may find during your travels.

Use the information in this chapter to make a list of what you want to carry based on your class and its abilities, then outfit your heroic self and head toward adventure!

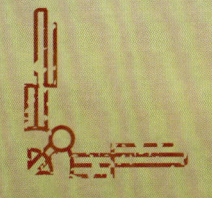

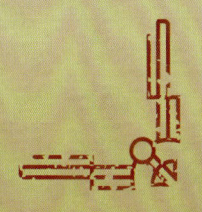

HATS
Headgear is available in a wide range of styles and sizes, from close-fitting rogue caps to huge, floppy wizard hats. Whatever the design, they're helpful for keeping sun and rain off the faces of weary adventurers trekking from dungeon to dungeon.

SHIRT
Some adventurers prefer loose shirts for mobility, and others like a more fitted garment that won't impede them while fighting. Either way, shirts can range from plain and rough to ultra-soft items made from the finest fabrics.

CLOAK
Part clothing, part blanket, a cloak is crucial for protecting you from bad weather, concealing you from enemies, and keeping you warm at night.

WAISTCOAT
Waistcoats are worn for reasons of warmth, style, and all those extra little pockets.

PANTS/SKIRT
Either pants or skirts are suitable for adventuring, so long as they are made from sturdy fabric and cut loose enough to allow a full range of movement. You can wear a skirt over leggings for added warmth.

FOOTWEAR
Boots are the most common footwear choice for adventurers, helping to protect your lower legs from water, slime, and ankle-biting beasts. Some adventurers prefer a soft-soled shoe that allows for extra-quiet footsteps.

CLOTHES: ANATOMY OF AN ADVENTURER'S OUTFIT

Clothing can say a lot about your character's personality, wealth, and social status. In turn, that affects how other characters, including allies and villains, respond to you. Fancy robes can help during negotiations with a local lord—or help you infiltrate that same lord's castle on a secret mission. Many magic users prefer long, loose garments with lots of hidden storage spots for their spell components and enchanted talismans. Some vestments are even covered with symbolic or magical designs. The tattered rags of a peasant might cause a warlock to hesitate when trusting you with an important quest—or allow you to pass through a crowd unnoticed by soldiers who are searching for you.

TRINKETS

Usually carried for sentimental reasons, trinkets are small objects that reflect your character's background and personality but aren't useful in combat (unless you're very creative!). They can also play a role in your interactions with other characters or provide the spark of inspiration for stories. Ideas include the following:

- A crystal that glows faintly in the moonlight
- A coin from an unknown land
- A tiny knife that belonged to a relative
- An empty vial that smells of perfume when opened

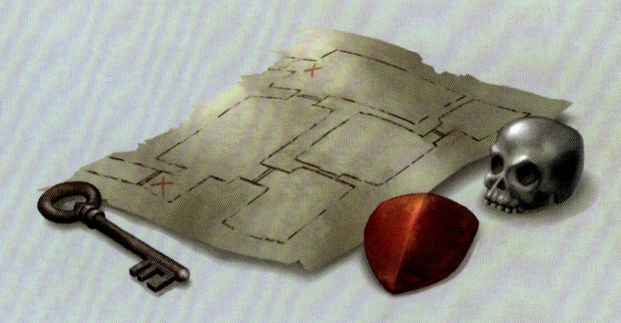

THE WARRIORS & WIZARDS COMPENDIUM

WHAT TO WEAR WHEN YOU'RE ADVENTURING!

Your choice of clothing can change how you move, how you fight, and how others interact with you. What you wear changes your style and strategy, so choose carefully.

THE CLASS MAKES THE CLOTHES

Although adventurers are free to wear whatever they like, each class leans toward clothing types that are most functional for their needs.

- **Combat classes** like barbarians, fighters, and warlocks value durable clothing that can fit under armor and withstand rough travel.

- **Clerics, monks, and paladins** often dress to reflect their faith and adorn their clothes with the colors or symbols of their deity.

- **Bards, druids, rangers, and rogues** often dress for their environment, from eye-catching stage attire to muted forest tones or shadowy blacks.

- **Spellcasters** such as wizards and sorcerers lean toward loose robes that won't hamper their magical gestures, with lots of pockets for spell components.

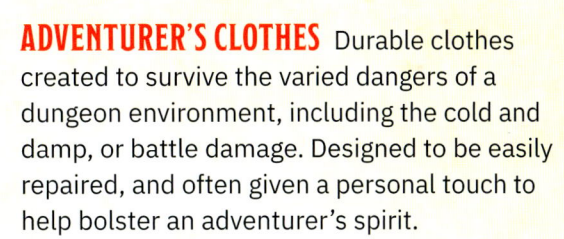

ADVENTURER'S CLOTHES
Durable clothes created to survive the varied dangers of a dungeon environment, including the cold and damp, or battle damage. Designed to be easily repaired, and often given a personal touch to help bolster an adventurer's spirit.

Wear this when trekking into dangerous environments—or to impress locals with tales of your past adventures.

Don't wear this when you need to stay out of sight. Adventurers attract attention, and not always the friendly kind.

FINE CLOTHES
Ornate attire made from expensive materials, which may even feature silk threads and gemstone decorations.

Wear this when you need to impress nobles, engage in diplomacy, or intimidate poor folks.

Don't wear this when you're out adventuring—fancy fabrics are too delicate for the dangers of a dungeon, and all that bling may attract nasty creatures!

TRAVELER'S CLOTHES
Sturdy, practical clothing in rough, but durable, fabric. Often features long cloaks for warmth and protection against the elements!

Wear this when you're traveling long distances or trying to find a spot at an inn.

Don't wear this to a fancy banquet, unless you want to upset your host.

THE WARRIORS & WIZARDS COMPENDIUM

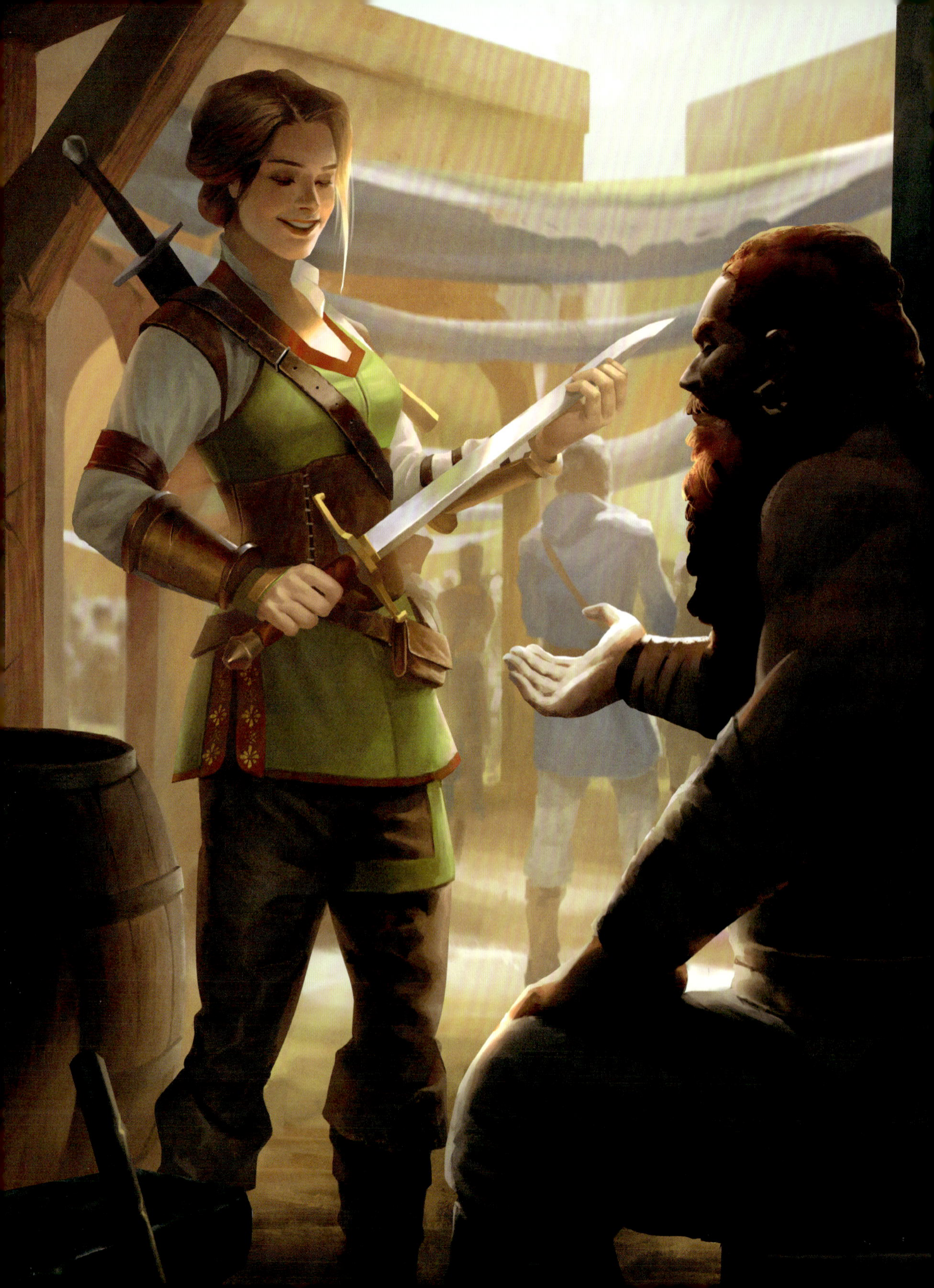

WEAPONS: BE READY FOR COMBAT

Whether you favor a longsword or a longbow, your weapon and your ability to use it effectively while adventuring will mean the difference between life and death. Your class and background can make you extra-effective with certain weapons or prevent you from using others, so you'll want to take both into consideration when making your choices.

Most people can use simple weapons without needing extra training. These include clubs, maces, and other arms often found in the hands of common folks. Martial weapons, including swords, axes, and polearms, require more specialized training. It's possible to injure yourself instead of an enemy if you attack with a weapon you don't know how to use, so watch out!

In addition to functionality, you should think about personal touches that make your weapons cool and unique. Is your axe engraved with dwarven runes? Does your dagger have a jeweled handle or a special scabbard? Was your shortbow's wood hewn from a sacred tree in far-off elvish lands? Your weapon will be your constant companion on the adventure ahead, so choose one you can trust!

SWORDS

The classic warriors' weapon, swords are made from a long piece of metal sharpened on both edges and mounted on a sturdy handle known as a hilt. They come in a range of lengths and weights and may be highly decorated or left plain, depending on the owner's wealth and taste.

Swords can be used to slash at enemies, puncture them with the sharp tip, and even deliver blunt strikes with the broadside or the hilt. The more ways your warrior can think of to wield their weapon, the harder it will be for enemies to dodge their attacks!

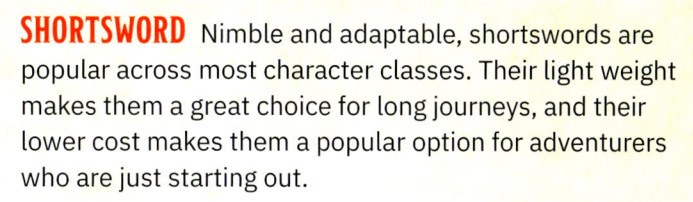

SHORTSWORD Nimble and adaptable, shortswords are popular across most character classes. Their light weight makes them a great choice for long journeys, and their lower cost makes them a popular option for adventurers who are just starting out.

As a one-handed weapon, shortswords allow their users to carry a shield as well—an important consideration for warriors who are restricted from some of the tougher armor classes. Don't underestimate the damage a skilled hero can do with one of these swift, sharp implements at their side.

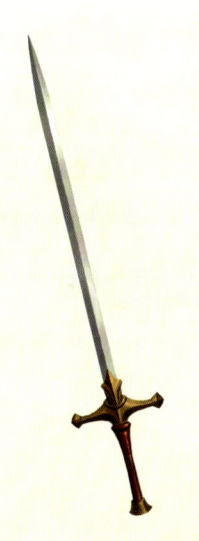

LONGSWORD The versatile longsword offers a great balance between the speed of a shortsword and the hefty power of a greatsword. As a one-handed weapon, it permits a hero to deliver swift, sharp strikes while allowing for a shield as extra protection. Used with both hands, longswords focus the full brunt of a warrior's strength into punishing blows.

The longsword is a great choice when you're not certain what kind of danger you'll be facing. Whether you tangle with lots of smaller opponents who need to be taken down quickly or a mighty beast that can only be defeated with powerful hits, the longsword is ready to deliver.

GREATSWORD The greatsword is a mighty weapon requiring immense strength and skill to use effectively. Any untrained heroes may wind up hurting themselves more than their opponents if they wade into battle with one of these.

A two-handed weapon, a greatsword can deliver powerful blows, even killing lesser creatures with a single strike. Due to their size and expense, greatswords are associated with paladins, fighters, and barbarians, although any trained warrior with sufficient might may find one to be a welcome ally on the field of battle.

THE WARRIORS & WIZARDS COMPENDIUM

POLEARMS

Polearms consist of a staff, typically made of wood, topped with a metal spike or blade. A classic battlefield weapon, its broad reach makes them a great choice against larger opponents. Armies often place rows of soldiers armed with polearms as their first line of defense against attacking cavalry, goblin hordes, giants, and other foes.

As close-combat weapons, polearms' longer length allows a wider swing than swords, increasing your range and building speed for a more brutal impact. Combined with a steady stance, a polearm can deliver crushing blows; paired with nimble footwork, the blade becomes a flashing blur of stabs and slashes. What fighting style will your warrior choose?

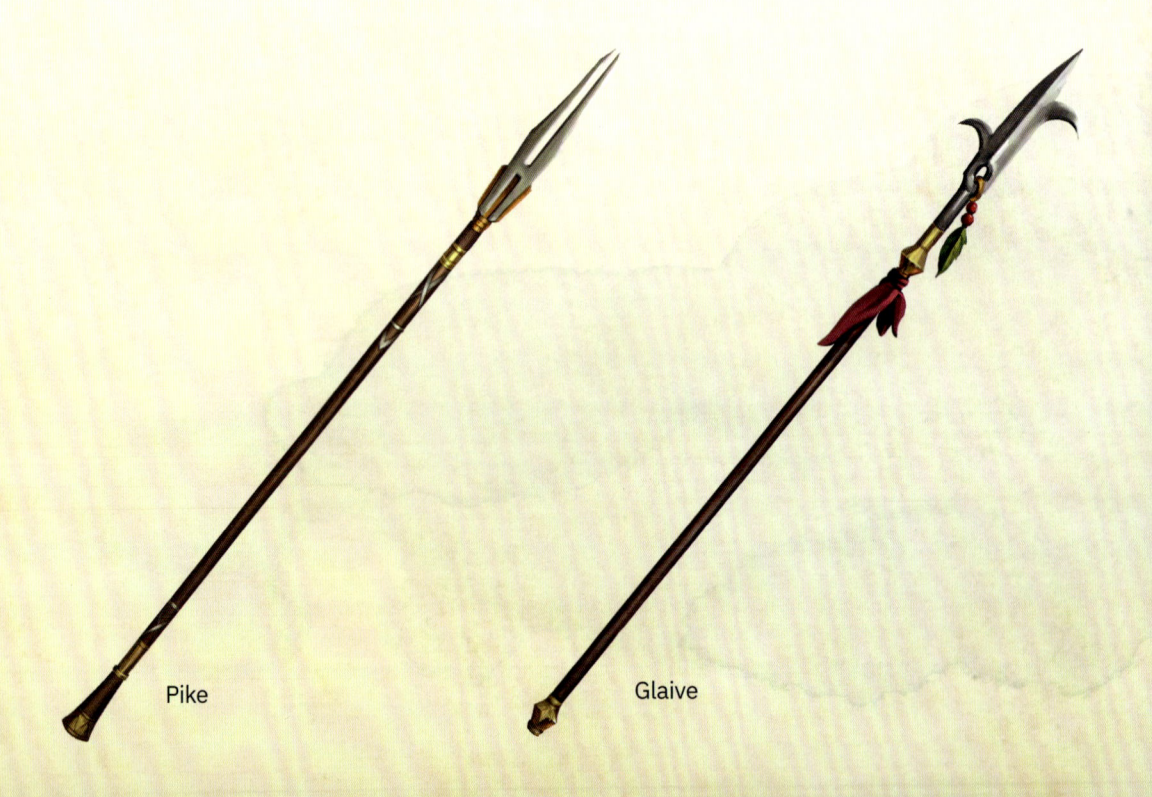

Pike

Glaive

PIKE Simple and effective, an inexpensive pike is a great weapon choice for starting heroes who find themselves short on gold. The spike delivers sharp stabbing damage to enemies, and can even be thrown if needed.

GLAIVE The curved hook of a glaive allows it to deal extra damage. You can even use it to snare opponents and pull them in close! The sharp edge of the blade can be used to stab or slash at foes for even more attack options.

HALBERD Combining the reach of a pike with the blade of an axe, a halberd opens up even more fighting techniques for a trained warrior. By gripping the staff near the base, you gain a wider range for your slashes, while holding it closer to the blade will deliver blows with a mighty impact.

FANG TIAN JI The complex blade of a fang tian ji is best placed in the hands of a highly trained fighter, for it takes years of experience to master the many attacks this weapon can achieve. Stabbing, slashing, even blunt impact from the flat side of the blade, this weapon will give you countless ways to overcome your foes.

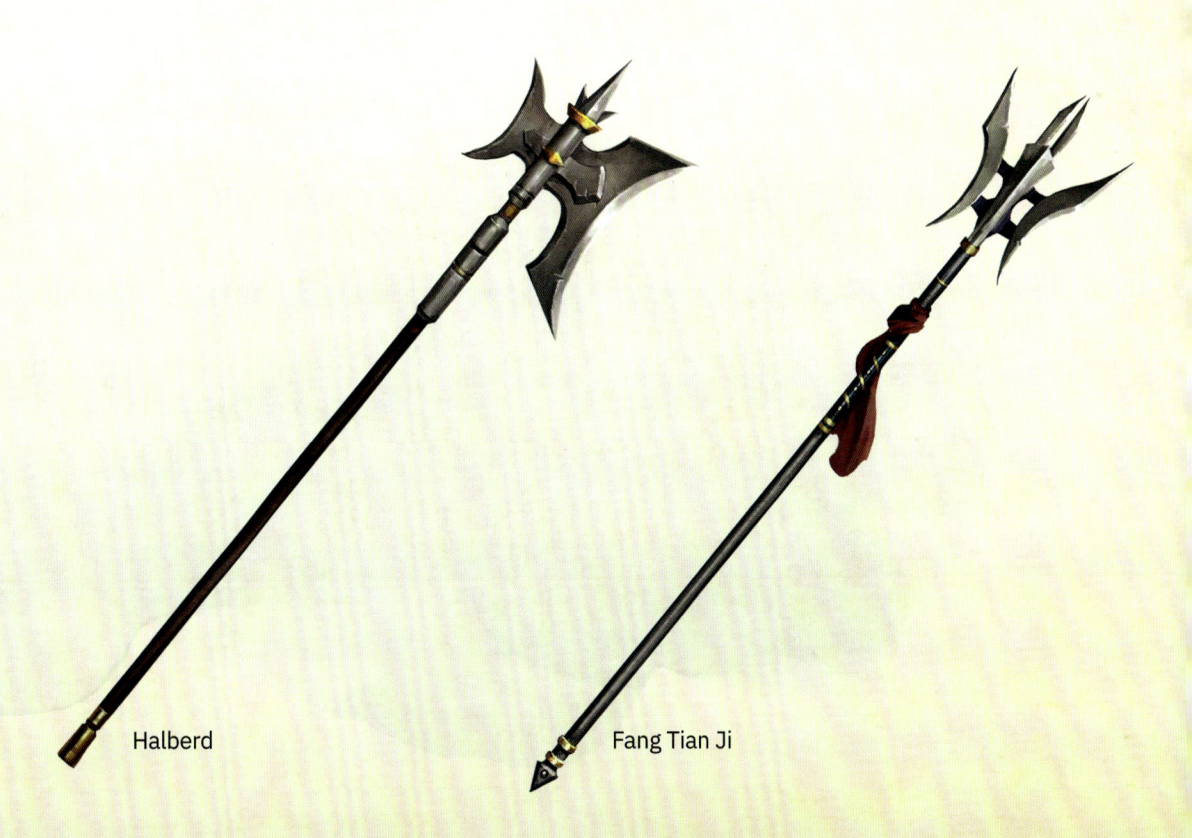

Halberd

Fang Tian Ji

THE WARRIORS & WIZARDS COMPENDIUM

OTHER MELEE WEAPONS

Swords and polearms are common choices of weapons for adventurers who like to get close to the enemy, but other options are available, including axes, hammers, and whips! These weapons are often very simple, but also very effective.

AXES Originally intended to cut down trees and split wood, axes first became a popular weapon among forest-dwellers. Axes range greatly in size and style. Some have one blade, and some have two; a pickaxe has a blade on one side and a pick on the other.

Hand axes can be used as both melee and thrown weapons, and some adventurers learn how to wield two hand axes at once. Most axes are still primarily tools, but some of the most stylish axes, like the long-handled pole axe, are designed specifically as weapons.

FLAILS Flails were originally farmers' tools used to beat grain for harvesting, but farmers adapted them as weapons to defend against attackers. Basic flails consist of two wooden batons linked by a chain or rope. Sophisticated versions might include a blade, a metal claw, or a spiked metal ball on one or both ends. Martial artists may train all their lives to master the use of a flail.

HAMMERS Intended as tools for construction, demolition, and metalwork, hammers have become favored weapons in some places, since they offer brutal power.

Hammers range in size from modest sledgehammers to huge iron mauls. Many are basic blunt instruments for striking enemies or denting armor, but warhammers are designed as impressive smashing weapons with long handles and small heavy heads to be wielded with speed and grace.

MACES Related to hammers, but conceived specifically as weapons, maces are metal bludgeons with spikes or blades designed to penetrate armor or pull a soldier off a horse. Because maces can be very ornate, they are sometimes the blunt weapon of choice for people of high status—but they can also be made from cheap raw iron and hit just as hard.

WHIPS Traditionally used for wrangling livestock, whips can be used as weapons by a highly trained expert. Some bullwhips extend as far as twenty feet, offering greater range than most melee weapons.

Other styles of whip have less reach but different advantages. Scourges are whips with multiple short tails that can be used to disarm an opponent. A riding crop can be carried discretely and delivers a stinging blow rather than lasting damage. Chain whips, made of metal rods linked by chains, are less flexible than other whips, but they hit very hard.

THE WARRIORS & WIZARDS COMPENDIUM

RANGED WEAPONS

Most ranged weapons were originally intended for hunting, but in a world of spellcasters, firebreathers, and terrible flying beasts, the ability to attack at long range can be a lifesaver. Bows and arrows are the most popular forms of ranged weapons, but they come in a few different styles, and there are some ranged weapons that might prove a better fit for your character.

BOWS Shortbows and longbows use the tension of a bowstring released by hand to propel an arrow toward a target. Shortbows are about three feet in height and can fire an arrow about eighty feet on average. Longbows are a couple of feet taller and can typically fire an arrow about one hundred fifty feet, but they're not as easy to carry around. All bows require some strength to use effectively.

CROSSBOWS Crossbows are simple mechanical weapons activated by pulling a trigger to release a catch on the bowstring, propelling a bolt toward a target. There are three popular types.

Hand crossbows are small and can be fired one-handed, but have a usual range of about thirty feet, and the string must be drawn back by hand. Light crossbows and heavy crossbows must be held two-handed, and a crank or lever is used to pull back the string. Light crossbows have a range of eighty feet, while a large and weighty heavy crossbow has a range of one hundred feet. Most crossbows can only fire one bolt at a time, and reloading can take several minutes.

DARTS (BLOW DARTS) Piercing darts can be thrown about twenty feet or shot from a blowgun to a distance of about twenty-five feet. Darts don't deliver much damage, so they are often tipped with dangerous or deadly poisons to make them more effective.

SLINGS A simple projectile weapon made of a pouch and cord, a sling is used to fling a small blunt projectile with great force an average of thirty feet. Hard metal projectiles called bullets are often used, but one great advantage of a sling is that they can also launch found objects such as rocks or even coins.

THROWING WEAPONS Daggers, shurikens, and other bladed throwing weapons have a range of twenty to thirty feet, depending on their weight and design. They require great finesse and aim to use effectively.

THE WARRIORS & WIZARDS COMPENDIUM

SPECIAL WEAPONS

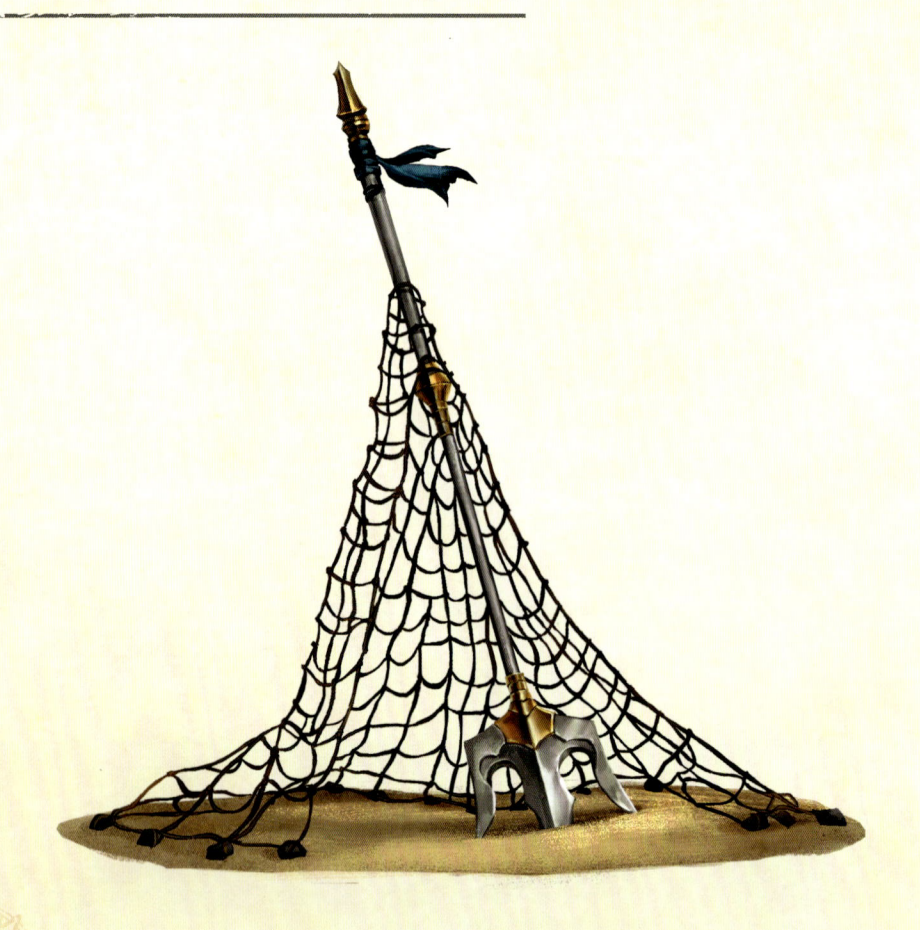

If a sword or axe isn't your style, there are other options to consider. A unique "signature weapon" that matches your fighting style or history is one way your character might stand out from other adventurers.

BOOMERANG A thrown hunting weapon made of wood or bone that delivers a bludgeoning strike to a target. Expert users can throw a boomerang so that it returns to their hand, but only if it hasn't struck a target.

CHAIN Heavy iron chains are challenging weapons to wield, but if you have the strength to haul and swing a length of chain, you can hit hard!

NET Weighted fishing nets can be hurled at opponents, tangling them up and leaving them vulnerable to follow-up attacks.

PICK A small, sharp spike with a handle, traditionally used for breaking up ice or stone. Easily concealed, and effective in close-quarters combat.

PUSH DAGGER Another easily concealed close-quarters weapon, comprising a small stabbing blade and a horizontal handle that rests in the user's palm.

SCYTHE Originally designed for harvesting crops, scythes are long-handled tools with a curved horizontal blade used in a sweeping motion. It is difficult to use as a weapon, but the blade can be reforged for use on a polearm or sword.

SICKLE A small one-handed version of a scythe. Its curved blade makes it a great choice for martial artists who strike at unexpected angles.

TRIDENT A spear with three prongs designed for spear fishing. A trident can be used as a throwing or thrusting weapon.

CRAZY COMBINATIONS

Instead of choosing a special weapon, you might take two familiar weapons and combine them in unusual ways. The only limit is your imagination! Here are some examples.

Dagger + Rope If you're an expert at throwing a dagger, adding a rope allows you to yank the dagger back.

Chain + Hammer A weighted chain with a bludgeon on the end creates an effective weapon for sweeping your enemies off their feet.

Crossbow + Axe Adding an axe blade to a crossbow creates a weapon that can be used for both ranged and melee combat.

Spear + Scythe Combining a spear and a scythe on either side of a pole creates a more versatile weapon for both forward and sideways attacks. Just remember to always check behind you!

Sword + Staff A sword can be hidden inside a staff or stick, giving you more options in combat and a chance to deliver a nasty surprise!

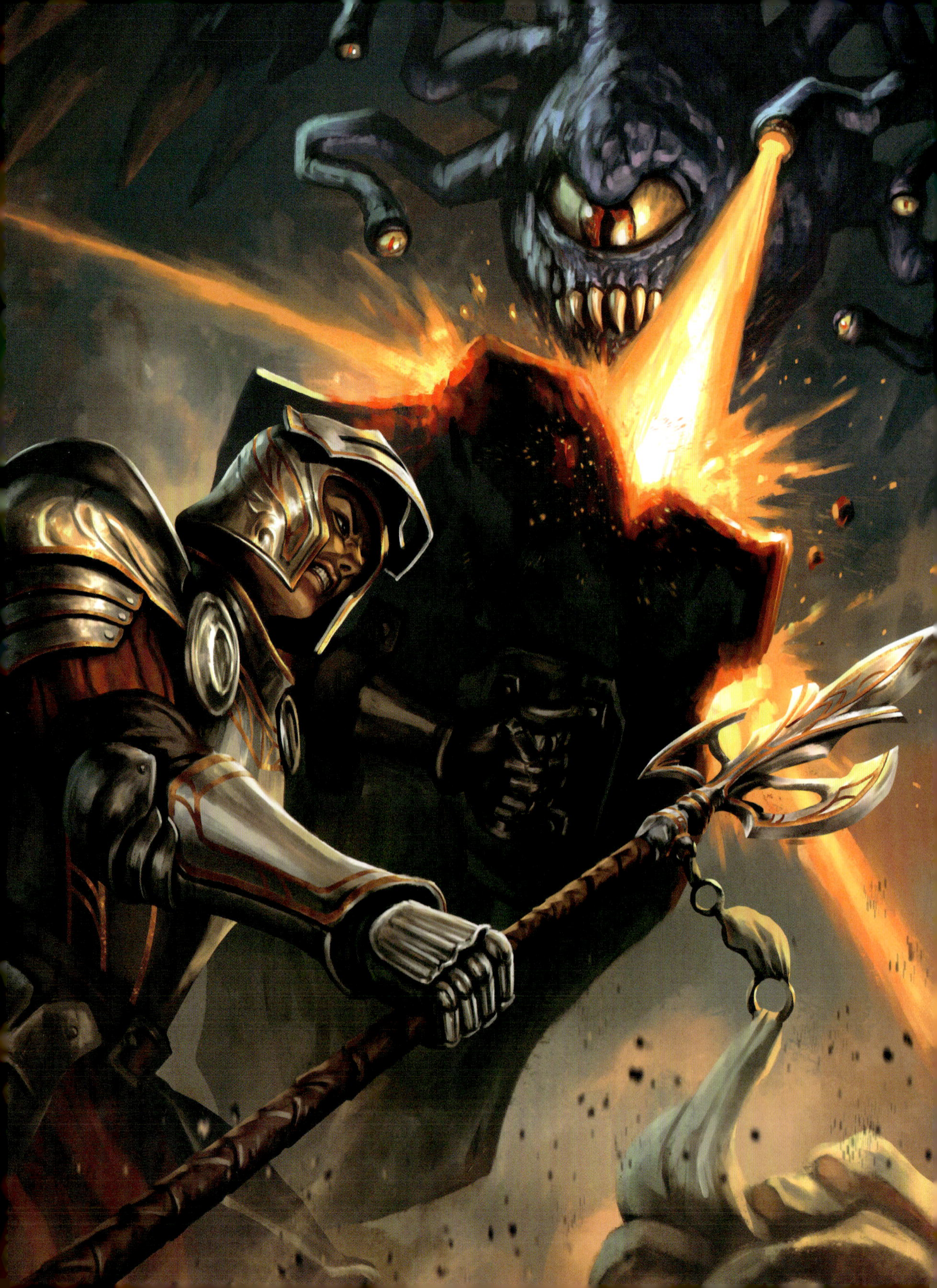

ARMOR: THE FOUNDATION OF DEFENSE

The toughest armor isn't always the best defense. Too much armor can slow down your character or even interfere with their magical abilities. Too little armor can leave you vulnerable to damage, especially if you tend to get up close and personal in a fight. Remember that some classes have restrictions on what kinds of armor they can use, so check what's available before you set your heart on that shiny suit of plate mail. Choose carefully if you want to survive the dangers ahead!

Budget is also a consideration for starting characters. Fancy metal armor can eat up all your savings, leaving you without the coins you'll need for food and additional gear. On the other hand, that homemade hide suit may be cheap, but it also won't offer much protection in a real fight. There's always a balance to be found when selecting armor.

GETTING IN (AND OUT) OF YOUR ARMOR

Putting on armor is no easy task. The speed with which you can go from normal clothes to full protection depends on the weight of your armor.

- **Light Armor** One minute
- **Medium Armor** Five minutes
- **Heavy Armor** Ten minutes

Make Your Choice Do you want to sit up for your turn keeping night watch in heavy, uncomfortable armor? Or, take the risk of having nothing but your weapon to protect you if there's an ambush? Luckily, it takes only a second to grab your trusty shield!

LIGHT ARMOR

Made from lightweight and flexible materials, light armor is the best choice for nimble adventurers. It will reduce damage from minor blows but might not be enough to protect you from stronger opponents.

PADDED ARMOR Made from quilted layers of cloth and batting, padded armor is lightweight and affordable, but not very strong. Be warned: This simple armor is bulky, which means your character is less stealthy than normal while wearing it.

Not ideal if you want to stay unnoticed.

LEATHER ARMOR The chest and shoulders of this armor are made of stiffened leather boiled in oil to increase its strength. The rest is made from softer materials that won't interfere with movement.

A great compromise between protection and weight, and pretty affordable too.

STUDDED LEATHER ARMOR This is leather armor that has been reinforced with rivets and spikes to help deflect blows.

Be careful, though—this type of armor is a lot more expensive than normal leather armor, and a lot heavier too. You don't want to wear this on a long trek unless you're quite strong.

CHOOSE WISELY

Remember, the more protection an armor provides, the more it interferes with your ability to move freely. If your character relies on being quick and agile, too much armor can actually be a bad thing.

THE WARRIORS & WIZARDS COMPENDIUM

MEDIUM ARMOR

Willing to sacrifice some mobility for extra protection? Medium armor may be just what you need. It's ideal for those who like to get into the thick of battle but possess more skills than just straightforward smashing to help them win the day.

HIDE Fit for a barbarian, this crude armor consists of thick furs and pelts that wrap around the body.

CHAIN SHIRT Made of interlocking rings, a chain shirt provides modest protection. It's great at deflecting sharp blades, but less helpful against bashing damage from maces or hammers. Its rings can be loud when they clink together, so to muffle the noise it's best worn as a layer between your regular clothing and a leather outer shell.

SCALE MAIL This armor is a mixture of leather and metal pieces overlapping like the scales of a fish—hence its name. With a coat, leggings, gloves, and sometimes an overskirt, it provides full-body protection for the intrepid adventurer.

BREASTPLATE Combining the solid toughness of a metal torso with the flexibility of leather armor, a breastplate helps protect your vital organs without weighing you down too much. Be careful, though, your chest may be safe, but your arms and legs are still exposed.

HALF PLATE Covering most of the wearer's body, these shaped metal plates are held together by leather straps to ensure the armor stays in place throughout the toughest fight. This type of armor is very strong but does have open gaps that leave weak spots for a skilled opponent to target.

HEAVY ARMOR

This tough stuff is your best bet for getting through a rough fight unscathed. However, the weight and bulk of heavy armor means that only the strongest and most experienced of warriors can wear it in combat without encountering speed or movement difficulties.

RING MAIL This is leather armor with heavy rings stitched across the surface. Metal makes it heavy to wear, but it's not as protective as chain mail because its rings are more spread out. On the plus side, it's less expensive than chain, making it a thrifty choice for beginning adventurers.

CHAIN MAIL The interlocking metal rings over a layer of quilted fabric in this armor provide solid protection against sharp-edged weapons such as swords and arrows. Be careful, though, you can still bruise beneath chain mail, and the tiny rings can be noisy when moving around.

SPLINT ARMOR Thin metal strips riveted onto leather backing create this tough, durable armor. Chain mail is added at the joints for extra protection at flexible spots, while thick padded fabric underneath keeps your skin from chafing.

PLATE MAIL The classic armor of knights and adventurers, this huge metal suit is designed to provide protection from head to toe. You'll need thick padding underneath to protect your skin, and well-fashioned straps to keep the weight properly aligned over your whole body. And plate armor is loud, so forget sneaking up on most creatures while wearing this.

THE WARRIORS & WIZARDS COMPENDIUM

SHIELDS

Often, a shield is an adventurer's best friend. Capable of stopping a wide range of attacks, from swords and arrows to warhammers and whips, shields are quick and versatile defensive tools. You can even use it as a bludgeoning weapon if you're backed into a corner and disarmed.

SHIELD MATERIAL AND PARTS Shields are made from many different materials, including wood, hardened leather, and metal. Wood and leather shields may have metal parts, like edges or spikes, to enhance their durability.

UMBO
A raised metal circle placed at the center of some shields, the umbo helps deflect blows aimed at the middle of the shield.

ENARMES
A leather-wrapped gripping handle attached to the back of the shield.

GUIGE
The long leather strap used to carry the shield across your back.

BUCKLER A small, round shield designed for basic personal protection, bucklers tend to be lightweight, inexpensive, and easy to carry and use. Their versatile design makes them the most common of all shields.

KITE Wide at the top and narrow at the bottom, kites are a longer shield that provides more coverage than a buckler. You can drive the pointed edge into the ground for added stability against an assault.

HEATER A smaller variation of the kite, a heater often has a peaked top to help defect sword blows. Its base is a little wider, giving more protection to the upper legs but potentially leaving your calves open to attack.

IMPROVISED Almost any object can become a shield with enough ingenuity— or desperation! Loose doors, coffin lids, metal serving plates, almost anything that's sturdy and in reach can help protect you from an enemy attack. You don't even need to be able to lift it—an overturned table or treasure chest makes a great place to hide from arrows! What kinds of improvised shields can you think of?

THE WARRIORS & WIZARDS COMPENDIUM

SURVIVAL GEAR

Whether crossing a desert, navigating a forest, or delving deep into a dungeon, there are certain things every adventurer needs to prepare for if they hope to survive, and that means bringing the right gear.

SHELTER The most basic form of shelter is a bedroll and a blanket but, if you can carry it, a weatherproof tarpaulin will help protect you from the elements. Better yet, bring a tent. Of course, some people are fine curling up in a tree or digging themselves a hole in the ground.

WATER A good waterskin is a vital piece of equipment for any adventurer, and you should take every opportunity to top up with clean drinkable water from a spring or stream.

FIRE Another vital piece of equipment is a tinderbox to light fires to keep you warm at night, cook food and boil water, and perhaps keep predators at bay. A tinderbox contains steel and flint, which can be struck together to create sparks, and some form of tinder, like wooden kindling or a flammable cloth, which can be used to ignite a fire.

LIGHT If you're navigating underground or by night, you'll need torches made from sticks wrapped in oil cloths that can be lit from a fire. Some adventurers have darkvision, allowing them to see in low light, but this ability won't allow you to see colors in the dark.

FOOD Adventure food needs to be compact and durable. Hardtack biscuits, made with just flour and water, are a popular choice. These crackers keep for a very long time but taste terribly plain. If you can't pack enough food for a long journey or want something flavorful, hunting and fishing equipment are very useful, so long as you know what to do with them! A guidebook to safe foraging is also helpful, plus a cooking pot in which to prepare your meals.

NAVIGATION A magnetic compass will help you find your way through unfamiliar territory, though remember that iron-rich caverns can throw off its accuracy. If a map exists for where you're going, it's a good idea to bring that too.

FIRST AID A basic healer's kit contains bandages, lotions, and splints, all of which are very useful if you forgot to bring a healer for your party—or if your healer is the one injured!

ADVENTURING GEAR

Defeat the monster, get the gold, avenge the people, save the day—adventuring is about more than just survival. Getting past every obstacle and facing off against every threat requires special equipment, so acquiring the right adventuring gear is very important.

Adventuring gear is just about anything that might help you get to your goal, aside from weapons, armor, trinkets, and magic items. These are some of the most popular examples.

Climber's Kit + Rope

Component Pouch

Hunting Trap

AMMUNITION If your weapon of choice is a sling, a bow, or a blowgun, make sure you pack enough shots, arrows, bolts, or darts for the journey.

BALL BEARINGS The thief's favorite. A handful of ball bearings tossed on flat ground can create an instant tripping obstacle for anyone chasing after you!

CLIMBER'S KIT Whether you're scaling a cliff, a tree, or a castle wall, you'll be safer with a climbing kit that includes pitons, gloves, and a harness.

COMPONENT POUCH A leather pouch that hangs from your belt, with separate compartments to hold the items needed for a spell.

HUNTING TRAP A heavy iron trap that you can set on the ground to catch big beasts (or unwary foes).

ROPE Rope is very useful for climbing, but you can also use it for setting traps, swinging across a chasm, or tying up prisoners.

THE WARRIORS & WIZARDS COMPENDIUM

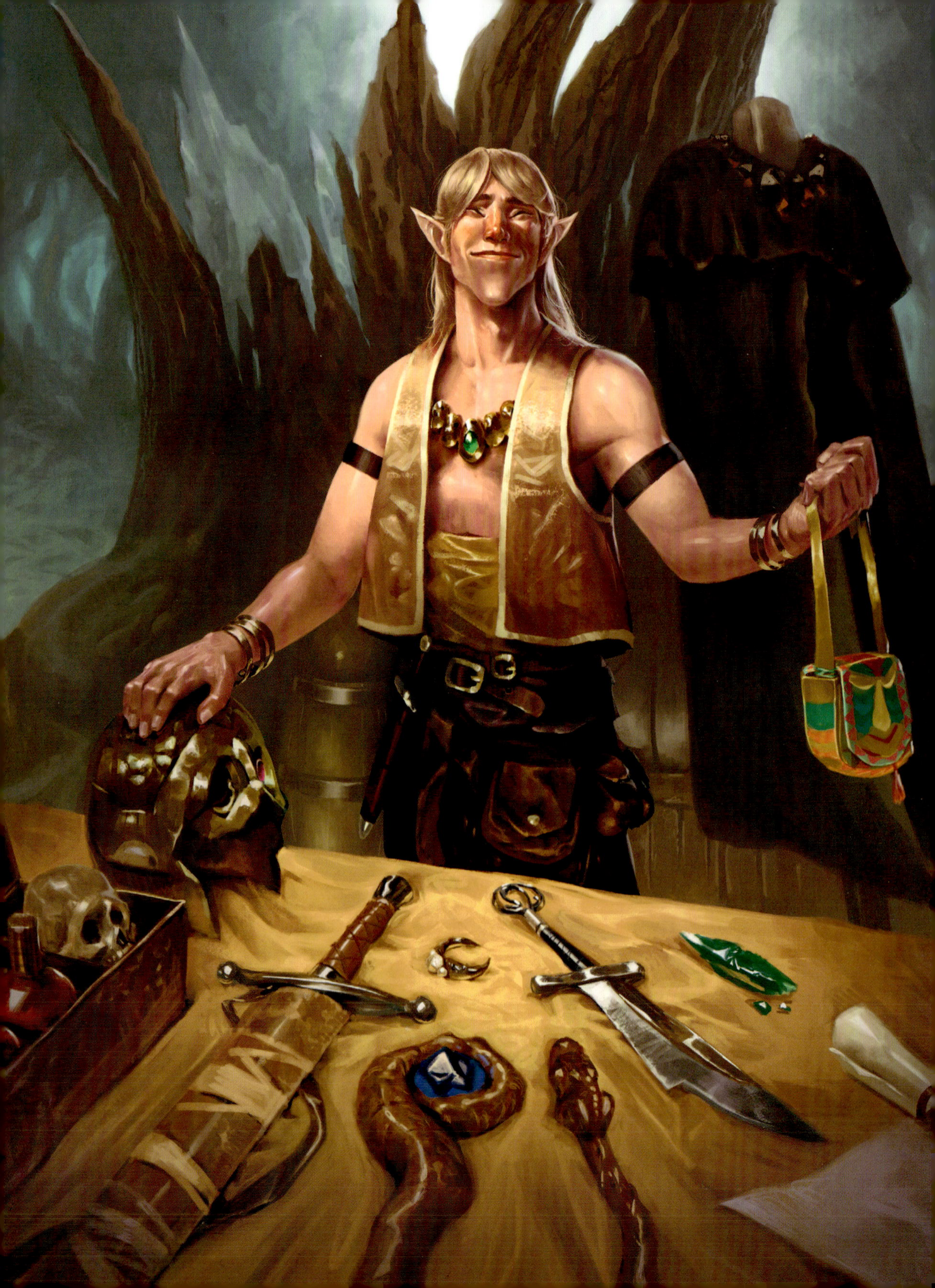

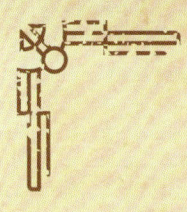

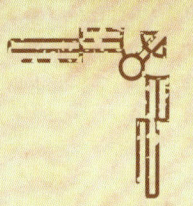

MAGIC ITEMS

There's one source of magical power that almost anyone can tap into: magic items. These rare and treasured objects come in near limitless forms and have near limitless uses. They include weapons such as swords and staves, spellcasting aids such as wands and rings, items of clothing such as cloaks and armor, and, of course, magic potions. By using such items, you might find you can walk on air, summon thunder, heal an ally, or even raise the dead.

Magic items are not easy to come by. You may uncover a powerful gemstone hidden deep in a dangerous dungeon, seize a magical sword from a vanquished foe, or receive a useful potion as a reward for a good deed. Gaining magic items requires a combination of courage and luck. Some magic items are common enough that you could buy them from a shopkeeper or a traveling salesperson on a lucky day; but beware, there are many counterfeits out there!

ATTUNEMENT

Most magic items require attunement, a special bond created when you spend an hour or more holding the item and focusing on its use. That may mean meditating on a magic ring, practicing with an enchanted sword, or studying a book.

You can only attune a maximum of three magic items at one time. The magic items on the following pages require attunement unless stated otherwise.

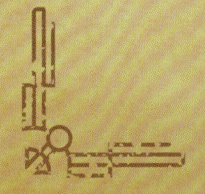

WEAPONS

Weapons are common and popular types of magic items, because even when the magic part doesn't come in handy, the weapon part just might.

Magic swords are especially celebrated. Many great heroes of legend carried famous swords that could sing, light themselves on fire, or never miss a stroke. However, there are magical versions of every type of weapon you might imagine, from bows and arrows to warhammers or hand axes.

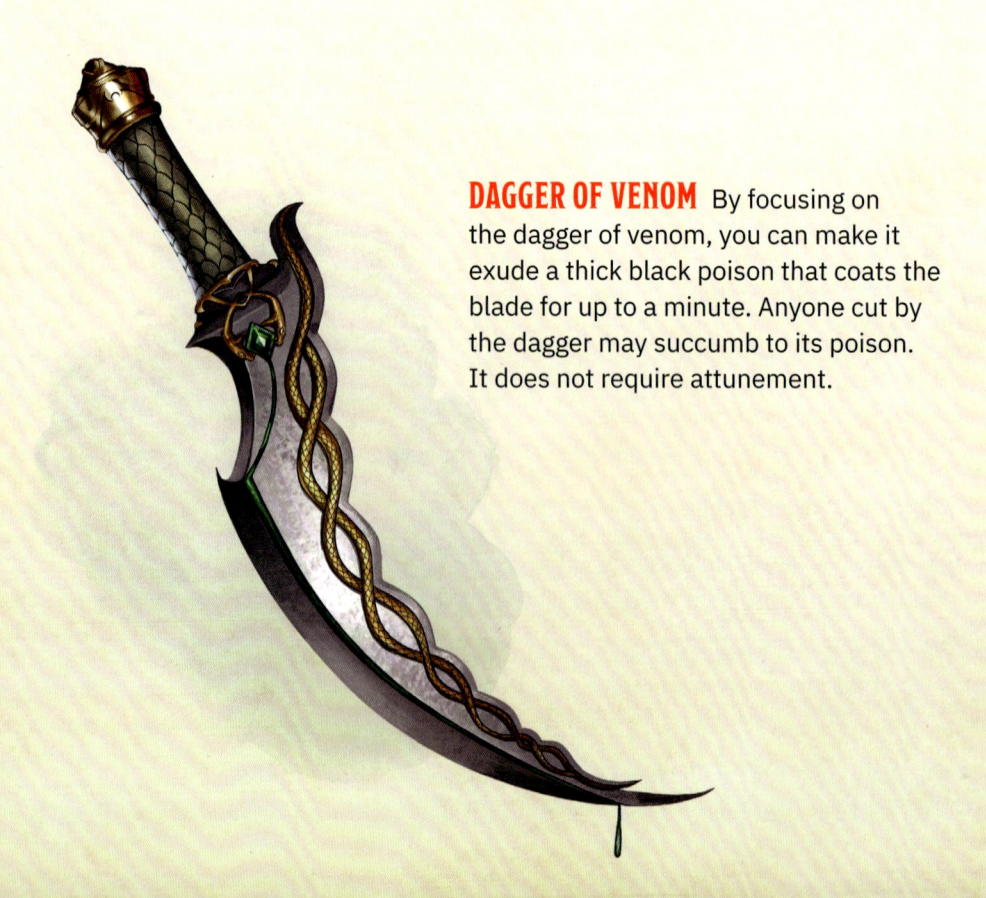

DAGGER OF VENOM By focusing on the dagger of venom, you can make it exude a thick black poison that coats the blade for up to a minute. Anyone cut by the dagger may succumb to its poison. It does not require attunement.

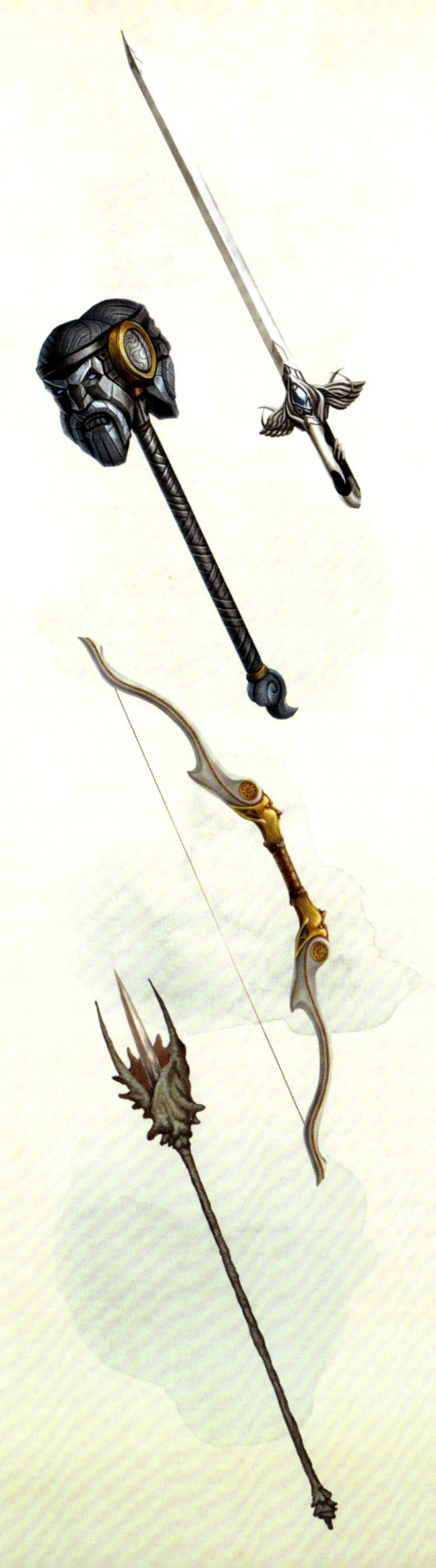

DANCING SWORD When hurled into the air, the dancing sword can be directed to strike like a missile at whatever nearby enemy you choose. If luck is on your side, it might attack up to four different foes before flying back to your hand.

HAMMER OF THUNDERBOLTS The hammer of thunderbolts gives you such great strength that you might survive going toe-to-toe with a giant! You can also use it to hurl thunderbolts at your enemies. However, the hammer's powers can only be accessed by someone wearing magical armor that gives them a giant's strength.

OATHBOW The oathbow is an elvish weapon that invites its owner to identify a "sworn enemy." Any arrow you fire will seek out that enemy, no matter the distance. However, the bow expects loyalty and, as long as your sworn enemy lives, you will find it difficult to use any other weapons.

WEAPON OF WARNING A weapon of warning can take many forms, but all types magically alert you to nearby danger. The weapon will even stir you from sleep when an enemy approaches, saving you from sneak attacks and deadly ambushes.

THE WARRIORS & WIZARDS COMPENDIUM

LEGENDARY WEAPONS

Legendary weapons exceed the usual benefits of magical weapons, delivering extraordinary powers worthy of the most illustrious adventurers. These armaments must be attuned to their user, forming a mystical bond, which means that only one adventurer can access the weapon's magic. In some cases this bond can flow both ways, causing the user to take on traits associated with the item's magic.

LUCK BLADE Every luck blade is infused with good fortune. Once per day, you can use the blade's luck to instantly retry a failed attempt to use the sword, giving you a second chance at success. Every luck blade contains up to three uses of a *wish* spell, the most powerful magic any mortal can wield. The luck blade retains the rest of its magic once its *wish* spells are used up. Luck blades can be greatswords, longswords, rapiers, scimitars, or shortswords.

NINE LIVES STEALER These blades are both cherished and feared by adventurers who seek to battle the most mighty of monsters, for legends are told of their ability to slay formidable beasts with a single blow. A nine lives stealer will, in the right circumstances, attempt to draw out the life force of its target. Should the blade succeed, the creature is instantly slain. This ability can only be used nine times for each sword. Characters who value goodness and morality may feel uncomfortable using the soul-shattering magic of a nine lives stealer.

TINDERSTRIKE This uncommonly sharp dagger contains a shard of Imix, the Prince of Evil Fire. The handle is always warm, and the blade smolders like hot coals for several minutes after each use. Tinderstrike grants fire mastery, allowing its holder to speak the language of fire elementals, command them, and resist fire damage. Within magical locations called fire nodes, the dagger can be used to create an elemental explosive device known as a devastation orb. Attunement to tinderstrike makes its wielder impatient and rash, causing them to act without thinking and to take needless risks until the magical bond is broken.

QUIVER OF EHLONNA Named for the goddess of woodlands in the realm of Greyhawk, this magic archer's case is especially prized by druids, although any adventurer may be attuned to it. The quiver of Ehlonna's three compartments connect to an extradimensional space, allowing it to store numerous items while never weighing more than two pounds. The shortest section of the quiver can hold up to sixty arrows or bolts, the middle one contains twelve javelins, and the largest holds six long objects, like quarterstaffs, bows, or spears. Non-archery items of a similar size can sometimes be stored in the appropriate compartment, although they may not always come back out.

LEGENDARY SWORD # THE SUNSWORD

The sunsword was once a particularly fine longsword with a blade made of magically resilient crystal, created by nobleman Sergei von Zarovich. Sergei was murdered by his envious brother, Strahd, who attempted to have the sword destroyed, but the hilt survived.

Imbued with magical will and possessed of a desire to seek vengeance on Strahd, the sword hilt generated its own blade of pure sunlight— the perfect weapon for destroying Strahd, whose hate and dark magics transformed him into a vampire lord. The sunlight blade also makes this sword a great weapon to use against any other undead you encounter!

The Sunsword is a swift weapon that cuts and blasts undead enemies with its radiant light. It can also act as a source of light in the dark. The sword possesses its own mind and can convey emotions to its wielder. For example, it might transmit a sense of fear if it senses danger nearby.

SUN BLADES

The true Sunsword is believed to be lost somewhere deep in the dark recesses of Castle Ravenloft, but other swords with a sunlight blade are known to exist. These swords are known as sun blades. By channeling daylight through their blade, they are capable of delivering deadly strikes against vampires and other undead monstrosities.

STAFFS

A magical staff is generally five to six feet long, about as tall as a regular human, and can be made from a wide range of materials, including wood, metal, or even crystal. They can be polished smooth or twisted and gnarled. Some staffs can be used as a melee weapon in combat, doubling as a quarterstaff. Even a non-spellcaster can use these artifacts to channel mystical power. Each staff has ten charges, which is the number of times it can be used before running out of power, and it regains one charge per day, usually at dawn.

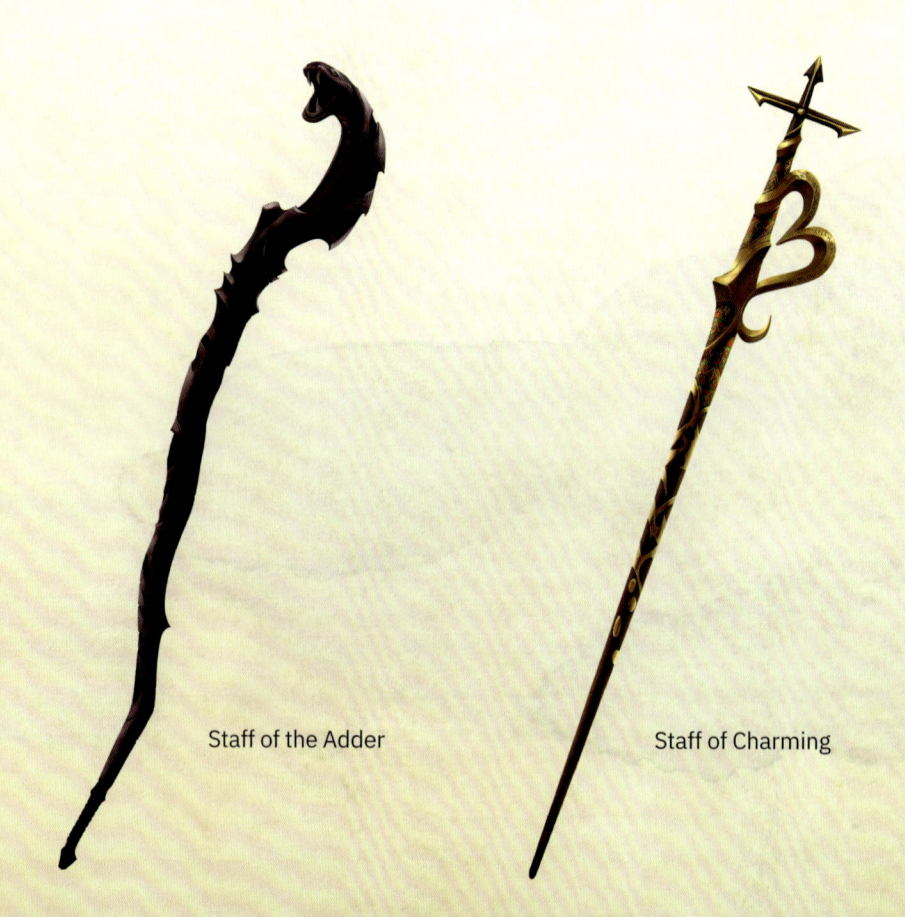

Staff of the Adder

Staff of Charming

STAFF OF THE ADDER When you speak a command word, the head of the staff of the adder comes to life, transforming into a poisonous snake that you can use to attack opponents. The effect lasts for one minute, so be quick.

STAFF OF CHARMING With the staff of charming, you can cast a spell that will charm another person, making them friendly toward you and willing to obey your commands. It also allows you to understand any spoken language.

STAFF OF FROST The wintery staff of frost grants you extra resistance to damage from cold and ice. You can also use it to cast a magical spell that will do freezing damage to your enemies.

STAFF OF WITHERING When you use the staff of withering to hit a foe, you can choose to inflict special withering damage that's harder to heal, along with the normal physical impact of your melee strike.

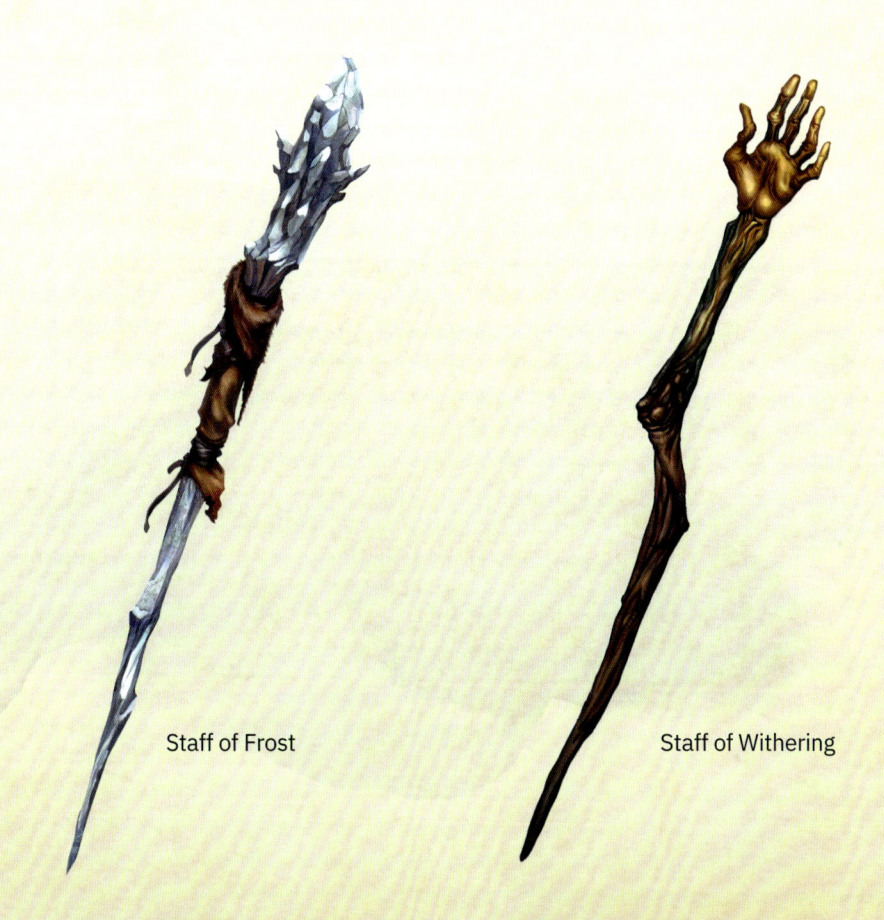

Staff of Frost

Staff of Withering

THE WARRIORS & WIZARDS COMPENDIUM

LEGENDARY STAFF

STAFF OF THE MAGI

The staff of the magi is a rare weapon that can be used as a standard quarterstaff in combat; however, its real value lies in its ability to cast and absorb magical attacks. When holding the staff, its possessor can use it to try and absorb any spell cast against them. If successful, the spell's energy is stored within the staff for future use, and the wielder is completely protected from the spell's effects.

The Staff of the Magi is capable of casting up to fifty spells, regaining one spell charge each dawn, along with any charges from spells that it absorbs. Magical attacks include casting fireballs, lightning bolts, ice storms, webs, and even a wall of fire. Its wielder can also use the staff to conjure an elemental servant, pass through solid walls, lift objects with psychic energy, detect magic, or cast an invisible shield to protect against evil.

In a desperate moment, the Staff of the Magi may be used for a single, explosive attack. By breaking the staff, all the magic stored within it is released at once. This retributive strike fills a thirty-foot sphere with explosive energy, wreaking untold amounts of damage and destruction. There is a chance that this explosion will cast the one breaking the staff into an alternate dimension.

WANDS

A magical wand is about fifteen inches long. They can be made from metal, bone, or wood and can be tipped with a charged piece of metal, crystal, stone, or some other material. Similar to staffs, each wand has seven charges that renew each day. If you run out of charges, the wand may be destroyed, so try not to drain it completely!

WAND OF LIGHTNING BOLTS A twisted metal wand, the wand of lightning bolts allows you to cast a lightning bolt (up to one hundred feet long and five feet wide) in any direction you choose. Be careful, though, because the lightning will set fire to anything flammable in its path!

WAND OF MAGIC DETECTION Each use of the wand of magic detection allows you to locate any magic power within thirty feet, causing enchanted items or locations to glow with a faint aura. The power lasts for up to ten minutes, but this powerful wand has only three charges, so use it wisely.

WAND OF PARALYSIS The wand of paralysis shoots a thin, blue ray that can hit a single target within a sixty-foot radius and paralyze them for up to one minute.

WAND OF POLYMORPH The creepy-looking wand of polymorph can transform its target from one type of creature into a different, less-dangerous type. The target is limited by the restrictions of its new form. For example, a human turned into a sheep would no longer be able to talk or walk upright. The effect lasts for up to one hour.

THE WARRIORS & WIZARDS COMPENDIUM

LEGENDARY WAND

WAND OF WONDER

One of the most powerful wands in all of existence, the wand of wonder can cast a staggering variety of magical spells. The effect is random and targets any one creature of the wielder's choice. Magical effects created by the wand can include the following:

Butterfly Swarm: A cloud of three hundred oversize butterflies forms around the target. The swarm makes it difficult for the victim to see or move through the space and lasts for ten minutes.

Darkness: A magical darkness surrounds the target in a fifteen-foot sphere. Not even darkvision or non-magical light sources can illuminate this gloom.

Gust of Wind: A strong wind pours out of the wand tip. All creatures in its path are pushed away, while torches and other flames are extinguished.

Heavy Rain: A sudden rainstorm falls around the target, obscuring vision and making everyone very, very wet.

Invisibility: Instead of striking a target, this effect works on the wielder, making them invisible to all creatures for up to one minute. The effect vanishes if the wielder attacks anyone.

Slowness: Causes the target to move at half their normal speed.

Stinking Cloud: A large sphere of yellow, noxious gas appears around the target, stinking of rotten eggs and skunk.

Thought Detection: The wielder can read the thoughts of their target for up to one minute.

USER BEWARE

Once in a while, the Wand of Wonder will not cast any outward spell. Instead, it simply stuns the wielder for ten seconds, leaving them convinced that something amazing has happened—even though it did nothing at all.

POTIONS

Potions are magical liquids made from enchanted herbs and other arcane ingredients, by experienced spellcasters who have spent years, if not decades, perfecting the art of capturing magic in a bottle.

A potion is a one-time-use magical item. You must drink the whole thing to get the special effect, so they can't be shared among multiple party members (unless you have multiple potions!). Once ingested, a potion takes effect right away, so be sure to save them for just the right moment.

POTION OF FLYING Drinking a *potion of flying* will allow you to fly for up to one hour. However, you can move only as fast as your character can walk on land. You can also hover in place. Be aware that you will start to fall the instant the potion wears off, so keep track of the time from ingestion.

POTION OF CLAIRVOYANCE
A *potion of clairvoyance* allows you to either see or hear what is happening in the moment at any location you have visited or seen before. You can also use it to see around corners or behind obstacles that are near your current location. The effect lasts for up to ten minutes, and you can switch between sight and hearing by focusing for six seconds.

POTION OF HEALING
An adventurer's best friend, a *potion of healing* will restore your body from damage sustained during a fight. Regular *potions of healing* repair minor wounds and bruises, while rarer types can do even more. Indeed, a *potion of supreme healing* will mend broken bones and fix deadly injuries in an instant.

POTION OF WATER BREATHING
The cloudy green *potion of water breathing* allows you to breathe underwater for sixty minutes. It smells—and tastes—as salty as the sea. Like the *potion of flying*, it wears off immediately once the hour is over, so don't let yourself get into deep waters without a plan of escape for when your time is up.

POISON POTION

Not all potions are friendly! Some nasty concoctions may look like a *potion of healing* but have effects that are the exact opposite. The unwary adventurer who imbibes this liquid will find themselves losing health fast. Only an *identify* spell, which can be learned by bards and wizards, is able to dispel the illusion that makes the *poison potion* look so sweet.

THE WARRIORS & WIZARDS COMPENDIUM

PARTICULAR POTIONS

Potions provide an easy-to-transport, easy-to-use means of accessing a dizzying array of magic effects. Although they can only be used once, a well-timed potion can be a powerful tool in an adventurer's arsenal.

POTION OF ANIMAL FRIENDSHIP If you've ever wanted to pal around with a dangerous critter, this is the potion for you. Drink it down and for the next hour, you'll be able to cast the *animal friendship* spell on one creature of your choosing. The beast must be able to see and hear you, and the spell will instantly break if you or your companions harm the creature. Otherwise, the animal is charmed by you for the next twenty-four hours. The potion works on creatures who walk, fly, swim, and slither, but be warned that very clever critters may be immune to its effects.

POTION OF FIRE BREATH This uncommon potion is sure to ignite fear in your enemies and awe in your allies. After drinking this flickering fluid, you'll be able to breathe a fiery blast at any target within a thirty-foot range (about the length of a school bus). This scorching experience inflicts a lot of damage, on top of being scary and cool. Your fire breath will last for one hour, or until you use it three times. Some potion-users have reported a smoky aftertaste, which can be fixed with a good teeth-brushing.

POTION OF GIANT STRENGTH
Prepare for a mighty flex once you guzzle this magic potion. For one hour after drinking, you'll have the same strength as a giant, packed into your regular-size body. You can use that strength to do all kinds of things, like lift heavy objects, fight powerful monsters, or beat all your friends at arm wrestling.

Just like giants, this potion comes in six varieties, with strength and rarity changing based on the giant type. Hill giant potions give the smallest gain, followed by frost, stone, fire, and cloud giants. Storm giant potions are powerful and rare enough to be considered legendary. That makes sense when you realize that every *potion of giant strength* requires a special ingredient—a fingernail sliver from the relevant giant type. Yum!

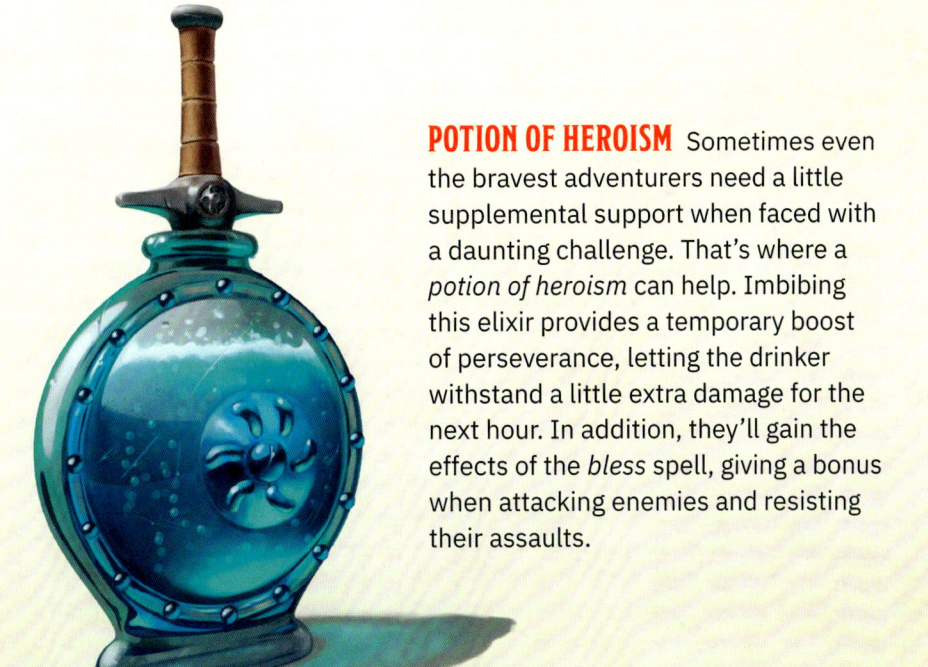

POTION OF HEROISM
Sometimes even the bravest adventurers need a little supplemental support when faced with a daunting challenge. That's where a *potion of heroism* can help. Imbibing this elixir provides a temporary boost of perseverance, letting the drinker withstand a little extra damage for the next hour. In addition, they'll gain the effects of the *bless* spell, giving a bonus when attacking enemies and resisting their assaults.

THE WARRIORS & WIZARDS COMPENDIUM

RINGS

Magical rings are a popular type of enchanted item, because they are small and discreet. As a result, your enemies don't always know you have them, or that you're about to use them, and you never need to be parted from them. (Nice jewelry can also really complete an outfit.)

A magic ring is like having a bonus spell at your fingertips—though it's really closer to your knuckle! Just remember that you can be attuned to only three magic items at once, so wearing a bunch of different rings doesn't necessarily mean you'll be able to access all their powers simultaneously.

RING OF THE RAM The ring of the ram generates a spectral battering ram that can smash through obstacles—including other people. Up to three times a day, you can use this ring like a long-distance super-punch to shatter doors or knock people off their feet.

RING OF ANIMAL INFLUENCE If you want to charm an animal to be your friend, frighten an animal to chase it away, or communicate with an animal so that you understand each other, wearing this ring will empower you to do any or all of these things. This ring does not require attunement.

RING OF REGENERATION An incredibly useful item for anyone who likes to dive into the thick of danger. The ring of regeneration allows its wearer to heal quickly from injury. Even if someone chops off part of your body, this ring will allow you to grow it back! (One important note: This kind of magical regeneration doesn't work if the part that's chopped off is your head.)

RING OF SHOOTING STARS This ring has several powerful effects. For example, it can generate dazzling light, or create balls of lightning that can shock anyone who comes near. However, its most useful effect is that it allows its wearer to fire shooting stars from their hands, which can burn anyone they strike! This ring can only be attuned at night.

THE WARRIORS & WIZARDS COMPENDIUM

CLOAKS

More than just clothing items to keep you warm and dry, magical cloaks can bestow wondrous powers upon their wearer. They can be worn by all character classes with no magical training required. Like all wearable magic items, cloaks are designed to be adjustable for all sizes, from tiny gnomes to towering dragonborn. Some cloaks even have, woven right into their fabric, the magical ability to change their size.

CLOAK OF DISPLACEMENT

The cloak of displacement casts an illusion that makes you appear to be standing just a little bit away from your actual location, making it much harder for enemies to hit you. If you *are* hit, the cloak's power stops working for a few seconds. If you are restrained, unconscious, or otherwise unable to move, the displacement illusion also stops functioning.

CLOAK OF ARACHNIDA
The spider-patterned cloak of arachnida allows you to climb as easily as you can walk, moving across vertical surfaces and upside down along ceilings. It also makes you resistant to poison and prevents you from being caught in webs. Once per day, you can create a sticky web up to twenty feet wide that can ensnare creatures.

CLOAK OF ELVENKIND
The cloak of elvenkind is an elvish garment that lets the wearer, when the cloak's hood is placed over their head, draw upon the natural stealth and perception of the elves. The cloak's power makes it harder for you to be seen when worn this way, while enhancing your ability to hide by shifting colors to provide camouflage.

CLOAK OF THE MANTA RAY
Worn with the hood up, the cloak of the manta ray grants you the ability to breathe underwater and swim as fast as a medium-size fish. The effects stop when the hood is lowered.

WONDROUS ITEMS

Wondrous magic items are ones that don't fall into any of the previous categories. They can range from wearable items, like boots and gloves, to uncommon jewelry such as circlets and brooches. Bags, ropes, carpets, crystal balls, musical instruments, and other uncommon objects also fall into this classification. This magical designation is limited only by your imagination!

MASK OF THE BEAST

These ornately beautiful masks contain a spell that can render an animal docile and friendly; most useful when the wearer wants to survive an encounter with a predator such as a big cat or a beast such as a charging bull. It's equally effective on less-threatening creatures, from fish to birds or even monkeys.

The wearer cannot directly command animals nor speak their language, but finds it easy to interact in ways not otherwise possible. For example, they might convince a lion to let them ride on its back, or ask a bear to attack an intruder. More powerful druids and sorcerers can target multiple creatures, and run with a pack of wolves or swim among sharks without any fear.

BAG OF HOLDING This bag appears to be relatively small, about two feet tall and four feet long, but it can hold up to sixty-four cubic feet worth of stuff. (That's about the size of four regular refrigerators.) Objects placed in the bag can weigh up to 500 pounds, but the bag itself will never weigh more than 15 pounds, similar to the weight of an average house cat. Overloading the bag causes its contents to vanish to another dimension, so keep track of how much you've stuffed inside.

BOOTS OF SPEED Click together the heels of a pair of boots of speed and your walking velocity will instantly double. On top of that, your reaction to attacks is increased, making it harder for enemies to get the jump on you. The magic wears off after ten minutes, and will not recover until you've had a long, eight-hour rest. You can turn the boots' magic off by clicking your heels together a second time, saving part of the magical charge for later use.

LANTERN OF REVEALING When lit, this lantern gives off a bright light that renders invisible creatures and objects visible. This light extends in a thirty-foot circle around the lantern. By lowering the lantern's hood, you can focus the light's range to five feet.

THE WARRIORS & WIZARDS COMPENDIUM

NOLZUR'S MARVELOUS PIGMENTS These very rare pigments allow you to create three-dimensional objects by painting them onto a flat surface. Each pot of paint can cover up to one thousand square feet, about the floor size of a small suburban house. When you complete the painting, the object or landscape becomes a real, physical object. Painting a door on a wall creates a real door you can walk through, for example. It is not possible to paint wealth or magic into being. Painted gold coins will turn out to be dull, worthless metal, and painted wands cannot be used for spells.

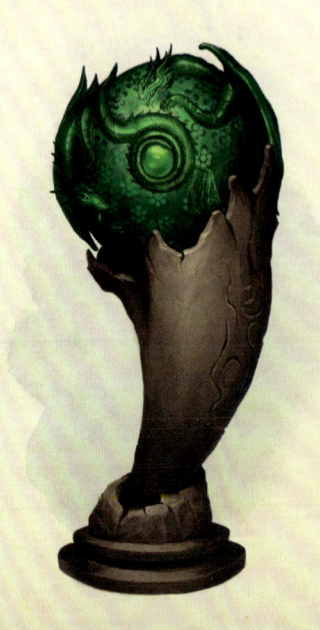

ORB OF DRAGONKIND The rare and wondrous Orbs of Dragonkind allow their user to *summon* a dragon. They don't grant any other control over the powerful beasts; all you're really doing is bringing one of the most formidable creatures in the world much *closer* to you. What they do when they arrive is up to them. Often, they'll want to punish the summoner! An orb grants other powers at random, such as healing or immunities; however, it also curses its wielder with unexpected weaknesses and disadvantages. Using an orb is very risky.

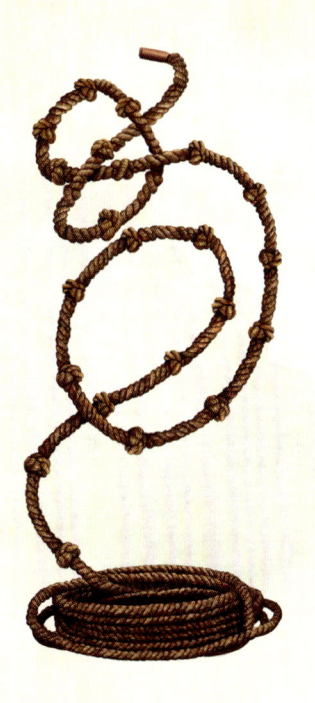

ROPE OF CLIMBING By holding one end of this magical rope and speaking a command word, the rope animates, moving toward the destination of your choosing. You can tell the rope to fasten itself (securing to an object), untie itself, or knot itself in one-foot intervals for easier climbing. The rope is sixty feet long and can hold up to 3,000 pounds in weight.

STACKING MAGIC ITEMS

Except in rare instances, a character can wear or use only one of each type of magic item at a time. Stacking multiple magic cloaks over your clothing, for instance, is not only very warm and bulky but can negate the effect of the magic.

For paired magic items, like boots or gloves, you must wear both the right and left items for the magic to work—so no sharing your boots of speed with a friend so you can both run double-time.

THE WARRIORS & WIZARDS COMPENDIUM

GUARDIAN GEAR

Survival is a key component of any successful encounter. Magic items such as the ones on this page are designed to help you not only challenge a powerful foe but also to live to tell the tale of your victory.

DREAD HELM Sometimes your best defense is to look really, really scary. That's where a dread helm comes in. This helmet's magic causes your eyes to glow red and hides the rest of your face in shadow, all without affecting your vision. The sharp spikes, sculpted side plates, and angular wings of the helmet add to the imposing effect. While a dread helm doesn't technically offer more protection than any other steel helmet, you're a lot less likely to get hit when your opponents are running away in fear.

HELM OF BRILLIANCE Each gem on this helmet is infused with a magic spell: *daylight* for opals, *fireball* for fire opals, *prismatic spray* for diamonds, and *wall of fire* for rubies. Casting a spell causes a gem of that type to disappear from the helm of brilliance. When all the gems are gone, the helm loses its magic. So long as the helm has one fire opal, you can command your weapon to burst into flame. If there is at least one diamond, the helm emits a dim light around undead creatures, dealing them additional damage. Avoid fire damage while wearing the helm, since there's a small risk it will activate all the gems at once, injuring everyone nearby and destroying the helm itself.

SCARAB OF PROTECTION This beetle-shaped medallion might be mistaken for an unusual piece of jewelry, until you hold it in your hand for a few seconds. Then an inscription will appear on its surface that reveals its magical nature. A scarab of protection grants its wearer a better chance of resisting spells of all kinds. When affected by necromantic spells or undead powers, adventurers can call upon this amulet to throw off any negative effects. This special ability can be used only twelve times, however, after which the scarab of protection crumbles into dust.

SPELLGUARD SHIELD Shields do a great job of protecting an adventurer from physical attacks. A spellguard shield goes a step further by protecting against magical harm as well. Spell attacks are less likely to work thanks to the shield's protective power. It is also easier to resist the effects of all kinds of magic while holding a spellguard shield. Such shields are usually decorated with mystical symbols, although that's not always the case.

CURATIVE CONTRAPTIONS

No matter how careful you are, the occasional injury is part of being an adventurer. Whether battling dangerous beasts, traversing rough terrain, tackling magical hazards, or dropping a heavy sack of treasure on your toes, there's plenty of ways to get hurt—or worse—during a quest. The magic items on these pages will help you alleviate the effects of all kinds of harm, from sickness and stubbed toes to death itself.

CAULDRON OF REBIRTH This tiny cast-iron pot is decorated with scenes of heroic adventures and can serve as a spellcasting focus to improve a wizard's or druid's magic. At the end of a long rest, use the cauldron to create a *potion of greater healing* that will last for twenty-four hours. The cauldron of rebirth can be increased in size, making it big enough for a medium-size creature to fit inside. Once every seven days, a dead humanoid can be placed inside the cauldron and covered with two hundred pounds of salt. Overnight, the salt will be consumed and the creature returned to life!

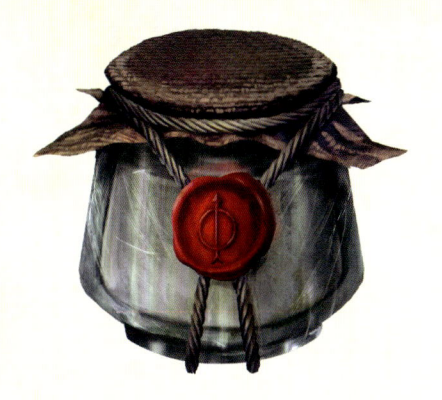

KEOGHTOM'S OINTMENT Developed by a legendary alchemist and explorer, Keoghtom's ointment is a thick, gloopy lotion that smells faintly of aloe. It can instantly cure any disease or poisoning and restore the health of the user. The ointment is stored in a glass jar that weighs about half a pound and holds up to five doses.

PERIAPT OF HEALTH This uncommon amulet features a red stone carved to look like a heart with two faces, one happy and one sad. When wearing a periapt of health, it is impossible to contract any disease, either by natural or magical means. If someone is already sick, they will not feel the effects of their illness as long as they are wearing the necklace. This works against all diseases, including those caused by monsters or magic, although it won't help against curses such as lycanthropy.

REINCARNATION DUST This purple dust inside a small pouch contains powerful but erratic magic. By sprinkling the dust on a dead humanoid—or even just a part of them—the target can be revived! The magic creates an entirely new body for the soul to inhabit. Curiously, this new body is often a different species than the original body. An elf revived by reincarnation dust may arise as a dragonborn or a human, for example. However, the dust will not work on anyone who has been dead for more than ten days or anyone who does not want to be revived.

THE WARRIORS & WIZARDS COMPENDIUM

INFUSED INSTRUMENTS

The idea that music is magic takes concrete shape through the enchanted instruments on these pages. Most can only be attuned by bards, although some instruments—like the *pipes of haunting*—can be played by anyone who possesses the right skills.

INSTRUMENT OF THE BARDS There are seven different types of these extraordinary instruments: the cittern, bandore, lute, lyre, mandolin, and two different types of harp. When played, the attuned musician can choose to cast one of seven different spells bound to the instrument. Four spells—*fly, invisibility, levitate,* and *protection from good and evil*—are common to all, while the other three spells vary depending on the instrument. The rarest instrument is the Ollamh harp, a legendary object capable of controlling the weather and summoning a fire storm.

LYRE OF BUILDING This small, U-shaped, stringed instrument lets you heal physical objects. While holding the lyre, you can cast the *mending* spell to repair a break or tear in any item that you touch. When a nearby object or building is damaged, you can also play it to temporarily protect the structure. Once per day, the lyre of building allows you to cast one of four different spells to do things such as create passages in walls, move large amounts of dirt, create finished objects from raw materials, and summon an enchanted construct.

PIPES OF HAUNTING Carved from bone and decorated with animal skulls, these creepy windpipes sound just as scary as they look. By expending a charge, the musician can play an eerie tune that frightens all nearby listeners. Creatures who succumb to the magic music find it harder to attack or approach the musician for one minute. You must know how to play wind instruments to use the pipes of haunting. An untrained player can create a dreadful sound with them, but it won't have the magic effect!

REVELER'S CONCERTINA This squeezebox-style instrument is similar to an accordion, although smaller and lighter, and produces a bright, upbeat sound. Just holding a reveler's concertina makes all your bardic spells a little more effective. While playing the concertina, you can cast the instrument's special spell—*Otto's irresistible dance*—against one nearby creature. The target immediately begins a comical dance that lasts for one minute, during which they are less able to attack or defend themselves. They also look very, very silly. The concertina can only create this effect once a day.

SNEAKY SUPPLIES

Stealth may be a rogue specialty, but any character can benefit from these magic items designed to help you access locked places, travel unseen, and move heavy items with relative ease.

CHIME OF OPENING The clear tone that this hollow metal tube makes when struck is capable of opening objects that would otherwise resist imposing physical force or the most skilled lockpicks. One lock or latch on the selected object opens with each note sounded, provided that the chime's sound can reach the object. If no locks or latches remain, the object itself opens. After sounding ten times, the chimes crack and become useless.

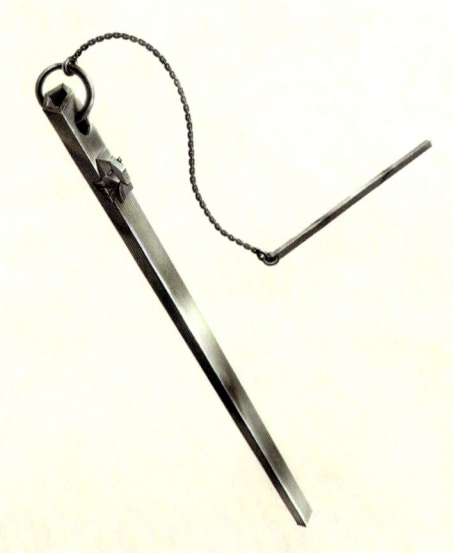

DUST OF DISAPPEARANCE This magic powder has the look and feel of very fine beach sand. When thrown into the air, all creatures and objects within ten feet become invisible. They cannot be seen, except by other creatures using magic or possessing extraordinary senses. However, those invisible will still make noise and leave tracks that might give away their location. The effect lasts for two to eight minutes, but can be broken if the user attacks or casts a spell. Unfortunately, the dust of disappearance doesn't reappear, which means each packet can only be used once.

IMMOVABLE ROD Imagine how useful it would be to defy gravity whenever you wanted. That's the magic of the immovable rod, which becomes stationary when the button on one end is pressed. No matter where you are when the button is pressed—falling through the sky, scaling an icy cliff, jumping over a sleeping dragon's hoard—the rod locks into place. Incredibly strong creatures might be able to move the rod a few feet with extreme effort, and loading the rod with more than eight thousand pounds will cause it to deactivate.

PORTABLE HOLE Carrying an extra-dimensional hole in your pocket can be surprisingly useful. This fine black cloth starts about the size of a handkerchief but unfolds into a six-foot round sheet that, when placed against a solid surface, opens up into a ten-foot-deep hole. You can fill the hole with almost anything that fits and close it back up by folding in the edges. Since everything inside is being stored in another dimension, the portable hole remains practically weightless.

There's only ten minutes of breathable air in the hole, so don't store living creatures inside for longer or they might suffocate! Trapped creatures can try to break out, reappearing within five feet of the hole's location if they succeed. It's a terrible idea to place one extradimensional container, like a bag of holding or a portable hole, inside a different one. The resulting blast will destroy both items and toss everyone nearby through a magic portal that promptly vanishes forever.

TREMENDOUS TOMES

Some adventurers believe that all books contain a little magic. With the tomes described here, there can be no doubt! Many magic books can only be used by wizards, who are trained to bring forth spells from written pages, although some tomes are accessible to everyone.

ATLAS OF ENDLESS HORIZONS Bound in dark leather, this thick book is crisscrossed with inlaid silver lines resembling a map or a chart. That's no coincidence, because this atlas contains a variety of spells capable of moving the user from place to place, or even between dimensions or planes of existence. The book has three charges (see page 168) and regains some used charges each dawn. The charges allow you to replace one of your memorized spells with a different spell from the book, or to teleport up to ten feet when hit by an attack.

FULMINATING TREATISE This thick spellbook reeks of smoke and ozone, with sparks of energy cracking along the edges of its scorched pages. It contains seven spells—among them *fireball, gust of wind, magic missile,* and *thunderwave*. The book has three charges and gains back some used charges each dawn. The charges allow you to replace one of your memorized spells with a different spell from the book, or to do additional damage to a creature who has already been injured by one of your spells.

MANUAL OF BODILY HEALTH This book contains detailed information on health and nutrition, written on magic-infused pages. By studying the manual of bodily health and following its advice for forty-eight hours over a six-day period, you will significantly improve your physical endurance. Similar manuals exist for increasing your dexterity (manual of quickness of action) and your strength (manual of gainful exercise). Magic manuals require one century to regain their power after being used.

TOME OF UNDERSTANDING This magic volume is filled with exercises to improve your intuition and insight. If you spend forty-eight hours during a six-day period reading the tome of understanding and practicing the exercises, you'll notice a decided increase in your wisdom. Related references exist for improving your charisma (tome of leadership and influence) and your intelligence (tome of clear thought). These magic books require one century to regain their power after being used.

THE WARRIORS & WIZARDS COMPENDIUM

USEFUL ODDITIES

Sometimes adventurers come across magic items that are so unusual it seems remarkable that anyone dreamt them up in the first place. These quirky creations often prove to be surprisingly useful, especially when you apply a little imagination to exploring their possibilities.

ABRACADABRUS This ornate wooden chest is studded all over with gemstones, with enough space inside to fit an average beach ball. To use, touch the closed lid and name an inexpensive, nonmagical object, which magically appears inside the abracadabrus. Conjured food is delicious and nourishing, but spoils after twenty-four hours. Gems and precious metals vanish after one minute. An abracadabrus has up to twenty charges, recovering a random number each dawn. If the chest runs out of charges, its gemstones might turn to dust, ending its magic forever.

BAG OF BEANS This heavy bag contains between four and twelve dried beans. If you plant a single bean in the ground and water it, a random magic effect pops up one minute later. Possibilities include a blue campfire, pink toads that turn into monsters, a giant beanstalk, or a sixty-foot pyramid with a mummy lord inside. If you dump all the bag's contents on the ground at once, the beans produce an explosion that damages everything within ten feet and ignites all flammable objects.

DAERN'S INSTANT FORTRESS Most adventurers make do with open campfires or simple tents when sleeping out in the wild. The ones lucky enough to possess this wondrous and rare magic item can, instead, take shelter in their very own fortress. With a command word, this one-inch metal cube expands into a square tower twenty feet wide and thirty feet high. Inside the fortress are two floors connected by a ladder. There are arrow slits on all the walls and a magic door that opens only at your command. Creatures in the way will be pushed aside as the building expands, sometimes being injured in the process. A second command word collapses Daern's instant fortress back into a metal cube, provided the tower is empty.

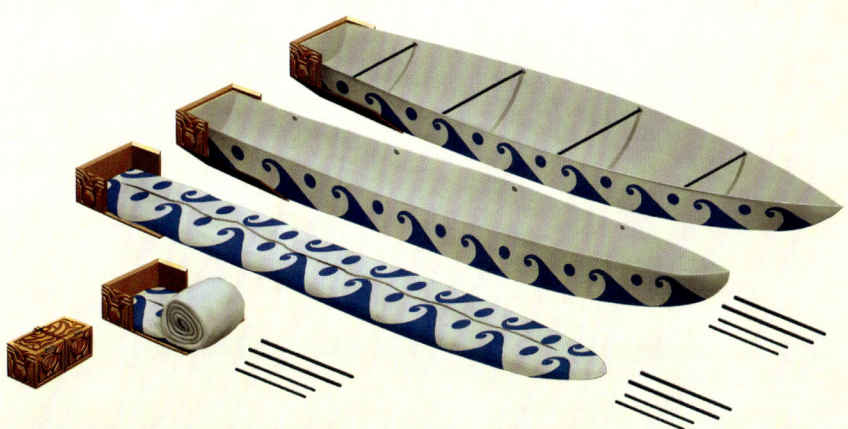

FOLDING BOAT This handy item is a welcome addition to any expedition party that travels over both land and water. In its basic form the folding boat appears as a rectangular wooden box about one foot long and weighing four pounds. Three different command words activate its magic properties. The first causes the box to unfold into a ten-foot boat capable of carrying four medium creatures. The second command produces a larger vessel with room for fifteen creatures. The final word collapses the folding boat back into its box form. This only works if no living creatures are inside the vessel, so you won't get dumped in the water if you accidentally say the command word while sailing.

THE WARRIORS & WIZARDS COMPENDIUM

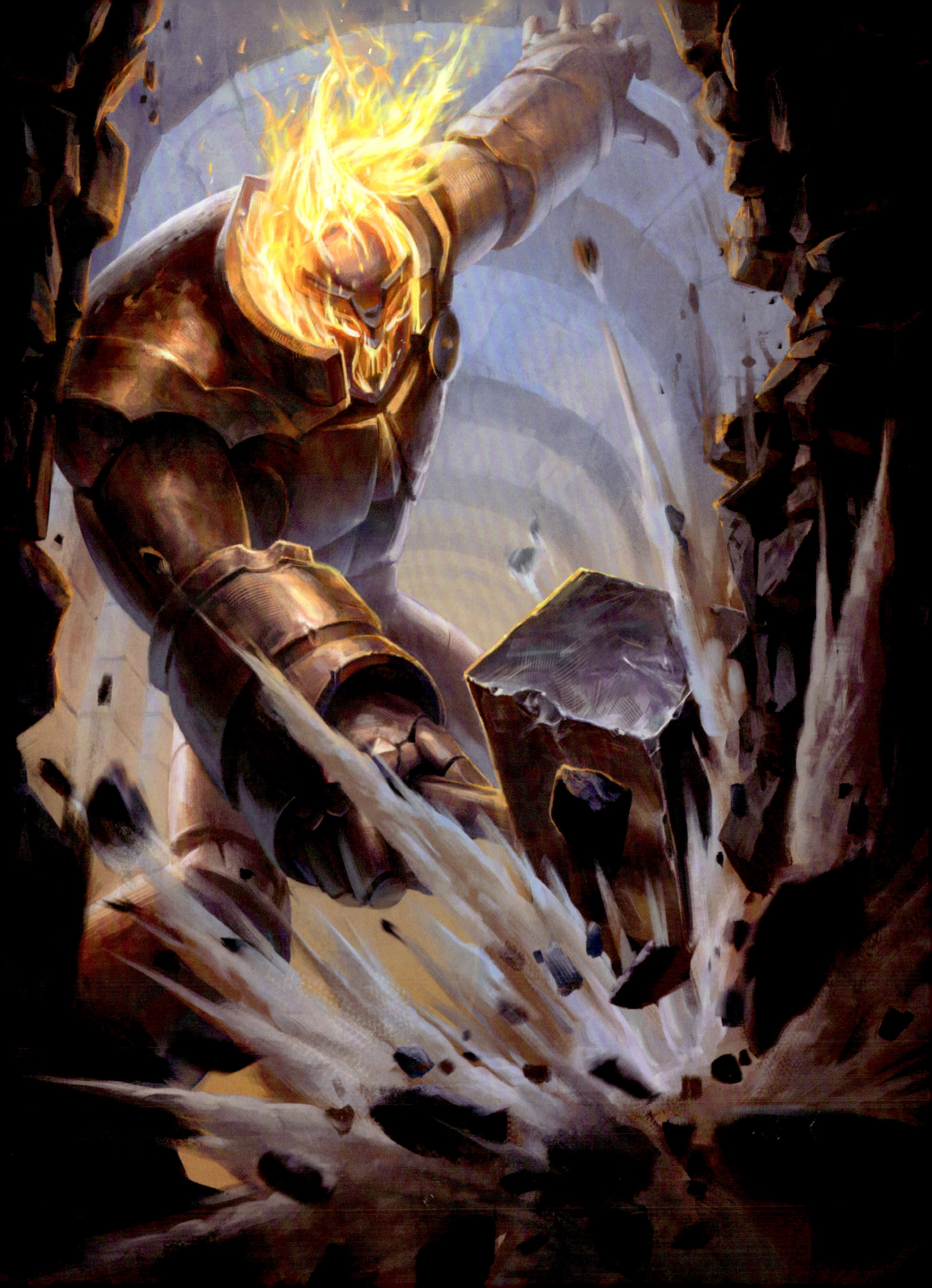

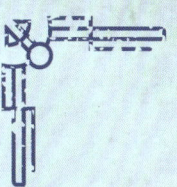

CURIOUS CONSTRUCTS

The adventuring party was not merely lost, they were trapped with no hope of escape. The artificer known as Dwallum had offered to provide them with weapons to protect their village from a young dragon that destroyed their neighbors. They only had to reach Dwallum at his forge, somewhere deep in the mines beneath the fortress of Ironslag—and bring him a gift from his daughter.

Somehow, the party had found themselves stuck in a room with no doors—a magical trap for unwary visitors. They feared they would never escape. Then they heard the *clang, clang, clang* of approaching footsteps. Heavy steps. Very heavy steps.

When the iron golem crashed through the wall, the adventurers immediately attacked in a desperate bid to survive. How could they have known that Dwallum himself had sent the golem to their rescue?

Constructs are unlike any other beings you might encounter on an adventure. Made from lifeless materials, they are animated by magic and infused with spirits that allow them to move and communicate. Often tough, strong, and possessing unusual immunities, constructs can be significant obstacles—or useful allies.

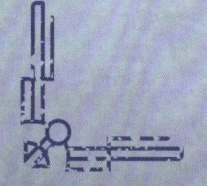

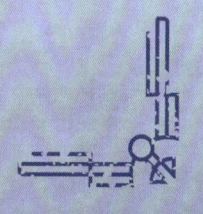

CONSTRUCTS OVERVIEW

In worlds dominated by magic, filled with entities such as unicorns, dragons, and giants, there are some who say constructs are the most disconcerting creatures that they have ever encountered—if they would call them "creatures" at all. Constructs are artificial beings made of inorganic or dead materials, like stone, clay, wood, or metal. Though they are created using magic, constructs require crafting expertise and engineering skills, making them products of science as much as magic. This fact can make them seem strange even to adventurers who are used to dealing with fey, lycanthropes, or the undead.

Artificers are experts when it comes to creating constructs—their technical approach to magic gives them all the skills they need to build and animate anything from a small clockwork assistant to an imposing stone defender.

FUNCTIONS

Constructs are always created to serve a purpose, and most of them fall into one of three categories.

Helpers: Constructs designed to assist their creator or act as a servant or companion. This includes the homunculi favored by artificers, and golems created by high priests.

Protectors: Constructs that guard locations, conduct patrols, or act as bodyguards to their creators. Many clockwork creations fall into this category. Golems can also perform this role.

Warriors: Constructs can be built to be very strong and very tough, and they follow orders without question, making them incredibly effective soldiers. The warforged are the most famous example of this type.

IMMUNITIES

Because constructs are inorganic, they are immune to certain conditions that affect organic life. They cannot be poisoned and do not require food, drink, air, or sleep. They are unaffected by psychic attacks and cannot be charmed or frightened. Constructs do not need to rely on ordinary senses.

GOLEMS

Golems are crafted from humble materials but possess incredible power and durability. These mindless servants have no independent thoughts and feel no pain, existing only to obey their creator's commands.

CLAY GOLEM Built by high priests who trap spirits in clay bodies, these golems are obedient servants and protectors of sacred sites. Some are beautifully carved by master artisans, while others are more roughly put together in forms only vaguely reminiscent of humans. Clay is not a strong vessel, so if the golem's form is seriously damaged, the spirit may escape, leaving the body to attack everyone around it indiscriminately. The golem must be destroyed or repaired to end its rampage.

Clay golems often outlive their creators, continuing to attend to their duties without thought or desire. If the creator used an amulet as a focus to control the golem, another adventurer can take over command by acquiring the amulet.

FLESH GOLEM The most disgusting form of golem, these constructs are built out of humanoid body parts stitched and bolted together. Flesh golems are enchanted with many of the same immunities as other constructs, but they are afraid of fire. A blast of lightning, however, can return them to full strength.

IRON GOLEM Larger and tougher than all other types of golems, iron golems have bodies constructed of wrought metal, usually shaped to resemble armor. Strong and heavy, they can crush enemies with a single punch or slice them in two with one swing of a sword. They can also vomit forth clouds of poisonous gas. Iron golems are almost unstoppable. Only magic items or weapons forged from a rare metal called adamantine stand a chance of doing any damage to their towering form.

SNOW GOLEM Like other types of golems, snow golems are elemental spirits trapped inside physical bodies, but in their case the bodies are made of snow. This provides excellent camouflage in snowy terrain, and most weapons pass harmlessly through them. However, snow golems are very vulnerable to fire.

STONE GOLEM Stone golems are much tougher than clay golems as they are carved from single blocks of dense, heavy stone. Often, they are carved in humanoid forms, but they can also be given beastly shapes, such as griffins, sphinxes, or lions. Stone golems are impervious to most forms of attack by magic or weapons, and they are surrounded by a time-distorting effect that can disorient and slow down attackers.

THE WARRIORS & WIZARDS COMPENDIUM

CLOCKWORKS

Clockwork constructs are complicated creations with impressive defensive and offensive abilities. The engineering skills of an experienced artificer are required to create one. Multiple copies of some constructs exist, like the gnomish bronze scouts. Others are so ambitious and elaborate that there may only ever be one of them, like the terrifying clockwork kraken.

BRONZE SCOUT Bronze scouts are built by gnomes to protect and defend their underground homes. Resembling giant centipedes, these creatures are capable of vicious attacks thanks to their sharp beaks, multiple blades, and ability to emit an electrical shock. Usually, they patrol the underground boundaries of gnomish territories, listening to the vibrations of creatures on the surface and occasionally extending their stalk-like eyes above the surface when they sense unusual activity.

The scouts can use their electrical powers to send a warning pulse to nearby gnomes before surging to the surface to attack. Like other constructs, they do not require food, water, or even air or sleep, which makes them excellent guards. Unfortunately for the gnomes, these creatures are very expensive to make, requiring huge amounts of bronze and gemstones.

CLOCKWORK KRAKEN The Clockwork Kraken is the unique and peculiar protector of an isolated and almost abandoned city. Rather than a single clockwork entity, the kraken consists of eight tentacles that move independently of each other. These tentacles use their flight and teleportation abilities to patrol the city, attacking any intruders they find. The only way to defeat the tentacles is to locate the engine of the kraken, which is kept in a secret location. The spirit that powers this monstrosity belongs to a kenku high priest whose remains are stored in the engine like a coffin. Only by cracking the engine open and removing the priest's remains can the kraken be deactivated.

STONE DEFENDER Stone defenders make excellent sentries for anyone with a fortress to protect. With the right spells in place, these constructs can stand motionless for years, decades, even centuries. They can camouflage themselves behind the giant stone slabs on their arms, making them virtually undetectable.

When alerted to intruders, they use those stone slabs to block attacks and to protect and defend the entrance. Their large, heavy stone bodies are resistant to most forms of attack. The stone slabs can also be used to strike back, and there aren't many adventurers who will get back up after being hit full force by these rocks.

HOUSEHOLD CONSTRUCTS

Not all constructs are created for travel or combat. Some find a place in the home, often in a protective capacity. Such constructs are easily mistaken for ordinary household items until they are activated by the touch or presence of an unfamiliar visitor.

BROOM OF ANIMATED ATTACK This household construct looks exactly like a normal broom until touched, at which point it activates and attempts to escape from being held. If successful, the broom immediately attacks whoever touched it, flying around them while whacking and thwapping their target with both bristles and handle. Some brooms of animated attack can be ridden as if they were a broom of flying, but only by their creators.

GUARDIAN PORTRAIT Have you ever felt like a painting was watching you? If the picture was a guardian portrait, it probably was! These constructs feature a realistic image of a specific person, often someone famous, with magic bound into the canvas and frame. Normally motionless, the image becomes animated when the portrait strikes. A guardian portrait can't make physical attacks, but it can cast spells that charm opponents, create visual hallucinations, move objects with telekinesis, and block the spellcasting of others.

RUG OF SMOTHERING Few things are quite so humbling as disarming a series of nasty traps and taking out watchful guards, only to be stopped by the very carpet beneath your feet. This construct can have many forms—from an ornately woven wool rug to a simple reed mat—but all rugs of smothering work the same way. When stepped on by an intruder, the rug springs to life, wrapping tight around its target and smothering them to death. An adventurer's allies will need to be careful while trying to free the victim from this bind, since half the damage done to the rug will actually be inflicted on the trapped person instead.

SKITTERWIDGET These surprisingly cute constructs resemble oversize metal cockroaches with dogs' heads, and speak a language made of high-pitched squeals. They are bound to a magical control ring, which allows the wielder to command up to seven of the constructs at once. They're mostly used for tasks such as cleaning, fetching tools, or delivering messages, although they can also be left to guard locations. Skitterwidgets can mate and breed, producing adorable offspring called kiddywidgets. They are dedicated parents, and even unrelated skitterwidgets will do their best to protect any nearby kiddywidgets.

THE WARRIORS & WIZARDS COMPENDIUM

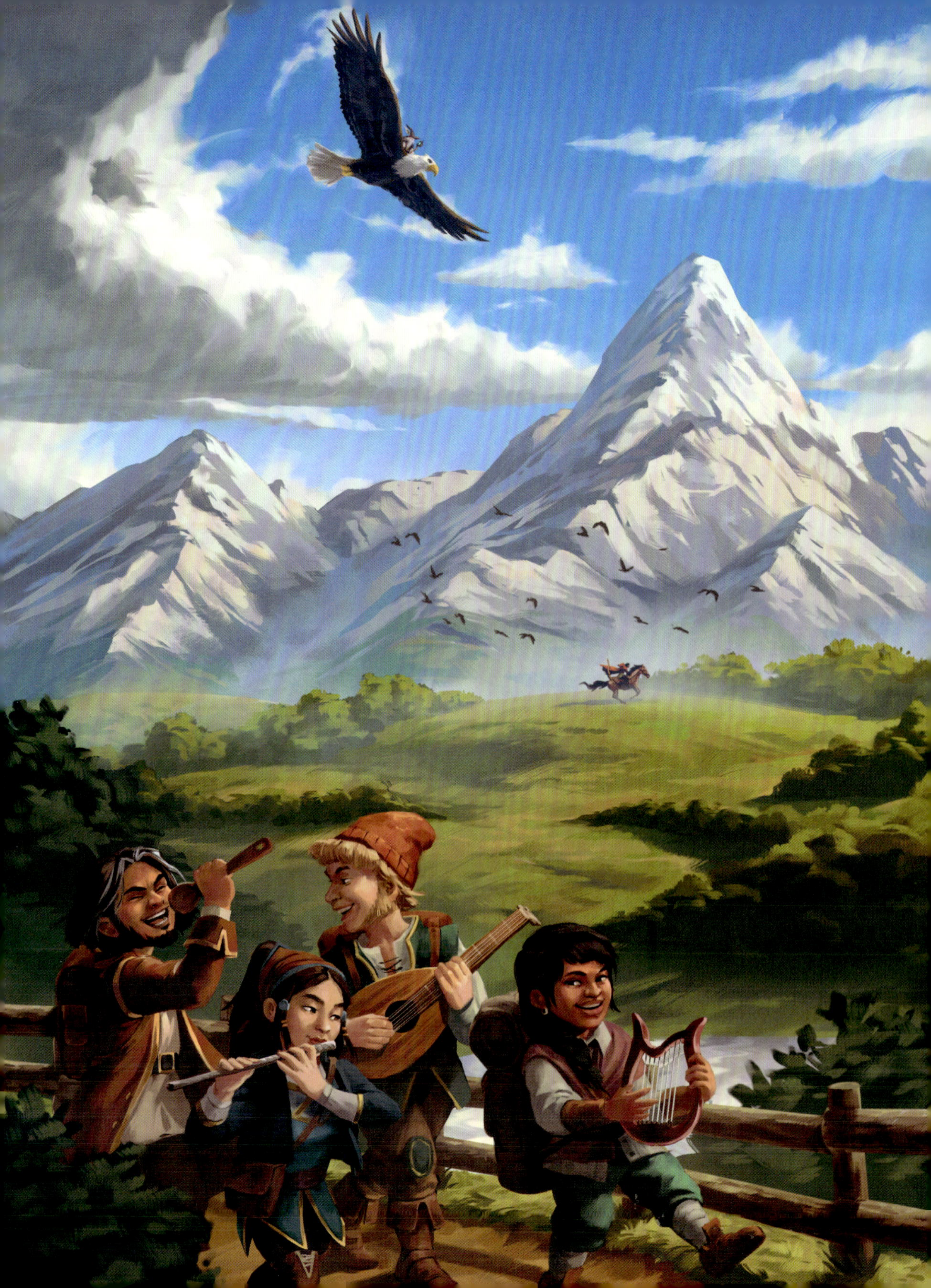

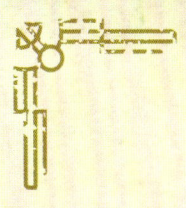

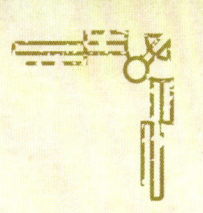

TRAVELING THE REALMS

The journey is at the heart of any great adventure. Every adventurer starts by leaving behind the world they know to encounter new places, new people, new opportunities—and new dangers. It is never just about the treasure at the bottom of the dungeon or the monster on the far side of the kingdom; it's about the paths that you take to get where you're going and the choices you make along the way.

Every choice changes the story—including whether to follow a map or follow the stars, whether to walk on foot or ride a mount, and whether to camp in the wilds or stay at an unfamiliar inn.

The journey is where your adventure takes shape—so approach each journey wisely!

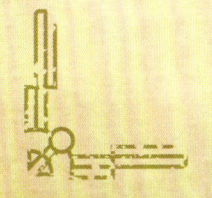

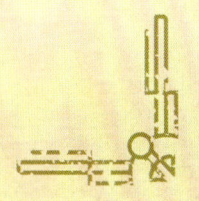

FINDING YOUR WAY

Navigation is the process of choosing and following a route. While rangers and minotaurs are naturally excellent at finding their way, everyone else can benefit from having a few useful tools in their inventory.

COMPASS A small magnet that always shows which direction is north, a compass is useful to work out your location. Experienced explorers familiar with an area can also use local landmarks in conjunction with a compass to determine their location. However, because compasses rely on magnets to indicate direction, they won't work on a magical plane that lacks a magnetic field. Large quantities of iron or steel also can distort nearby magnetic readings and affect the accuracy of a compass, especially in mines.

LODESTONES Lodestones are minerals that are naturally magnetic, so a lodestone hung on a string or suspended in a liquid can act as a natural compass. Rare and highly sought after by spellcasters for use in certain spells, lodestones can be expensive to buy—and valuable to find.

STAR CHARTS Star charts are maps of the night sky that show the position of constellations in relation to each other at a certain time of year. Navigators and explorers have relied on these charts for centuries, especially when at sea with no landmarks to provide direction. Such charts are essential for anyone traveling at night. Sometimes, multiple charts are collected in books called star atlases that show how stars change positions throughout the year. Some charts even allow navigators to select the time and date of their travel for greater accuracy.

MAPS

Combined with a compass, star chart, or other navigational techniques, maps allow you to travel toward a destination with relative accuracy. Maps note useful features, like roads and bridges, along with terrain such as lakes, hills, and swamps. Within the game setting, maps can be found, earned, purchased, or even stolen. Adventurers who travel through uncharted lands—or who are unable to find a map before starting their journey—may need to create their own maps as they go, or risk becoming lost.

Maps can be useful to give players a sense of the area that they're exploring and their position relative to allies and enemies alike. The Dungeon Master may share a pre-made map with the group, or players can draw their own maps as they investigate the region (see Cartography, page 252, and Terrain Symbols, pages 254 to 255).

Remember, maps show you what the mapmaker *wants* to show you. Traps or hidden treasures may have been intentionally left out. Sometimes a map itself is carefully planned bait designed to lure you into trouble.

TRAVEL METHODS

Knowing where you're going or where you are on a journey is vital, but just as important is the method you use to get there. Many adventuring parties travel on foot, especially when faced with difficult or uncertain terrain. For longer trips, faster travel, or journeys across difficult regions, you will want to consider all your options.

MOUNTS

A mount allows a rider to travel on its back, typically doubling an adventurer's travel speed while also allowing more stuff to be carried. A mount can be any willing animal larger than the rider. A gnome or a halfling might ride on the back of a dog or a giant rat, while a giant might be more comfortable riding on a mammoth. The most popular mount is a horse. Horses are used for travel, battle, leisure, and even sport. Warhorses are trained for combat, and pack horses are trained to carry as much weight as possible.

Some mounts are particularly good at navigating difficult terrains, like goats climbing steep rocks or wolves moving across frozen wastelands. Flying mounts, including wyverns, giant eagles, and giant bats, can travel great distances or soar over high mountains. Other mounts, such as dolphins, sharks, and giant seahorses, can travel underwater.

Mounts sometimes excel in combat, allowing adventurers to move swiftly and nimbly, though riding a griffon or a large armored warhorse can also make you a bigger target. Choosing the right mount can be a great way to help define your character. Imagine the sort of adventurer who rides on the back of a bear, or a lion, or a giant frog.

CAN I RIDE A DRAGON OR A UNICORN?

A mount usually needs training, either by the rider or by a professional handler. Rangers can sometimes quickly train a wild animal to act as a mount, and spellcasters can use magic to temporarily achieve the same effect.

However, some potential mounts are intelligent enough that they must be reasoned with—or bribed—to become your steed. They are also smart enough to abandon you if you don't treat them well! You can't tame a dragon, centaur, or pegasus; you can only negotiate with them or use magic to control them.

Unicorns are particularly picky. You can't ride one if the unicorn thinks you're a bad person—and unicorns really do *know* if you're nice or just faking it.

VEHICLES

Mounts are fast and can adapt quickly to circumstances, but they won't solve every transportation problem during your adventures. That's where vehicles, either water-ready or land-based, can help keep your adventures going.

BOATS AND SHIPS Sometimes the call to adventure takes you far from familiar shores and across vast oceans. Perhaps you will visit a strange land filled with mysterious cults, lost treasures, or living dinosaurs, or maybe your adventures will happen on the high seas, exploring underwater cities and fighting pirates. Before setting out to sea, think about how far you need to travel and how many people are in your group. Do you need a huge oceangoing ship with a thirty-person crew, or can you all fit in a small boat that only needs to travel along the coast?

Barges: Ideal for narrow waterways such as rivers or canals, barges float on the water but are pulled by animals walking on a path alongside the course. Barges can be as simple as a plain wooden raft or more complex structures with space for both passengers and cargo.

Galleys: Huge ships powered by crews of up to eighty dedicated rowers. They can carry a lot of cargo, people, or equipment and are well-armed to protect against pirates.

Keelboats: Slow sailboats that can be piloted by a single adventurer, with room for cargo or a small crew.

Longships: Fast-moving vessels typically used for military transport, with troops that act as the crew and power the boat by rowing.

Rowboats: Small and humble boats for crossing lakes and rivers.

Sailing Ships: Designed for fast travel to take cargo or passengers across the sea at maximum speed. They carry enough weapons and armor to defend against attackers.

Warships: Heavily armored and heavily armed ships designed for battle at sea, with crews of soldiers and sailors.

CARTS AND WAGONS It's a good idea to pack light for a journey, but sometimes that's not possible. Whether you need to carry weapons or trade goods, escort a VIP or transport a sick person to a healer, there are times you'll need to carry more than a single mount can handle. Pick carefully. Do you need something fast, something sturdy, or something with lots of room? Think about the animals that will pull your vehicle. Even if your options are limited to horses, some horses are fast and some are strong, and only the most expensive are both.

Carriages: A carriage is a wagon designed to transport passengers in comfort. Common features include seating inside and a cover to protect travelers from bad weather and potential attacks.

Carts: These smaller modes of conveyance, often two-wheeled vehicles, can be as simple as a wooden platform for carrying cargo or as fancy as a covered two-seater vessel for a driver and passenger. They can be drawn by one or two animals.

Sleds: A sled has runners that glide over ice and snow. Pack animals, such as reindeer, horses, or dogs, usually pull a sled.

Wagons: Four-wheeled vehicles that can carry heavy cargo or a lot of people, wagons offer more space and stability than carts. They're also heavier and may require two, four, or more animals to pull the weight. Large groups traveling together in multiple wagons form a wagon train or caravan.

INNS & WAYSTATIONS

Inns, taverns, and trading posts are places on the road where you can stop to rest, restock, and meet new faces. You may find allies who can warn you about threats ahead and help your party strengthen its bond. It's not an interruption in your journey but an opportunity to regroup and move forward.

These inns—offering bedrooms, stables, and food and drink—are found at key locations along popular thoroughfares, especially crossroads and junctions, or just before dangerous terrain such as deserts, dense woodlands, swamps, or valleys.

You may also find trading posts at these locations where you can buy and exchange goods and services from a potion seller, a fur trader, a blacksmith, or guides for hire. Those working at these posts often settle in the area, leading to the creation of small towns.

LOCAL CUSTOMS

Every small town has its own customs and traditions that distinguish it from its neighbors; understanding those details is vital to safe travel. For example, one town insists that everyone be indoors when night falls. What are they so afraid of in the dark? Another town has a festival where they chase away stray cats. How did the festival begin and what does it represent?

At one seaside tavern, they tell visitors to swallow a fish to protect against storms. What happens if you refuse? Another inn has magical markings etched in the flagstones under the rugs. Are they there to protect you?

DO THIS

Pay your bills. Innkeepers can be intense about collecting their debts.

Watch your pockets. Inns are the hunting ground of pickpockets. You may not notice you've been robbed until you're back on the road.

DON'T DO THIS

Don't get fancy. You might be tempted to spend all your coin on the nicest inn you can find, but all you usually need is food, water, and shelter.

Don't overstay your welcome. Always keep the adventure moving.

MAKING CAMP

You won't always find a comfortable place to stay on your travels. However, rest is essential and long journeys may require you to make camp out in the wild. Setting up camp also gives you a chance to review your progress and make new plans. Here are six tips for success in making camp.

- Think about safety when choosing a camping spot. Is your space vulnerable to floods, fires, tumbling rocks, falling trees, or dangerous animals?

- Choose flat ground where your party can stay close together and share warmth if necessary.

- Find or build a shelter to protect your group from wind, rain, snow, or the blazing sun.

- Light a fire to cook, boil water, and keep warm.

- Hunt and forage for food and a source of clean water.

- Set up watch where everyone takes turns staying awake and keeping an eye out for threats.

DO THIS

Check your surroundings. Look for signs of bandits, big predators, magic traps, or small houses. (You don't want to set your bedroll on a fairy village.)

Protect your belongings. Thieves may try to sneak into a camp at night.

DON'T DO THIS

Don't leave a fire unattended. Always watch your campfire and make sure it's extinguished when you leave.

Don't fall asleep on watch. Something very bad may happen if you do.

RESTING AND KEEPING WATCH

Every member of an adventuring party needs regular rest to stay ready for whatever comes—even elves, who do not sleep but need a certain period of meditative trance to be at their best.

Eight hours of rest are often necessary for spellcasters to recharge their spells and for other adventurers to recover their strength. A period of rest can include a couple of hours on watch for each adventurer so long as nothing goes wrong.

Are you a night owl or an early bird? A light sleeper or a heavy sleeper? Those aspects of your character may help you decide which shift in the watch you take.

THE WARRIORS & WIZARDS COMPENDIUM

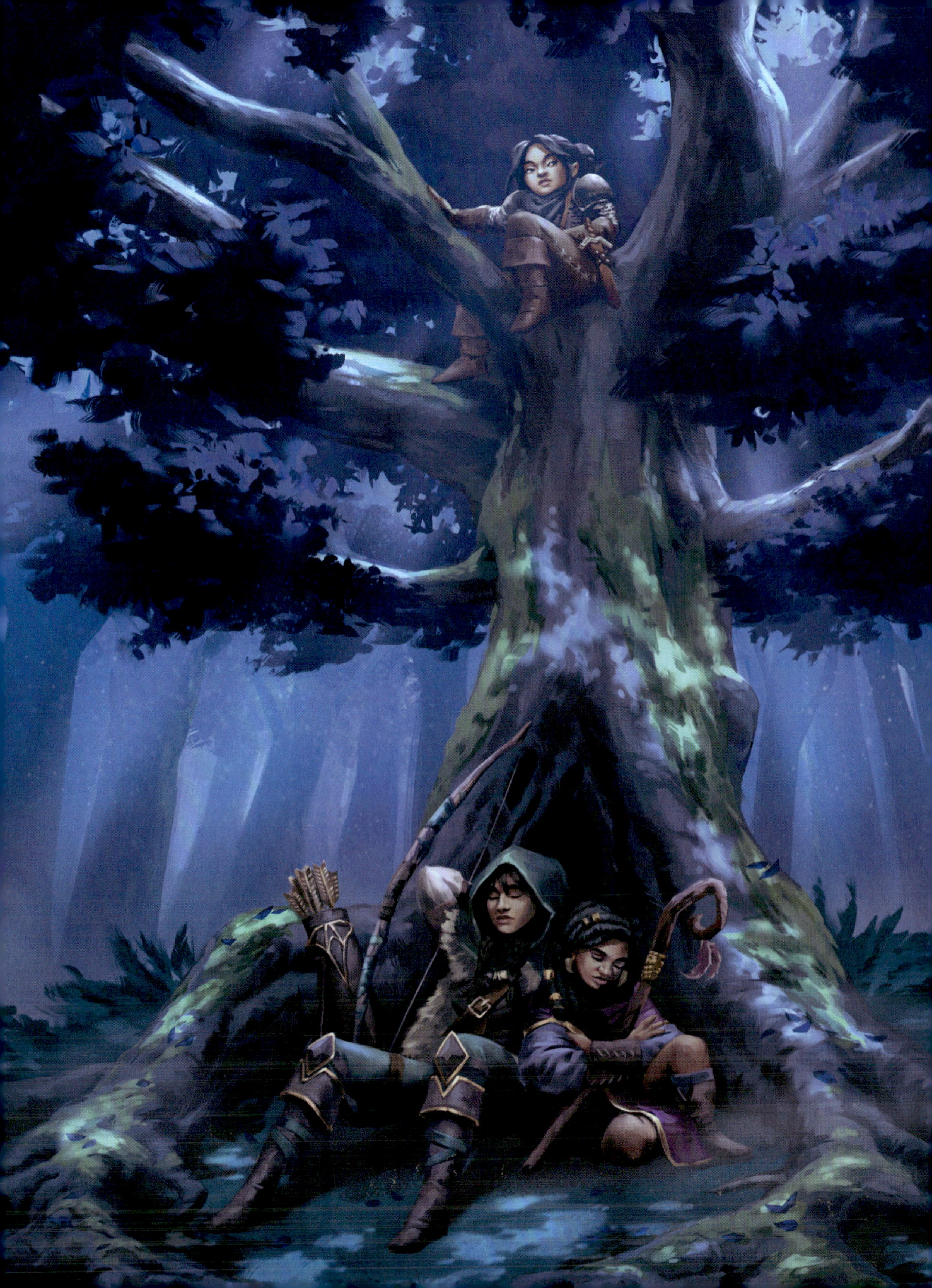

ENCOUNTER

WHICH WAY TO GO?

A difficult river crossing cost the adventurers several hours of daylight. Exhausted, the three travelers made camp in the hollow of an old tree where they could take turns keeping watch from a perch with a clear view of the road ahead.

On first watch, Manju the ranger was alarmed to see a family of owlbears sniffing around for food. She kept very quiet until the creatures moved on and then watched them retreat into a cave on the southern road that was almost completely hidden by a fallen tree.

On second watch, Shana the wizard held her breath as a unicorn charged down the northern road with panic in its eyes, trailing ribbons of light as it ran. She wondered what could possibly be so awful to cause such a powerful creature to flee in fear.

On third watch, Fen the fighter offered bread to an old woman traveling alone, and the old woman advised her to stay off the roads for fear of bandits. She told Fen to follow a path of bluebells through the woods, which would keep them safe. It was a rough track along which no cart could travel.

As morning came and the wayfarers prepared to move on, a caravan of wagons arrived behind them—a traveling circus. The circus owner said her group planned to take the northern road, and she invited the party to travel with them. There is strength in numbers.

Which is the right path to take? Manju, Shana, and Fen face a difficult choice; they all have different information from their time on watch. How much should they share with each other and the circus? Are the owlbears on the southern road less of a threat than the unknown danger on the northern road? Should they trust the old woman who recommended the bluebell path, or would they be safer traveling with the circus? Which way would *you* go? The choice is yours!

FORAGING & HUNTING

If your adventure involves a lot of time in the wilds of nature, you must plan for what you will eat and drink. Some adventures won't require you to spend much time on meal details, especially if you're traveling only a short distance; for other endeavors, food will be central to the experience.

FORAGING

If your character does not eat meat or if game is scarce, foraging for plants is an important skill needed to provide food. Foraging is the practice of gathering edible plants—including fruits, nuts, seeds, roots, flowers, leaves, and fungi—in the wild.

Anyone can forage, but your chances of success depend on your wisdom and experience. This is an area of expertise where rangers and druids excel. A field guide to plants, berries, and mushrooms is a useful tool for foraging, especially as a means to avoid eating anything poisonous or magical. The first rule is: If you don't recognize something, don't eat it.

HUNTING

Hunting for food is a specialized skill. It can involve setting traps, fishing, and tracking animals or luring them to your location. Rangers are often good hunters because of their familiarity with nature and their expertise in stealth and tracking. On a long trek, a ranger can be the most important member of your adventuring party.

HUNTING EQUIPMENT

Adventurers have to be careful not to overpack; too much stuff can slow you down. Since you can't bring along every piece of hunting gear, you'll want to choose wisely based on your character's skills and destination.

Camouflage: Magic spells such as *invisibility* can provide excellent camouflage, but otherwise you may need clothing to help blend into the environment.

Fishing Tackle: Rod, line, hooks, and everything needed to catch a fish.

Hunting Trap: A metal device that traps an animal.

Knives: Swords are not designed for preparing meat. Hunters always carry a hunting knife.

Lures: Scents that attract animals, or whistles that imitate their call. Each lure attracts one type of animal.

Snares: Wires that tighten around the leg of an animal when it steps on the trap.

DO THIS

Only use what you need. Leave enough for others, just as you'd want them to leave enough for you.

Respect nature. Nature has some dangerous defenders, so tread carefully.

DON'T DO THIS

Don't get caught trespassing. If anyone owns the land you're hunting or foraging on, or if it's sacred land, you could get into a lot of trouble.

Don't get hunted. There's always something bigger than you and just as hungry lurking out in the wild.

THE WARRIORS & WIZARDS COMPENDIUM

DANGERS ON THE ROAD

Trouble is a fact of life for an adventurer—if you don't encounter *any* difficulty, you're not really on an adventure. Here are some forms of trouble that you might face.

BANDITS Bands of thieves and rogues travel the wilds looking for people to rob.

GUARDS AND PATROLS People have a tendency to be territorial, and guards are very suspicious of strangers.

MAGICAL HAZARDS Some areas you enter may carry a curse or enchantment, where the truly unexpected happens. Your magic won't work as desired, perhaps, or ghosts may emerge from the fog, or you could suddenly start floating away!

MONSTERS Dangerous creatures lurk everywhere, and they're likely to attack if you enter their territory.

NATURAL HAZARDS Rockslides, quicksand, volcanoes, earthquakes, ice, and even dangerous plants are just some of the ways the natural world can ruin your plans.

TRAPS Outlaws and hunters are known to set out traps, ensnaring unsuspecting travelers in hidden pits and falling nets.

DO THIS

Travel in groups. There is strength in numbers.

Listen. Pay attention to hiding places, weather, and each other.

DON'T DO THIS

Don't draw attention. Showing off treasures or boasting about your skills are good ways to put a target on your back.

Don't split up the party. You don't want trouble to find you while you're separated from the group.

WEATHER

Bad weather can have a serious impact on your journey's progress and likely make you struggle in certain conditions.

- Extreme cold weather will wear you down if you're not wearing warm clothing or are not immune to cold.
- Extreme hot weather will hit you harder if you're wearing heavy armor, especially metal types that trap heat.
- Strong wind interferes with ranged weapons, open flames, and flying creatures.
- Heavy rain or snow can put out fires and limit your ability to see and hear well.

The weather on other worlds or dimensions is sometimes even more extreme, such as searing heat or raging storms on the Elemental Planes, or unpredictable conditions in realms where powerful beings manipulate the elements.

ALLIES ON THE ROAD

Many of the creatures you encounter on your travels are dangerous. However, some may become allies or friends, especially if you help each other out. Others that appear monstrous at first are not all that they seem—so long as you respect their territory.

Centaurs: Part human and part horse, these nomads travel great distances across plains and deserts. Centaurs avoid contact with others but may trade with you or help you find your way.

Dryads: Fey spirits bound to trees and protectors of the forests. Dryads watch travelers closely to make sure all is well; if you're respectful of nature, they may help you.

Pixies: These fairies with beautiful wings are eager and excitable. They love to make new friends but also like to play tricks. Keep your sense of humor and they may be friendly.

Satyrs: Half human, half goat, and 100 percent the party people of the deep woods. They are usually happy to help, but you may need to dance and sing with them first.

TAMING PETS

During your adventures you may want an animal friend at your side—a cat, dog, monkey, or even a pseudodragon. Your ability to tame an animal depends on two things: the animal's nature and your skill at animal handling. If the animal is too wild, suspicious, or aggressive, or if you lack the wisdom to train them, you're unlikely to make them your pet.

Druids and rangers who work with animals can train a beast companion to obey their commands.

Spellcasters who master the ritual to find a familiar can bind a spirit to the form of an animal, with all of that animal's characteristics.

DO THIS

Seek out help. Not every encounter is hostile—you'll meet helpful people on your travels.

Be kind to strangers. Most people that you meet are trying their best to survive.

DON'T DO THIS

Don't be gullible. Some people take advantage of kindness. Be careful and ponder a stranger's motives.

Don't disrespect the ways of others. An ally can become an enemy if you cross them.

THE WARRIORS & WIZARDS COMPENDIUM

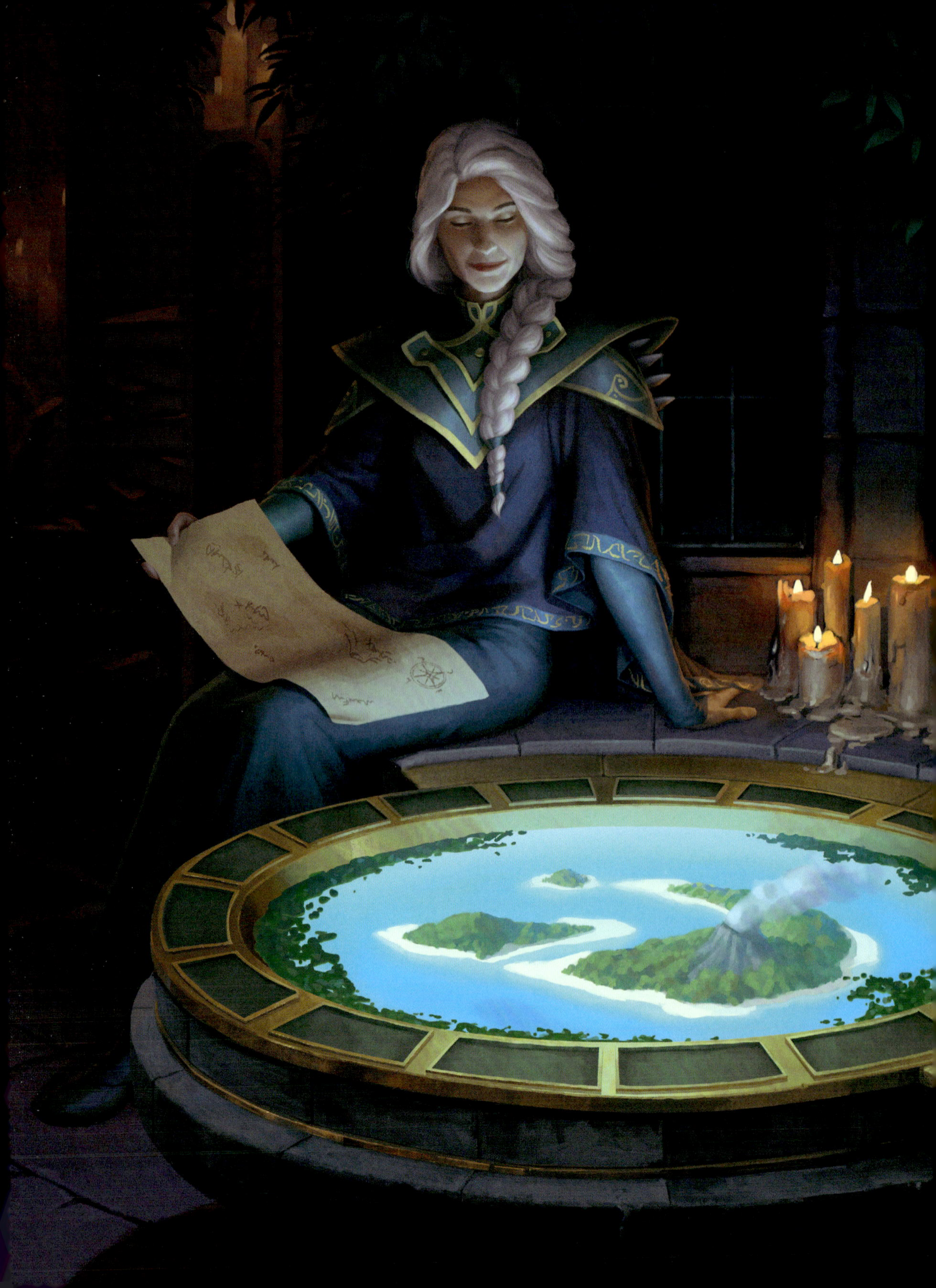

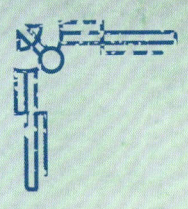

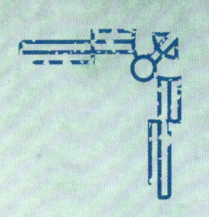

A REALM OF YOUR OWN

Once you've created a character, it's time to start thinking about the world they live in and explore. The right fantasy world can help you generate endless adventures and memorable stories! Fantasy realms are limitless, constantly changing and growing, but it all starts with your own creativity. From initial concept to world building, every element—dungeons to cities, terrain to language, history to technology—is yours to design by yourself or in collaboration with friends.

When you close your eyes, what kind of places do you see? Ornate dungeons laden with traps, or twisting caverns made from rough-hewn rock? Soaring mountains and steaming volcanoes tucked away in remote places, or vibrant kingdoms and towns filled with citizens going about their lives?

You could start with a single dungeon and add details as your game goes along, inventing your world in response to your players' adventures. You could also start with a grand vision for your players to discover, building up a geography and history before your first session. There's no wrong approach, so long as you are having fun and exploring your imagination.

In a world where magic and monsters are real, there are no limits, only new destinations to explore.

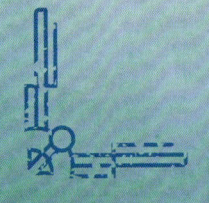

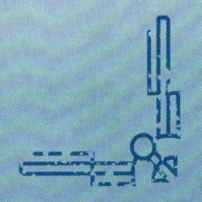

DUNGEON CONCEPT

When you set out to create your own dungeon, think about its function and the distinct features you can use to engage adventurers as they explore it. A goblin village isn't the same as a cloud giant's stronghold or a white dragon's lair. Each one would look different, feel different, and carry their own unique threats.

LOCATION

Figuring out where your dungeon is located will instantly start to narrow your focus and generate other ideas. Look to the following list of dungeon locales for inspiration, or come up with your own. The options are endless!

- Behind a waterfall
- Beneath a graveyard
- Floating in the sky
- In a cliff face
- In catacombs beneath a city
- In the desert
- Inside a volcano
- Underwater

CREATOR

Knowing who built this dungeon will also help you understand the size and scope of the place you're creating. And remember, whoever constructed it doesn't still have to be dwelling there. Many dungeons are abandoned and reused over the centuries.

Use any of the following potential creator options, or come up with something of your own invention.

- A forgotten civilization
- A wizard
- An evil cult
- Dwarves
- Elves
- Goblins
- Smugglers
- No creator at all (natural formations)

PURPOSE

Dungeons are built to fulfill an objective. Knowing what that is will help you define important areas within. Also, keep in mind that dungeons can be repeatedly abandoned and then repurposed by different occupants. A shrine can fall into ruin and become a lair, or a castle may have been struck by a dark plague and become a tomb.

Death Trap: A way to guard treasure or a competition to test the skills of warriors and wizards alike, a death trap is built to destroy any who enter.

Lair: A monster's living quarters and also a place where it can hoard its valuables. Be careful, a creature confronted in its home tends to fight with even more intensity than usual.

Mine: An active mine where rare ore, gemstones, or metals are harvested, or an abandoned mine occupied by creatures who thrive in the dark.

Stronghold: A secure base of operations for villains or monsters. A fortress like this is built with defense in mind, so a successful delve may involve infiltration rather than charging at the front entrance.

Temple or Shrine: Whether still active or now abandoned, this place was intended for worship and ritual.

Tomb: A resting place for the departed, along with their secrets and treasures.

POPULATING YOUR DUNGEON

What's a dungeon without monsters to fight? Start by choosing a few of your favorite foes, then use the following guidelines to help you decide on the rest.

ECOLOGY

Areas where people or creatures gather have their own ecosystems. Creatures who live there need to eat, drink, breathe, and sleep. A king needs a throne room, but also a bedroom. Worshippers need places to pray. Soldiers need barracks and storage areas for their equipment. Are there areas still under construction or that have been closed off due to collapse, mold, or other issues that have arisen? When you set out to design a dungeon, you should think about the internal logic of the spaces you're creating and what the occupants need in order to carry out their day-to-day tasks—food preparation will probably be close to food storage, a guardhouse should be near the prison cells it watches over, or a hatchery placed by the sleeping area of a protective mother.

INHABITANTS

A dungeon is sometimes dominated by a single monster or a large group of intelligent creatures, but they don't have to be the sole occupants. Fungi, vermin, scavengers, and various predators can all coexist in the same space with the main inhabitants.

- Do the creatures controlling this dungeon have pets? If so, where are those pets kept and how are they fed?

- Do the occupants of this place take prisoners? Are those captives potential allies to you if they're freed?

- If a dungeon is quite large, are there multiple factions within vying for control?

The ways in which all the dungeon's inhabitants interact will give you any number of story ideas.

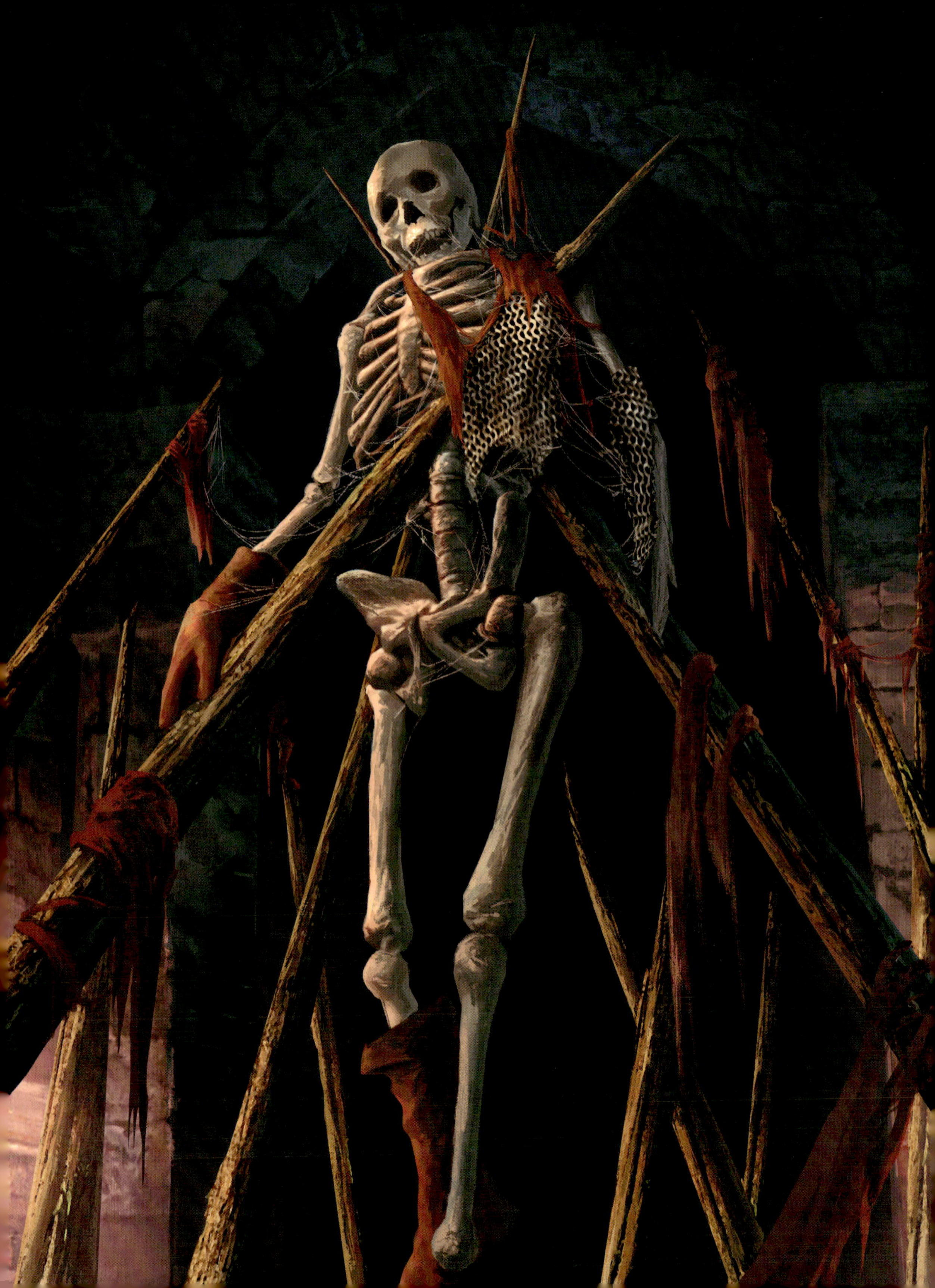

TRAPS

Intentional and dangerous, traps are created to fool the unwary and stop their progress through a dungeon. These devices may be built to hurt or to hold, but they're always constructed to cause trouble.

Like the dungeon itself, when creating traps you must first decide who built them and what purpose they serve. It's rare that a trap would be set up in a space where denizens need to travel often, so think carefully about why it's been placed there and what lies beyond that's worth protecting.

Second, decide if the trap will be mechanical or magical in nature. Mechanical traps include basic ambush material such as pits or falling blocks, but can ramp up in complexity to whirling blades, flying arrows, flooding rooms, or clockwork puzzles. Magical traps cast a spell when activated and the effects can be almost anything you imagine: A floor trap could teleport the person who sets it off to another part of the dungeon.

Third, determine how the trap is triggered, what the effect will be, and how a group of adventurers might detect it if they were careful enough: Opening a door improperly could prompt a blast of magical fire to erupt into the hallway. Intelligent creatures who place traps in their lairs need ways to get past them without harming themselves. A trap might have a secret switch that disables its effect or an alternate route that adventurers can take to bypass it entirely.

CATACOMBS

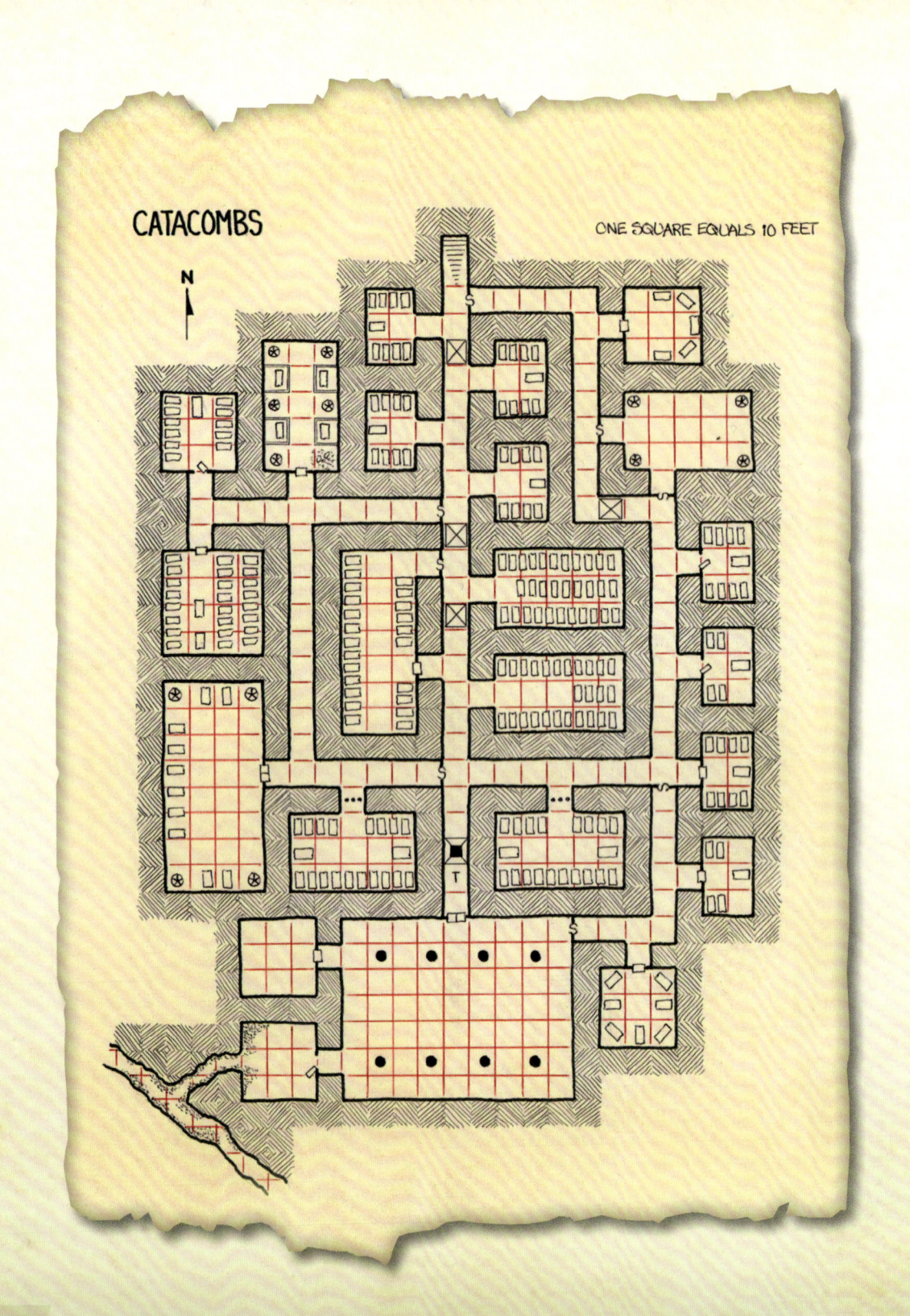

ONE SQUARE EQUALS 10 FEET

N

MAPMAKING

Having a concept, knowing the occupants, and creating a list of different areas are the perfect ingredients for building a dungeon. Now you need to start making a map!

A dungeon is most easily mapped on graph paper, with each square representing a standard measurement, such as five or ten feet per square. Use your key areas as starting points, then connect them with other features. As you plan, keep these points in mind.

- Symmetry is boring. If a group of adventurers explores one half of a dungeon, they'll rush through the second half if the layout is the same. Don't make your maps too predictable.

- Even if a dungeon is manually constructed, there are ways to incorporate indigenous features as well. Waterfalls, chasms, falling rocks, and other natural elements can provide interesting obstacles for your players.

- Using the grid is a nice way to get straight hallways and rectangular rooms, but don't be afraid to switch things up by varying the shape, size, and direction of your dungeon areas.

- Think about furniture and storage. How are the denizens using this space and what is needed to carry out daily tasks?

- Even though your map is two-dimensional, think in three dimensions. Use stairs, ramps, platforms, ledges, and balconies to add height or depth. It will make your dungeon more interesting than just having an endless series of level rooms.

- The ultimate goal within your dungeon will usually be as far from the entrance as possible, forcing adventurers deeper into danger and heightening the drama.

MAP SYMBOLS

Here are a series of standardized symbols you can use on your graph-paper maps to denote specific dungeon features. Mix and match them to bring to life the hidden places you've always imagined.

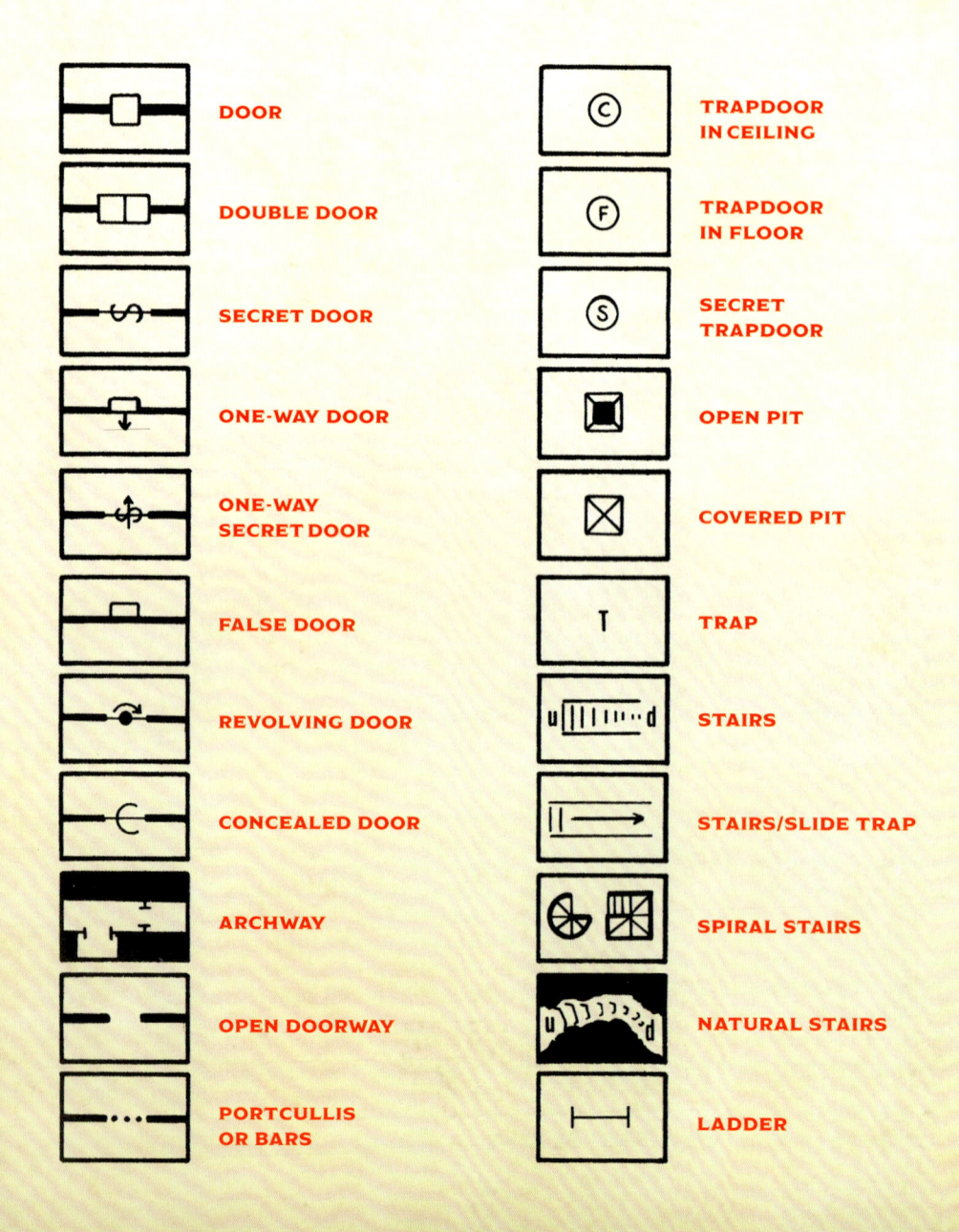

Symbol	Name	Symbol	Name
	DOOR		TRAPDOOR IN CEILING
	DOUBLE DOOR		TRAPDOOR IN FLOOR
	SECRET DOOR		SECRET TRAPDOOR
	ONE-WAY DOOR		OPEN PIT
	ONE-WAY SECRET DOOR		COVERED PIT
	FALSE DOOR		TRAP
	REVOLVING DOOR		STAIRS
	CONCEALED DOOR		STAIRS/SLIDE TRAP
	ARCHWAY		SPIRAL STAIRS
	OPEN DOORWAY		NATURAL STAIRS
	PORTCULLIS OR BARS		LADDER

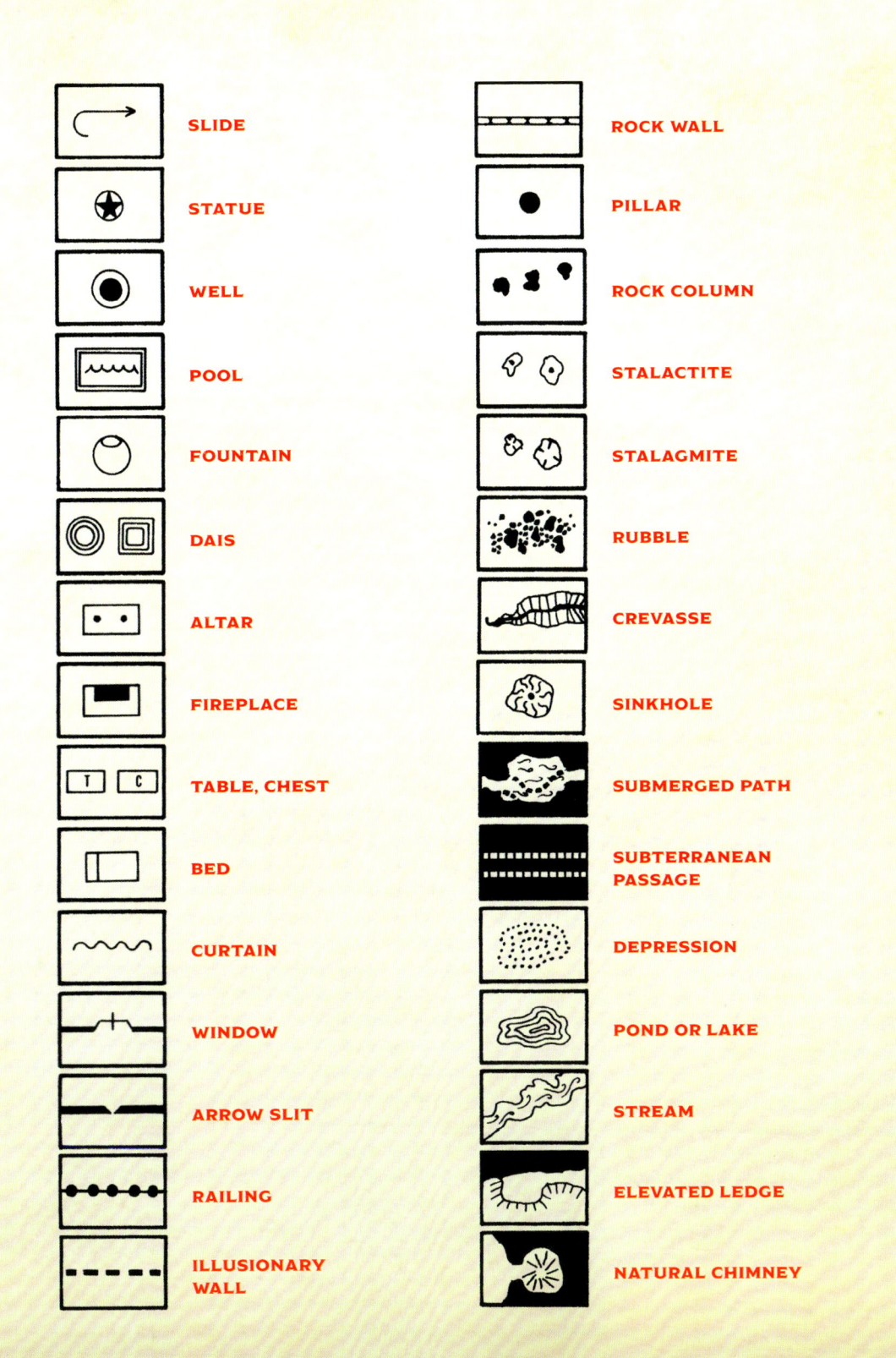

Symbol	Name	Symbol	Name
➔	SLIDE	▬▬▬	ROCK WALL
★	STATUE	●	PILLAR
◉	WELL	•••	ROCK COLUMN
~~	POOL	◦ ◦	STALACTITE
○	FOUNTAIN	❊ ❊	STALAGMITE
◎ ▣	DAIS	░░░	RUBBLE
••	ALTAR	〰	CREVASSE
▬	FIREPLACE	❀	SINKHOLE
T C	TABLE, CHEST	❀	SUBMERGED PATH
▭	BED	∙∙∙∙∙	SUBTERRANEAN PASSAGE
∿	CURTAIN	⦾	DEPRESSION
⊥	WINDOW	⦿	POND OR LAKE
⊤	ARROW SLIT	～	STREAM
• • • • •	RAILING	◠	ELEVATED LEDGE
‒ ‒ ‒	ILLUSIONARY WALL	◉	NATURAL CHIMNEY

THE WARRIORS & WIZARDS COMPENDIUM

MAP EXAMPLES

The shrine of an evil cult where worshipers gather to make sacrifices, or a holy place of worship overrun by invading hordes that need to be cleared out by brave adventurers? You decide which one your adventuring party will face!

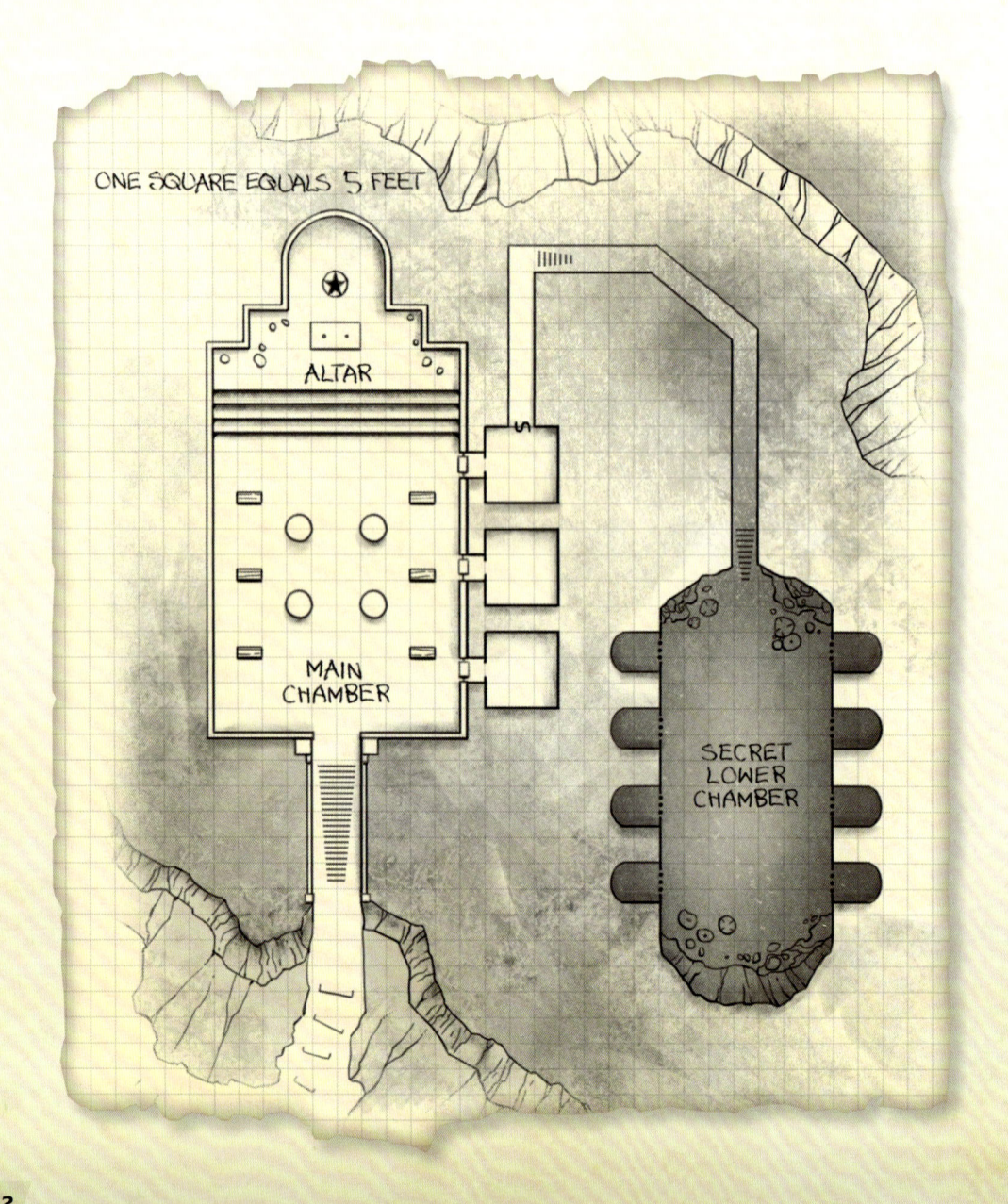

A haunted ship sailing through ghostly waters, or a pirate boat manned by cut-throat villains who have been terrorizing innocent farmers along the shoreline? Every map contains multiple possibilities, depending on how you decide to customize it!

EXPLORATION & QUESTS

How a dungeon experience begins and how it ends can contribute a great deal to making the journey through the space a memorable one. Epic fantasy stories don't start with someone merely opening a door and walking down a hallway. Use the entrance of your dungeon as a way to set expectations and to build excitement about the dangers and delights that lay ahead.

- What kind of journey is required to get to the dungeon? Is it close by or in a remote and inhospitable location?

- Is the entrance hidden? If so, what clues or methods must the adventurers use to find it?

- Is the entrance guarded? Who watches over this space and what will it take to get past them?

- Is the entrance locked? Is there a key, a magical phrase, or a trick used to gain access?

- Is the entrance magical? A teleportation circle may transport adventurers directly into the heart of a dungeon, or a permanent illusion may hide the safest entrance to a creature's lair.

- Is there more than one entrance? A fortress has a main gate, but there may be other smaller entry points for servants, shipping, or garbage disposal that adventurers can use to make their way inside. A cave may have a large opening at the base of a mountain, but there may be smaller tunnels at higher points as well.

Once a group has plumbed the depths of your dungeon, you'll want to make sure the final encounter is worthy of their time and effort. What kind of big set piece can you use and what foes can they face that will engage and excite them? What final obstacle must they overcome for their quest to be declared a success?

Are there any other tasks you can add to the final encounter beyond merely fighting a villain? Freeing prisoners, stopping a ritual, activating an ancient artifact, or undoing a curse can split the adventuring party's attention in a way that feels frantic and exciting. Maybe the final battle ends with the entire room crumbling as the floor gives way, sending the heroes plummeting toward an underground river that threatens to wash them away. Whatever you decide, make it exciting; because if you do, you and your friends can build stories together that you'll always remember.

TREASURE

At the end of every quest there must be a reward, a reason for adventurers to go through trials and tribulations while risking their health and happiness. For a cleric, that reward may be a renewal of faith after serving the needs of their deity. For a paladin, it may come in the form of pride from vanquishing evil. Along with satisfaction, conviction, and an overall sense of a job well done, the most common and appreciated form of compensation in a world of sword and sorcery is treasure. When you build your dungeon and populate it with dangers aplenty, you'll also want to decide what kind of wealth is available for plundering. Here are some ideas to get you started.

Art Objects: Idols or other sculptures, paintings, rare musical instruments, and even finely crafted dinnerware may be found and have value.

Coins: Simple and to the point. Gold, silver, and copper coins are the most common, but there are also rarer electrum and platinum ones to be considered as well.

Gemstones: Diamonds, rubies, sapphires, emeralds, amethysts, and dozens of other gems, plus brand-new crystal fascinations you come up with from your own imagination.

Jewelry: Necklaces, earrings, rings, bracelets, and other trinkets. Some may be kept and worn by adventurers while others can be traded or sold.

Knowledge: Rare books or scrolls, spell books, or alchemic recipes. For researchers and spellcasters, there may be information worth more than mere gold can purchase.

Magic Items: Wondrous items and enchanted objects are the kind of treasure many adventurers crave. Create your own or look to the Magic Items chapter (page 161) for specific items to use.

New Adventure: A map to another destination, a mysterious code to be solved, or a journal detailing a villainous plot—sometimes the most valuable thing an explorer can find is a reason to keep exploring.

HOW MUCH IS TOO MUCH?

Receiving riches is a thrill, but be careful not to overload your dungeon with too much treasure. Magic items are less enchanting if a hero has a backpack full of them, and the desire to take on new expeditions can fade quickly if characters have more money than they know what to do with.

Keep in mind that the life of an adventurer does come with financial obligations. Armor needs to be repaired, clothes replaced, and weapons sharpened, and there are always local peasants in need who could use some of that newly unearthed gold to better their own lots in life. As a hero's legend begins to grow, their needs and expenses will rise to match their reputation.

BUILDING YOUR WORLD

There are many ways to approach world building in Dungeons & Dragons. You could make changes to an existing realm or design a whole new one from scratch. You can start with a small region and expand only as needed in your campaign. Or you can dream up a vast geography and history before your players roll a single die. It's up to you!

Whatever your approach, consider the core aspects of how your world functions. Setting basic guidelines for your world makes it feel more real and believable by creating a sense of consistency.

Talk to your players to get an idea of the kinds of adventures that they enjoy, and make sure your world gives them plenty of opportunities to have fun. If they're interested in fighting evil monsters and gaining treasure, stock your world with lots of bad guys. If they're more excited by exploration and discovery, develop a landscape filled with cool ruins, hidden nooks, and lots of unusual beasts. If they hope to save innocent people in classic heroic fashion, provide plenty of interesting characters for them to protect.

The possibilities for your world are as big as your imagination. What kind of place will you bring to life?

QUESTIONS ON WORLD BUILDING

Is your world magical or mundane? How common is magic, and how do average residents feel about it? Are monsters an everyday sight or something rare and wonderous?

Is your world tamed or wild, known or unknown? Will your players deal with unfamiliar landscapes devoid of civilization, or find adventure in a vast, long-established empire?

Is your world new or ancient? Are your players the first adventurers of a rising civilization, or part of a tradition going back centuries? If traces of past kingdoms are still visible, how do people feel about them?

How structured is society, and how is it run? If there are conflicts between certain groups, how are those disputes resolved?

Does your world have a god or gods? Do divine forces intervene, and, if so, how often? (Clerics and paladins can still channel divine magic, whatever you decide!) How important are fate and destiny?

Does your world obey the same physical laws as the real one, or does it have any unique quirks?

MAPPING YOUR WORLD

Making maps of your world helps you and your players to better picture where their adventures happen and where they must travel to reach their goals. You may prefer to start locally, mapping the area where your journey will begin before expanding outward, or you may want to start by designing whole continents before zooming in on smaller areas. Some Dungeon Masters find it helpful to make two versions of their maps, one with information for the players to know when the game begins and one with all the secret details to be discovered along the way. Others prefer a single map with written notes to remind them where the hidden elements are located.

Whatever your approach, you'll likely need maps of several different scales (see Scale, page 253). Province maps use a one-mile scale and represent an area that your players can travel in about a day. Kingdom maps use a six-mile scale and represent several days to a week of in-game travel, depending on the terrain. Continent maps use a sixty-mile scale and show only the largest landscape features, such as mountains, coastlines, major cities, and political boundaries.

Your first step for any map is deciding what your world's environment looks like. Are there forests or deserts? Mountain ranges or glaciers, islands or volcanoes? Is it warm in the middle region and colder to the extreme north and south, or does the world's magic affect its temperature and terrain? Let your imagination run wild with all the possibilities!

Once you've decided on the landscape of your world, sketch out the biggest features, like lakes, hills, mountains, craters, and oceans. Next add grasslands, forests, swamps, and so on, plus rivers that connect lakes and flow into the ocean. Figure out the best place for settlements, which are typically located near such resources as good farmland, hunting, or mining spots. Communities benefit from access to natural travel routes such as rivers or oceans as well as roads that link them.

If appropriate, add ruins, ghost towns, mysterious landmarks, and ancient temples to your world. These provide a sense of history and encourage your players to explore. Even small details help bring your world to life and become the starting point for unexpected adventures.

CARTOGRAPHY

Cartography, the study and practice of making maps, records a physical landscape in a smaller, usually two-dimensional format. Drawing on paper is a simple, classic way to create maps. If you enjoy computers, there are different kinds of cartography software options you could explore. Crafty Dungeon Masters may even enjoy building three-dimensional versions of their maps with paper-mâché or other modeling materials to really bring their world to life.

Whatever your approach, the following basic cartography principles will help make your maps as clear and easy-to-use as possible.

SCALE

When making a map, all the grids on the paper should represent an equal amount of physical space. This ratio is known as the map scale. In a dungeon, one square of map almost always represents either five or ten feet of terrain. Outdoors, one map section usually represents one mile, six miles, or even more, depending on how much area you're mapping. A smaller scale is best for a detailed map where you need to locate specific spots, like old ruins or monster lairs, while a large scale is more useful for traveling between cities or other far-flung locations.

MAPPING PAPER

Grid paper, which is already divided into sections of equal size, is useful for drawing maps. Dungeon maps are often built using square-grid paper, while a hexagon (six-sided) grid is a better choice for outdoor maps. The six sides reflect the wider choice of directions that characters have when moving through an open landscape. That said, any paper that can be divided into equal sections will work just fine.

RECORDING LANDMARKS

There are plenty of ways to record points of interest on your map. Some people rely on words where needed, such as writing "mountain" or "danger: snakes." Those with artistic inclination and lots of time may develop realistic illustrations to bring the landscape to life. Most fall in between these two approaches, using a mix of words and standard map symbols, like those on page 254.

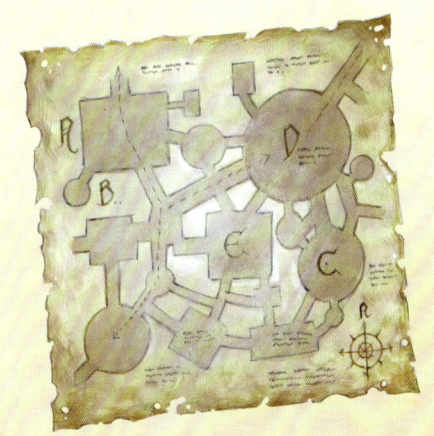

TERRAIN SYMBOLS

Here are some standardized symbols to use to indicate specific landscape features on your maps. Mix and match them as needed or create your own for any elements not shown here.

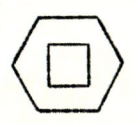

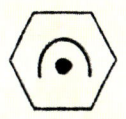

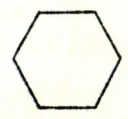

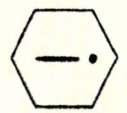

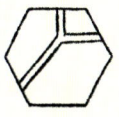

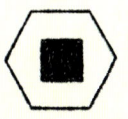

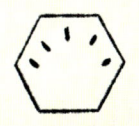

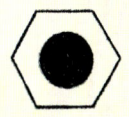

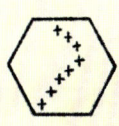

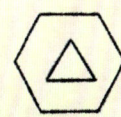

Symbol	Name	Symbol	Name
	BARREN OR BROKEN LAND		JUNGLE
	BORDER		MOUNTAIN
	CAPITOL		PLATEAU OR CLIFF
	CASTLE		RIVER
	CAVE		ROAD
	CITY		RUINS
	CLEAR		SWAMP
	DESERT		TOWN
	FOREST		TRAIL
	GRASSLAND		VOLCANO
	HILLS		WATER
	ICE FLOE		

THE WARRIORS & WIZARDS COMPENDIUM

INHABITANTS

All kinds of beings may populate your world—from humanoids and tame animals to dangerous beasts, mysterious plants, and perhaps even living objects. The inhabitants of your world, along with how and where they live, will help shape the adventures available to your players.

SETTLEMENTS

Communities, from small villages to sprawling cities, form the basis of civilization in a Dungeons & Dragons world. You get to decide what these communities look like, where they're located, how they function, and the ways they interact with outsiders. Here are some questions to consider when designing a settlement.

WHAT IS THE SETTLEMENT'S PURPOSE IN YOUR GAME?

- Is it a home base for your players' characters, a way station, a source of information, or the site of the adventure itself? Will characters be defending this place, or trying to drive out an evil that has taken over?

WHO LIVES HERE?

- Are the inhabitants mostly people of a single background or a broad mixture? What is the common language? What are the values, customs, and religions? Are residents welcoming or suspicious toward strangers?

WHY DOES THE SETTLEMENT EXIST?

- Is it located near natural resources, like good farmland, forests, or mines? Do rivers or roads connect it to other towns? Is it a hub for travelers and merchants? Is it growing and thriving or on the decline?

HOW DOES THE SETTLEMENT LOOK AND FEEL?

- Is it a tiny hamlet or a metropolis? Do the buildings and streets have a distinctive style? Does it have protections, like guard posts or walls? How does it smell and sound? What's the weather like? What mood do you want your players to feel when they arrive?

MONSTERS & LAIRS

While you can always surprise your players by placing creatures in unexpected locations, most monsters and beasts have preferred landscapes that best suit their needs. Certain monsters are powerful enough to scare off other creatures from living nearby, while others opt to live in packs or tribes for companionship and safety.

The practical aspects of monsters' lives can also spark ideas for adventures. Without enough prey, hungry beasts can threaten travelers and nearby settlements. Lakes and wells could be infested by water monsters. The space demands of a growing population might put them in conflict with farmers or villagers. Challenges like these can inspire your players to come up with creative solutions that go beyond a straightforward attack.

Even when a monster is defeated or driven away, their lair remains. Other monsters might move in to fill the vacant space, creating a new problem. The lair of a red dragon killed ten years ago might now be home to a tribe of goblins, an owlbear family, or even a mix of several different creatures. Humanoid settlements can also be converted by monsters into functional lairs, either by moving into abandoned places or driving away the residents of an active village. Adapting old lairs and ruins in this way can give a sense of history to your world.

CREATURE LOCALES

Monster profiles should include information about a creature's preferred habitat. Here are a few suggestions to get you started.

Forests: Owlbears, displacer beasts, unicorns.

Hills and Mountains: Goblins, orcs, hill giants.

Lakes and Rivers: Merrow, green dragons, water elementals.

Swamps: Giant lizards, yuan-ti, black dragons.

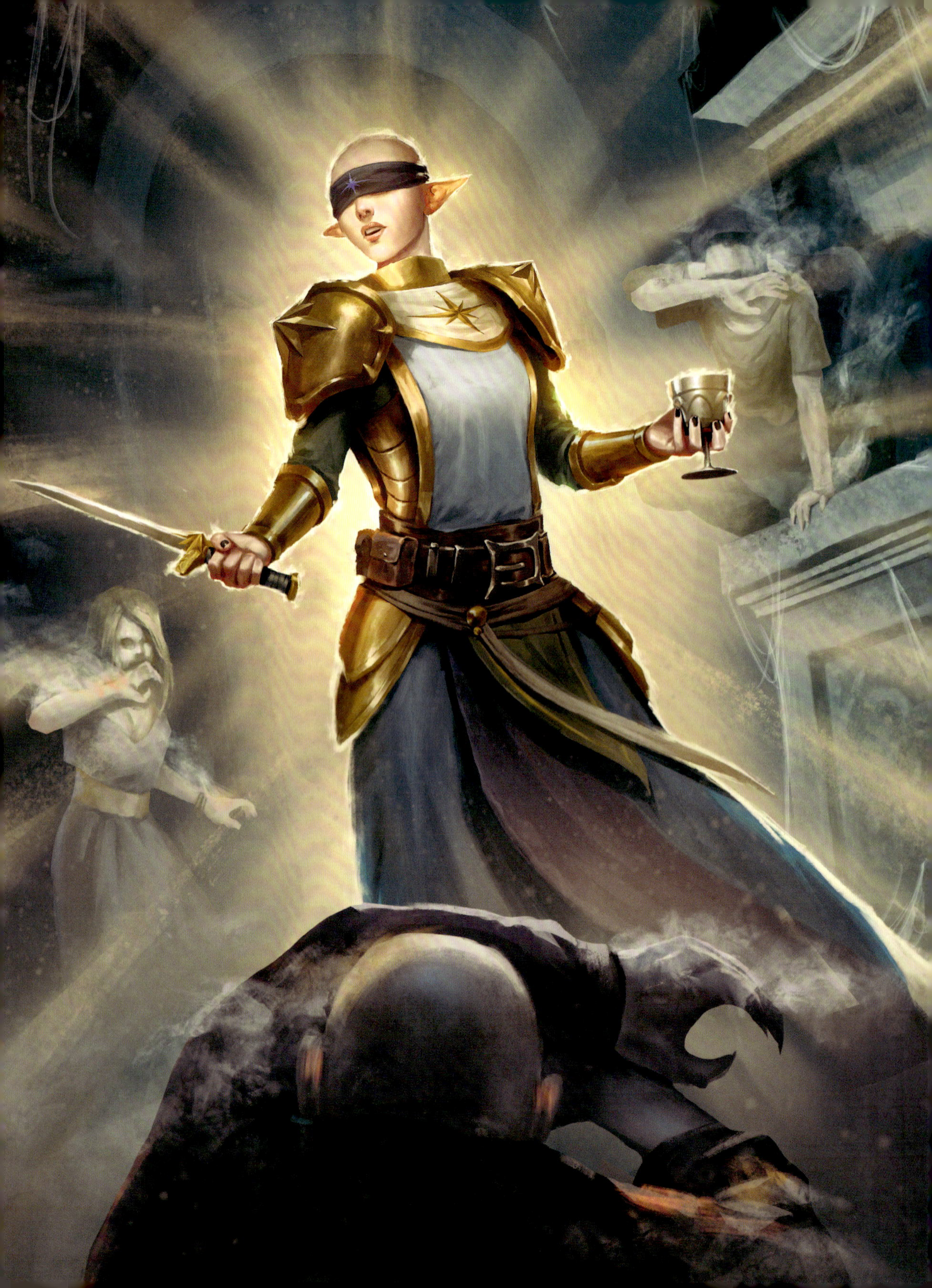

USING CHARACTERS
TO TELL YOUR OWN STORIES

Bel Vala could hear footsteps on the cold stone floor and smell touches of exotic fragrances used to mask the stench of death, but there was no breathing to match the animalistic movement she detected.

Undead.

The unliving were her most hated enemies, and she would do anything to destroy their evil blight.

The cleric's hands clenched tightly. She could feel the familiar touch of Giver, her enchanted dagger, and Taker, the silver chalice. These linked items would not seem like much to a casual observer, but those with the ability to see the flow of magic energy between them would be awestruck by their potent aura.

The vampire spawn began to move closer in unison as a spindly female from their ranks broke the silence of the room with a hissing threat, her tongue pressed against sharp fangs.

"Lord Strahd has marked you for death."

Bel Vala smirked and her hands quivered for a moment as she felt the divine power of her god Corellon surging from within.

Pure sunlight exploded from Bel Vala's frail body and the vampires screamed in agony.

Reading about adventure is a great way to stir your imagination, and creating a character of your own is an important first step in composing your personal stories. Building a new character is about discovering who they are at the beginning of their journey and then finding out who they become as their legend grows across the land.

Your idea might start with a single hero or a small group of adventurers, but from there it can go *anywhere*: a creature's lair, the village nearby, cities and dungeons, caverns or skyscapes. You get to choose all the ingredients and stir them together. To help you as you develop your story, here are some questions to keep in mind:

WHO ARE YOUR CHARACTERS?

- Are they like you or different? Young or old, human or something else?

WHERE DOES YOUR STORY TAKE PLACE?

- At the top of a mountain, in a serene forest, deep underwater, or in a creepy boneyard?

WHEN DOES THE STORY HAPPEN?

- At night or during the day, in the middle of a thunderstorm or right before the bells toll to ring in the new year? Think about time passing as your story unfolds.

HOW DO THINGS CHANGE AS THE STORY PROCEEDS?

- Do your adventurers succeed or fail? Do they find somewhere new or explore somewhere old?

WHAT SHOULD SOMEONE FEEL AS THEY EXPERIENCE YOUR STORY?

- Do you want them to laugh or get scared? Cheer or be grossed out?

WHY ARE YOUR CHARACTERS GOING ON THIS ADVENTURE?

- Knowing what their goals are will help you create a compelling tale of courage and exploration.

Remember, you don't have to answer all these questions by yourself! DUNGEONS & DRAGONS is a collaborative game where you work with your friends to create your own stories. One person acts as a narrator, called a Dungeon Master, and the other players in the story each take on the role of an adventurer, called a Player Character, in an adventuring party.

The Dungeon Master sets up a scene by describing a place and any threats that may exist, and then each player contributes ideas by explaining their character's actions. With each scene created by the group, the story moves forward in unexpected and entertaining ways.

If you don't feel confident starting from scratch, you can go to your local gaming store and play a DUNGEONS & DRAGONS demonstration session. Demos can be a quick way to learn how the game is played and possibly make some brand-new friends at the same time.

After you've read through all the character options in this heroic handbook, there's even more DUNGEONS & DRAGONS material out there to ignite your imagination. *The Monsters & Creatures Compendium* is bursting at the seams with beasts and beings for you to discover, including werebeasts, giants, and dragons—plus a guide to help with creating new monsters of your own!

You know who your adventurer is and have equipped them for their journey. Now find out what dangers lurk in the darkness and *answer the call to adventure!*

TEN SPEED PRESS
An imprint of the Crown Publishing Group
A division of Penguin Random House LLC
1745 Broadway
New York, NY 10019
tenspeed.com
penguinrandomhouse.com

Copyright © 2025 Wizards of the Coast LLC. All rights reserved.

Penguin Random House values and supports copyright. Copyright fuels creativity, encourages diverse voices, promotes free speech, and creates a vibrant culture. Thank you for buying an authorized edition of this book and for complying with copyright laws by not reproducing, scanning, or distributing any part of it in any form without permission. You are supporting writers and allowing Penguin Random House to continue to publish books for every reader. Please note that no part of this book may be used or reproduced in any manner for the purpose of training artificial intelligence technologies or systems.

TEN SPEED PRESS and the Ten Speed Press colophon are registered trademarks of Penguin Random House LLC.

Wizards of the Coast, Dungeons & Dragons, D&D, their respective logos, and the dragon ampersand are registered trademarks of Wizards of the Coast LLC in the USA and other countries. All characters in this book are fictitious. Any resemblance to actual persons, living or dead, is purely coincidental. All Wizards of the Coast characters, character names, and the distinctive likenesses thereof, and all other Wizards trademarks are property of Wizards of the Coast LLC.

Most of the text and illustrations in this work were originally published in various volumes of the Young Adventurer's Guide series published by Ten Speed Press, an imprint of Crown Publishing Group, a division of Penguin Random House LLC.

Typefaces: Capita by Dieter Hofrichter, IMB Plex Sans by Mike Abbink, Johnstemp by Georg John, Tiamat Condensed by Jim Parkinson, and Tiamat Text by Jim Parkinson

Library of Congress Cataloging-in-Publication Data is on file with the publisher.

Hardcover ISBN: 978-0-593-83970-6
Ebook ISBN: 978-0-593-83971-3

Publisher: Aaron Wehner
Editor: Shaida Boroumand | Production editor: Sohayla Farman | Assistant editor: Kausaur Fahimuddin | Designer: Betsy Stromberg | Production designer: Claudia Sanchez
Production: Dan Myers | Copy editor: Shoshana Seid-Green | Proofreaders: Kate Bolen and Katy Miller | Publicist: Maya Bradford | Marketer: Paola Crespo
Illustrators: Conceptopolis, LLC, and Goodname Digital Art Studio

Manufactured in China

10 9 8 7 6 5 4 3 2 1

First Edition

Cover illustration by Goodname Digital Art Studio

The authorized representative in the EU for product safety and compliance is Penguin Random House Ireland, Morrison Chambers, 32 Nassau Street, Dublin D02 YH68, Ireland, https://eu-contact.penguin.ie.